Conceptualization and

Measurement of

Organism – Environment

Interaction

Conceptualization and

Measurement of

Organism – Environment

Interaction

Edited by
Theodore D. Wachs
and Robert Plomin

American Psychological Association
Washington, DC

Published by the
American Psychological Association
1200 Seventeenth Street, NW
Washington, DC 20036

Copies may be ordered from the
APA Order Department
P.O. Box 2710
Hyattsville, MD 20784

This book was typeset in Times Roman by Harper Graphics, Waldorf, MD.

Printer: Braun-Brumfield, Inc., Ann Arbor, MI
Cover designer: Grafik Communications Ltd., Alexandria, VA
Copyediting: Christine P. Landry and Olin J. Nettles
Production coordinator: Christine P. Landry

Library of Congress Cataloging-in-Publication Data

Conceptualization and measurement of organism-environment interaction
  / Theodore D. Wachs, Robert Plomin, editors.
      p.   cm.
   Based on papers presented at a conference sponsored by the
American Psychological Association, Purdue University, and
Pennsylvania State University, held in November 1989.
   Includes bibliographical references and index.
   ISBN 1-55798-126-4 : $40.00 (acid-free paper)
   1. Environmental psychology—Congresses. I. Wachs, Theodore D.,
1941–   . II. Plomin, Robert, 1948–   . III. American
Psychological Association. IV. Purdue University. V. Pennsylvania
State University.
BF353.C65 1991   70456
155.9—dc20   91-18356
                                                                     CIP

Printed in the United States of America
First edition

CONTENTS

CONTRIBUTORS

Lee J. Cronbach, 850 Webster Street #623, Palo Alto, CA
Byron Egeland, *Institute of Child Development, University of Minnesota*
Scott Hershberger, *Center for Developmental and Health Genetics, College of Health and Human Development, Pennsylvania State University*
Robert B. McCall, *Office of Child Development, University of Pittsburgh*
Andrew Pickles, *Institute of Psychiatry, London, England*
Robert Plomin, *Center for Developmental and Health Genetics, College of Health and Human Development, Pennsylvania State University*
Michael Rutter, *Institute of Psychiatry, London, England*
Gene P. Sackett, *Regional Primate Research Center, University of Washington*
L. Alan Sroufe, *Institute of Child Development, University of Minnesota*
Theodore D. Wachs, *Department of Psychological Sciences, Purdue University*

FOREWORD

The relative contributors of "natural" and "environmental" determinants of behavior are not easy to assess. Controversy continues among behavior scientists as to how best to accomplish this and indeed whether it can be done at all. Of particular interest currently is the measurement of genetic, experiential, and interactive conditions controlling behavioral outcomes.

This volume presents findings reported at a November 1989 conference on how behavior scientists conceptualize and measure the synergistic influence of organismic and environmental factors. A major goal of this conference, which was cosponsored by the Science Directorate of the American Psychological Association, Purdue University, and Pennsylvania State University, was to create recommendations that developmental researchers would find useful in understanding organism–environment interactions. The American Psychological Association is pleased to have sponsored this conference and now to make these original research presentations available in book form.

Federal research agencies stopped most support of investigator-initiated state-of-the-art research conferences in scientific psychology over a decade ago. During this period, however, scientific psychology has continued to grow, and scientific psychologists have adapted their talents to diverse areas. Yet, there have been few opportunities for investigators in new and promising research areas to convene in special settings to discuss their findings. As part of its continuing effort to enhance the dissemination of scientific knowledge in psychology, the APA established in 1988, in its Science Directorate, the Scientific Conferences program. An annual call for proposals is issued by the APA Science Directorate to solicit conference ideas. Proposals from all areas of psychological research are welcome. From the inception of this program through mid-1991, 19 conferences have been funded, with a total outlay of more than $250,000.

A list of the conferences funded through this program follows:

Researching Community Psychology: Integrating Theories and Methodologies, September 1988

The Psychological Well-Being of Nonhuman Captive Primates, September 1988

Psychological Research on Organ Donation, October 1988

Arizona Conference on Sleep and Cognition, January 1989

Socially Shared Cognition, February 1989

The Role of Experience in Modifying Taste and Its Effects on Feeding, April 1989

Perception of Structure, May 1989

Suggestibility of Children's Recollections, June 1989

Best Methods for the Analysis of Change, October 1989

Conceptualization and Measurement of Organism–Environment Interaction, November 1989

Cognitive Bases of Musical Communication, April 1990

Conference on Hostility, Coping/Support, and Health, November 1990

Psychological Testing of Hispanics, February 1991

Study of Cognition: Conceptual and Methodological Issues, February 1991

Cardiovascular Reactivity to Psychological and Cardiovascular Disease: A Conference on the Evidence, April 1991

Developmental Psychoacoustics, August 1991

Maintaining and Promoting Integrity in Behavioral Science Research, October 1991

The Contributions of Psychology to Mathematics and Science Education, November 1991

Lives Through Time: Assessment and Theory in Personality Psychology From a Longitudinal Perspective, November 1991

Lewis P. Lipsitt, PhD
Executive Director for Science
Science Directorate, APA

Virginia E. Holt
Manager, Scientific Conference Program
Science Directorate, APA

PREFACE

In November 1989, the American Psychological Association, Purdue University, and Pennsylvania State University, whose deliberations are summarized in this book, cosponsored the conference on the conceptualization and measurement of organism–environment interaction. In organizing the conference around these particular issues, our ultimate intention was to develop a set of recommendations that would be useful to developmental researchers. The number of participants was limited to individuals who were actively engaged in the field so as to facilitate and encourage informal (although not unstructured) roundtable discussion.

As organizers of the conference, we designed a format that centered around the three specific topic areas that we felt were essential to the study of organism–environment interaction: environmental contributions, organismic contributions, and design and analytical strategies. Prior to the conference, we requested that participants circulate brief papers among themselves outlining their current approaches to the study of this topic. We emphasized that these brief outlines were to be regarded as jumping-off points for amplification and further discussion. Specifically, L. Alan Sroufe and Theodore D. Wachs focused on environmental contributions; Robert Plomin and Gene P. Sackett discussed organismic contributions; and Lee J. Cronbach, Robert B. McCall, and Michael Rutter dealt with design and analysis considerations.

The first session of the conference centered on discussion of the commonalities and differences among participants concerning the definition of *organism–environment interaction*. The second session focused on environmental contributions. The third focused on organismic contributions. The fourth centered around design and analytical strategies, particularly those that are most likely to reveal interactions. The final session involved a summarization of the main issues raised in the preceeding sessions and an attempt to answer some of the following questions: (a) What are the most appropriate conceptual models for approaching the study of organism–environment interaction? (b) What aspects of the organism or environment are most likely to be sensitive to interactions? (c) What are the most appropriate design features for revealing organism–environment interactions? (d) What statistical or analytical procedures might be particularly useful in testing organism–environment interactions?

The chapters in this book reflect these discussions, in terms of both format and, more critically, substance. Each chapter was written after the conference, so it reflects not only the authors' initial ideas but also the impact of the focused group discussion on the authors' current thinking. In chapter 1, Wachs and Plomin discuss the current status of organism–environment interaction in developmental studies, distinguishing between organism–environment *covariance*, *transaction*, and *interaction*.

In chapter 2, Sackett discusses the importance of the developmental history of the organism. He emphasizes that developmental studies may yield either main effects or interactions depending on a complex combination that involves outcome variables, the temporal period under study, and the developmental history of the organism.

Plomin and Hershberger, in chapter 3, approach the study of organism–environment interaction from a behavioral genetics viewpoint. Their chapter centers on how genetic theories and methods not only aid the researcher in defining genetic contributions to the study of organism–environment interaction but also how they may be useful in illustrating environmental contributions.

In chapter 4, Wachs approaches the problem from an environmental perspective. The emphasis of this chapter is on how the nature of the population studied defines the most appropriate means of assessing environmental contributions.

In chapter 5, Sroufe and Egeland emphasize the multiplicity of processes, including interaction, that can act to influence development. Using attachment as an illustration, Sroufe and Egeland emphasize prior developmental history of the child as an individual characteristic that can influence developmental outcomes both through organism–environment covariance and organism–environment interaction.

Cronbach, in chapter 6, emphasizes the nature of the relation between interactions and main effects, the role of power considerations when analyzing organism–environment interactions, and the use of alternative statistical and design strategies.

In chapter 7, Rutter and Pickles illustrate the different types of organism–environment interaction and discuss analytical procedures that are appropriate for different interaction processes.

In chapter 8, McCall focuses on design and analytical questions from a developmental rather than a measurement perspective. Developmental trends in the appearance of interaction versus covariance, the need for extreme group studies, and the problems encountered when using traditional approaches such as analysis of variance or regression form the major focus of his chapter.

In the final chapter, Wachs attempts to synthesize the various themes presented in the book, with specific reference to the question of which measures, designs, and analytical strategies are most promising for future research. This chapter was submitted to all participants in order to obtain their reactions and suggestions. As a result, it includes areas of agreement and disagreement.

In addition to expressing our gratitude to the cosponsors who provided funding for this conference, we wish to acknowledge the participation of three psychology graduate students who were selected in a nationwide competition: Mariana de La Flor (Indiana University), Jody Ganiban (University of Rochester), and Anne Ricciuti (University of Virginia). The suggestions of Virginia Holt of the Science Directorate of the American Psychological Association concerning conference organization and the heroic efforts of Elana Pyle, Pennsylvania State University's administrative officer, in taking charge of the day-to-day conference requirements were highly instrumental in making the conference run smoothly.

Whether this conference will actually influence the nature of future research investigations on organism–environment interaction is a question that will only be answered in time. At least on the basis of the enthusiasm demonstrated by the conference participants, we are optimistic that the results presented here will in fact promote understanding and stimulate further discussion and studies concerning issues of conceptualization and measurement in this area of research.

Theodore D. Wachs
Robert Plomin

CHAPTER 1

OVERVIEW OF CURRENT MODELS AND RESEARCH

THEODORE D. WACHS AND ROBERT PLOMIN

Like the auto salesperson's concept of "preowned," *interaction* is a term with many meanings. For example, a recently published book on interaction (Bornstein & Bruner, 1989) included chapters on culturally based knowledge transmission from adults to children; biological or psychological mechanisms used by the child to integrate knowledge presented by adults; the interrelation of genes and cultures across time; the interrelation of behavior units across time; the role of context in understanding the meaning of individual attributes; and the differential reactivity to environmental stimulation of individuals with different genotypes. The Bornstein and Bruner book does not represent an isolated example. A similar multiplicity of definitions is seen in the various chapters of the earlier Magnusson and Allen (1983) book on interaction. This conceptual hodgepodge when discussing interaction means, in practice, that all too often the same term—interaction—is used to denote completely different processes. Before discussing conceptual or methodological aspects of organism–environment interaction, we think it critical to specify exactly what we mean by the term *interaction*. Specifically, it is essential to distinguish between the processes of interaction, transaction, and covariance.

Organism–environment interaction, as defined here, is used in the statistical sense of interaction: differential reactivity by different individuals to similar environmental stimulation. Note that differential reactivity does not have to be governed by genes; differential reactivity may also be a function of prior environmental history or nongenetic biological factors such as nutrition. In contrast, *organism–environment covariance* refers to the process by which children with

1

different characteristics either actively or reactively elicit different types of experiences from the environment, thus creating covariance between the environment and characteristics of the organism (Plomin, DeFries, & Loehlin, 1977). Finally, *organism–environment transaction* is defined as the developmental interrelationship between child and environment, with child influencing environment and environment influencing child across time (Rutter, 1983). Organism–environment transaction encompasses organism–environment covariance but carries it further temporally, in the sense that the environment that has been previously influenced by the child in turn now influences the child. The critical point is that all of these distinctly different processes are often referred to under the rubric "interaction." Organism–environment transaction is what is most often referred to as an interaction by behavioral scientists; however, interaction as transaction is clearly different from interaction as differential reactivity. In part, this may reflect the fact that interaction involves different individuals differentially reacting to similar environments, whereas transaction involves both different individuals and different environments.

Transaction studies rarely go beyond main effects statements about the role of the environment on the child (e.g., the effect of parental behavior on children) or the role of the child on the environment (e.g., the effect of child characteristics on parental behavior). Such studies have limited relevance to the study of organism–environment interaction per se. When transaction research moves beyond main effects, both interactions and correlations are considered in the interplay between organism and environment. Furthermore, transactions connote a developmental, specifically longitudinal, perspective on the interplay between organism and environment. Although a developmental perspective is valuable for the investigation of any process, this is not intrinsic to our definition of interaction. In sum, transaction is a much broader and looser term than interaction as defined earlier. In this book we focus on interactions as we have defined them rather than on transactions, although a developmental perspective on interactions is well represented in the following chapters.

The distinction between covariance and interaction is important in terms of differentiating between two major processes that influence developmental outcomes. Specifically, it may be important to determine if individual or group differences in environment–development relations are attributable to differential reactivity (organism–environment interaction), to different environments being provided for different individuals or groups (organism–environment covariance), or to a combination of interactions and covariance. For example, in studies of sex differences in reactivity, boys appear to be more adversely affected than girls by parental divorce (Bergman, 1981; Hetherington, Cox, & Cox, 1982) or day care (Gamble & Zigler, 1986). However, those same studies also suggest the possibility of differential treatment of boys and girls by the custodial parent or by day-care providers, making it difficult to establish whether the developmental mechanism is interaction, covariance, or a combination of the two. A similar situation exists in studies of children who have difficult temperaments. Although research suggests that difficult children react differently than do nondifficult children to differences in parental discipline styles (Gordon, 1983) and environmental stress (Barron & Earls, 1984), these studies cannot eliminate the possibility that difficult children also may be treated differently by their parents. Although organism–environment covariance is an essential process in development, the major focus of this book is on organism–environment interaction, as defined earlier.

It should also be noted that we do not discuss the conceptualization and measurement of individual differences per se. There is rich empirical and conceptual literature describing both major domains of individual differences and what factors lead to individual differences. Rather, our focus is on a related but different domain: how individual differences act to mediate the impact of the environment on development.

The idea that unique characteristics of the organism govern the way in which individuals respond to the environment (organism–environment interaction) has been around since at least the time of Aristotle:

> It would seem then that a study of individual characters is the best way of making education perfect, for then each has a better chance of receiving the treatment that suits him. (Aristotle-Nicomachean Ethics, Book 10, chapter 9, cited in McKeon, 1941).

The concept of organism–environment interaction is an intuitively appealing one that has received support from a variety of sources. For example, over the past 15 years a number of theoretical papers have emerged that have a common theme: The impact of the environment on development will depend on the nature of the organism on whom the environment impinges (e.g., Horowitz, 1987, Plomin et al., 1977; Rutter, 1983; Thomas & Chess, 1976; Wachs, 1986). Within the biomedical literature, individual differences in reactivity to specific drugs are commonplace (Neims, 1986; Rapport, Stoner, DePaul, Birmingham, & Tucker, 1985; Stubbs, Budden, Jackson, Terdal, & Ritvo, 1986), as are individual differences in physiological reactivity to stress (Falkner & Rogonessi, 1986; Kasl & Cobb, 1970; Magnusson, 1988; Mason, 1968a, 1968b) and diet (Kawasaki, Delea, Barter, & Smith, 1978). At a behavioral level, for infrahuman populations, differential reactivity to objectively similar environments is seen as a function of species differences (Henderson, 1980; Hinde & Stevenson-Hinde, 1973), strain differences within species (Freedman, 1974; Fuller, 1967; Sackett, Rupenthal, Fahrenbruch, Holm, & Greenough, 1981), or differences in nutritional history of the organism (Findley, Ng, Reid, & Armstrong, 1981; Weinberg, Dallman, & Levine, 1980). The concept of individual differences mediating the impact of environment is also derived from the increasing amount of research in areas such as behavioral genetics (Plomin & Rende, 1991), resilient children (Rutter, 1985), temperament (Thomas & Chess, 1977), and reactivity to psychotherapy (Dance & Neufeld, 1988) or to educational interventions (Cronbach & Snow, 1977). Much of this research suggests that the approaches to understanding development that do not systematically include individual-difference factors may be incomplete.

Given this pattern of evidence from diverse areas, it is surprising that there is so little emphasis on the process of organism–environment interaction in studies of human development. In part, the problem is theoretical. The predominant emphasis of the majority of development research and theory is universal processes of development, with a corresponding neglect of individual differences (Feldman, 1980; Horowitz, 1969). Given the predominance of the experimental model in developmental research and theory (McCall, 1977), the potential relevance of individual differences as a mediator in the developmental process is all too often simply dismissed (Cronbach, 1957; Kopp, 1978).

Although it is perhaps not surprising to find the study of individual-difference mediators minimized in areas that emphasize "universal" processes of development, such as in the study of learning and memory (Feldman, 1980), what is surprising is a similar neglect in areas that consider nonuniversal developmental processes. For example, in the study of environmental influences on development, some environmentally oriented researchers have emphasized the mediating impact of individual-difference factors (e.g., Wachs & Gruen, 1982). However, the study of environmental influences on development has been conceptualized primarily as a main effects, global question: "What are the good and bad aspects of the environment that can either facilitate or hinder development?" (Wachs, 1986). This main effects model is seen most vividly in early intervention studies, in which the impact of intervention was determined by looking at an overall group mean and not at the range of reaction within the group. Environmental psychologists have been reluctant to accept the idea of organism–environment interaction because the existence of interaction would make it difficult to use a global main effects model. The classic response of environmental psychologists has been to essentially ignore the possibility of individual differences in reactivity, both in their designs and in their models (Wachs, 1983).

Similarly, in the field of behavioral genetics, although some behavioral genetic researchers emphasize the interaction of organism and environment (e.g., Kendler & Eaves, 1986), a major assumption shared by most behavioral genetic researchers is that gene–environment interactions are minimal at best (Wahlsten, 1990). Behavioral geneticists have been reluctant to deal with organism–environment interaction because (a) it is not easily encompassed or assessed in the components of variance approach and (b) environmental measures typically have not been included in behavioral genetic research (Plomin et al., 1977). The traditional response of behavioral geneticists faced with interaction has been to rescale the data to eliminate variance attributable to interaction (e.g., Mather & Jinks,

1982) or to ignore the interaction and attempt to deal only with main effects (Wahlsten, 1990).

The lack of interest in organism–environment interaction is more than a conceptual problem, however. It is also attributable, in part, to the lack of systematic evidence for replicable, specific organism–environment interactions. This is not to say that there is no evidence available showing that different children react differentially to similar environmental stimulation (Cronbach & Snow, 1977; Wachs & Gruen, 1982). Rather, the problem is one of finding a consistent pattern of evidence for organism–environment interaction in human development studies (Cronbach & Snow, 1977; Plomin & Daniels, 1984). It is this inability to find a consistent pattern of results that led Plomin and Daniels (1984) to their pessimistic conclusion: "It is considerably easier to talk about interactions than it is to find them" (p. 161).

However, the evidence just cited does not allow researchers to simply drop the concept. Organism–environment interaction is commonplace in the biomedical field and for infrahuman populations. The reactions of infants and children are not uniform for a variety of natural or imposed experiences (Garmezy & Rutter, 1983; Hanson, Gottesman, & Meehl, 1977; McKay, Sinisterra, McKay, Gomez, & Lloreda, 1978; Rutter, 1985; Stevenson, Parke, Wilkinson, Bonnevaux, & Gonzalez, 1978; Walker & Emory, 1983; Williams, 1977). Although ignoring the possibility of organism–environment interaction may lead to more parsimonious theory, the cost for this apparent parsimony may be the neglect of a potentially major influence in development. However, being sensitive to the possible existence of organism–environment interaction does not help researchers understand why specific, replicable organism–environment interactions are so difficult to find.

An attempt to deal with the question of why specific organism–environment interactions are so hard to isolate was a focus of a symposium, organized by Wachs and Plomin, for the 1985 meeting of the Society for Research in Child Development. One major conclusion drawn from this symposium was that different conceptual and methodological approaches to interaction may well account for differences between studies. A second conclusion was that there are few guidelines about the most appropriate methodological strategies for investigating the nature of organism–environment interaction in human development. One major, unresolved research issue that arose from this symposium was how to decide, a priori, which characteristics of organisms and environments, outcome variables, or ages are more likely to be sensitive to interaction influences. Addressing these types of issues is critical for researchers hoping to study the role of organism–environment interaction in human development. Unfortunately, the brevity of the symposium format did not allow participants to formulate a comprehensive approach to dealing with these issues. This book allows us to go beyond the restricted format of a symposium and thus develop a set of recommendations that would be useful to developmental researchers interested in the conceptualization and measurement of organism–environment interaction. These recommendations are summarized in chapter 9.

References

Barron, A., & Earls, F. (1984). The relation of temperament and social factors to behavioral problems in three year old children. *Journal of Child Psychiatry and Psychiatry, 25,* 23–33.

Bergman, L. (1981). Is intellectual development more vulnerable in boys than in girls? *Journal of Genetic Psychology, 138,* 175–181.

Bornstein, M., & Bruner, J. (1989). *Interaction in human development.* Hillsdale, NJ: Erlbaum.

Cronbach, L. (1957). The two disciplines of scientific psychology. *American Psychologist, 12,* 671–684.

Cronbach, L., & Snow, R. (1977). *Aptitudes and instructional methods.* New York: Wiley.

Dance, K., & Neufeld, R. (1988). Aptitude treatment interaction in the clinical setting. *Psychological Bulletin, 104,* 192–213.

Falkner, B., & Rogonessi, S. (1986). Psychosocial stress and reactivity as risk factors of cardiovascular disease. *Journal of the American Academy of Child Psychiatry, 25,* 779–784.

Feldman, D. (1980). *Beyond universals in cognitive development.* Norwood, NJ: Ablex.

Findley, E., Ng, K. Reid, R., & Armstrong, S. (1981). The effects of iron deficiency during development on passive avoidance learning in the adult rat. *Physiology and Behavior, 27,* 1089–1096.

Freedman, D. (1974). *Human infancy: An evolutionary perspective.* Hillsdale, NJ: Erlbaum.

Fuller, J. (1967). Experiential deprivation and later behavior. *Science, 158,* 1645–1652.

Gamble, D., & Zigler, E. (1986). Effects of infant daycare. *American Journal of Orthopsychiatry, 56,* 26–42.

Garmezy, N., & Rutter, M. (1983). *Stress, coping and development in children.* New York: McGraw-Hill.

Gordon, B. (1983). Paternal perception of child temperament and observed mother-child interaction. *Child Psychiatry and Human Development, 13,* 153–167.

Hanson, D., Gottesman, I., & Meehl, P. (1977). Genetic theories and the validation of psychiatric diagnosis. *Journal of Abnormal Psychology, 86,* 571–588.

Henderson, N. (1980). The effects of early experience on the behavior of animals. In E. Simmel (Ed.), *Early experience and later behavior* (pp. 45–78). New York: Academic Press.

Hetherington, M., Cox, M., & Cox, R. (1982). Effects of divorce of parents on children. In M. Lamb (Ed.), *Nontraditional families* (pp. 233–288). Hillsdale, NJ: Erlbaum.

Hinde, R., & Stevenson-Hinde, J. (1973). *Constraints on learning.* San Diego, CA: Academic Press.

Horowitz, F. (1969). Learning, development, research and individual differences. In L. Lipsitt & H. Reese (Eds.), *Advances in child development and behavior* (pp. 84–127). San Diego, CA: Academic Press.

Horowitz, F. (1987). *Exploring developmental theories.* Hillsdale, NJ: Erlbaum.

Kasl, S., & Cobb, S. (1970). Blood pressure in men undergoing job stress. *Psychosomatic Medicine, 32,* 19–38.

Kawasaki, T., Delea, C., Barter, F., & Smith, H. (1978). The effect of high sodium and low sodium intakes on blood pressure and other related variables in human subjects with idiopathic hypertension. *American Journal of Medicine, 64,* 193–198.

Kendler, K., & Eaves, L. (1986). Model for the joint effects of genotype and environment on liability to psychiatric illness. *American Journal of Psychiatry, 143*, 279–299.

Kopp, C. (1978). Individual differences and intervention for infants and young children. *Journal of Pediatric Psychology, 3*, 145–149.

Magnusson, D. (1988). *Individual development from an interactional perspective.* Hillsdale, NJ: Erlbaum.

Magnusson, D., & Allen, V. (1983). *Human development: An interactional perspective.* San Diego, CA: Academic Press.

Mason, J. (1968a). A review of psychoendocrine research in the pituitary adrenal cortical system. *Psychosomatic Medicine, 30*, 567–607.

Mason, J. (1968b). A review of psychoendocrine research in the sympathetic-adrenal-medullary system. *Psychosomatic Medicine, 30*, 631–653.

McCall, R. (1977). Challenges to a science of developmental psychology. *Child Development, 48*, 333–344.

McKay, H., Sinisterra, L., McKay, A., Gomez, H., & Lloreda, T. (1978). Improving cognitive ability in chronically deprived children. *Science, 200*, 270–278.

McKeon, R. (1941). *The basic works of Aristotle.* New York: Random House.

Mather, K., & Jinks, J. (1982). *Biometrical genetics* (3rd ed.). London: Chapman & Hall.

Neims, A. (1986). Individuality in the response to dietary constituents: Some lessons from drugs. *Nutrition Review Supplements, 21*, 237–241.

Plomin, R., & Daniels, D. (1984). The interaction between temperament and environment: Methodological considerations. *Merrill-Palmer Quarterly, 30*, 149–162.

Plomin, R., DeFries, J., & Loehlin, J. (1977). Genotype–environment interaction and correlation in the analysis of human development. *Psychological Bulletin, 84*, 309–322.

Plomin, R., & Rende, R. (1991). Human behavioral genetics. *Annual Review of Psychology, 42*, 161–190.

Rapport, M., Stoner, G., DePaul, G., Birmingham, B., & Tucker, S. (1985). Methylphenidate: Reactions of hyperactive children. *Journal of Abnormal Child Psychology, 13*, 227–244.

Rutter, M. (1983). Statistical and personal interactions: Facets and perspectives. In D. Magnusson & V. Allen (Eds.), *Human development: An interactional perspective* (pp. 295–321). San Diego, CA: Academic Press.

Rutter, M. (1985). Resilience in the face of adversity. *British Journal of Psychiatry, 147*, 598–611.

Sackett, G., Rupenthal, G., Fahrenburch, C., Holm, R., & Greenough, W. (1981). Social isolation rearing effects in monkeys vary with genotype. *Developmental Psychology, 17*, 313–318.

Stevenson, H., Parke, T., Wilkinson, A., Bonnevaux, B., & Gonzalez, M. (1978). Schooling, environment and cognitive development: A cross cultural study. *Monographs of the Society for Research in Child Development, 175* (43, Serial No. 175).

Stubbs, E., Budden, S., Jackson, R., Terdal, L., & Ritvo, E. (1986). Effects of fenfluramine on eight outpatients with the syndrome of autism. *Developmental Medicine and Child Neurology, 28*, 229–235.

Thomas, A., & Chess, S. (1976). Behavioral individuality in childhood. In L. Aronson, E. Tobach, D. Lehrman, & J. Rosenblatt (Eds.), *Development and evolution of behavior* (pp. 529–541). San Francisco: Freeman.

Thomas, A., & Chess, S. (1977). *Temperament and development.* New York: Brunner/Mazel.

Wachs, T. D. (1983). The use and abuse of environment in behavior genetic research. *Child Development, 54*, 396–408.

Wachs, T. D. (1986). Models of physical environment action. In A. Gottfried & G. Brown (Eds.), *Play interactions* (pp. 253–278). Lexington, MA: Lexington Books.

Wachs, T. D., & Gruen, G. (1982). *Early experience and human development*. New York: Plenum Press.

Walker, E., & Emory, F. (1983). Infants at risk for psychopathology: Offspring of schizophrenic parents. *Child Development, 54*, 1269–1285.

Wahlsten, D. (1990). Insensitivity of the analysis of variance to heredity-environment interaction. *Behavior and Brain Sciences, 13*, 109–161.

Weinberg, J., Dallman, P., & Levine, S. (1980). Iron deficiency during early development in the rat. *Pharmacology, Biochemistry and Behavior, 12*, 493–502.

Williams, T. (1977). Infant development and supplemental care: A comparative review of basic and applied research. *Human Development, 20*, 1–30.

PART ONE

INDIVIDUAL AND ENVIRONMENTAL CONTRIBUTIONS

CHAPTER 2

TOWARD A MORE TEMPORAL VIEW OF ORGANISM– ENVIRONMENT INTERACTION

GENE P. SACKETT

INTRODUCTION

Over 20 years ago Denenberg and Whimbey (1963) and Denenberg and Rosenberg (1967) published seminal papers concerning an important temporal source of variation in postnatal development. Handling rats of a grandmaternal generation (F_0) during their infancy affected the postnatal exploratory behavior of their non-handled offspring (F_1) and nonhandled grandchildren (F_2). Subsequent studies showed that handling grandmothers before mating or during pregnancy also affected the behavior of nonhandled F_1 and F_2 rats (Insel, 1972; Wehmer, Porter, & Scales, 1970). A similar effect was found for malnutrition prior to mating and during pregnancy. Newborn rat offspring (F_2) of protein-restricted grandmothers had lowered brain cell numbers (Zamenhof, van Marthens, & Grauel, 1971) and adult reversal learning deficits (Bresler, Ellison, & Zamenhof, 1975), even though neither they nor their mothers had experienced malnutrition. These results have been largely ignored in the human developmental literature. Overlooking these studies is unfortunate because they have helped establish the important concept of nongenetic intergenerational effects on biological and behavioral development.

The research reported in this chapter was supported by United States Public Health Service grants HD-08633 and HD-02274 from the National Institute of Child Health and Human Development Mental Retardation Branch and RR-00166 from the Animal Resources Branch. The editorial assistance of Kate Elias is greatly appreciated.

11

Due to their two-group experimental designs, those seminal studies revealed only main effects of intergenerational environmental experience. However, other handling studies also demonstrated a major temporal principle, one involving organism–environment interaction: A specific experiential variable can have different effects depending on an individual's maturational stage at exposure. Thus, prenatal handling inhibits postnatal exploration, but postnatal handling facilitates later exploration (Denenberg & Zarrow, 1971). The same interaction is found for intergenerational effects. Premating and prenatal F_0 handling reduces F_2 exploration, whereas postnatal F_0 handling increases F_2 exploratory behavior.

This interactional principle also operates in rodent protein malnutrition studies. Fetal brain effects differ markedly depending on the period of gestation during which the mother experiences malnutrition (Zamenhof & van Marthens, 1978). However, the intergenerational consequences of this interaction between malnutrition and prenatal maturational stage are not known because effects on future generations were not studied.

It is true, of course, that genetic differences are a major source of intergenerational effects, even if one knows little about the actual biology of gene expression effects on behavior. As shown by Cavalli-Sforza, Feldman, Chen, and Dornbusch (1982), culture also provides powerful and measurable nongenetic intergenerational influences on human development. An important question raised by Cavalli-Sforza et al. relates to the temporal principle just stated: Do the effects of cultural transmission from different sources (e.g., parents, teachers, friends) interact with age at acquisition and age at performing activities involving the transmitted information? The Cavalli-Sforza et al. study, being cross-sectional, could not answer this inherently longitudinal, temporal question.

In this chapter I raise similar questions concerning a different set of nongenetic intergenerational effects. Like the rodent studies described previously, these questions concern the existence of transgenerational environmental effects on organismic processes and the interaction of these processes with environmental variables at particular developmental stages. One purpose of this chapter is to present some nonhuman primate data serving as a model for how nongenetic organismic intergenerational effects might influence human development.

A second issue addressed here concerns prenatal factors. Clearly, maternal–placental–fetal processes are critical for the organization of postnatal development at many levels. Studies of maternal exposure to alcohol, drugs, and other teratogens show that fetal development is exquisitely sensitive to environmental poisons and toxins. However, as expected from the temporal interaction principle, most of these effects interact with gestational age at exposure (Porter & Hook, 1980; Vorhees & Mollnow, 1987). Evidence for the popular hypothesis that psychosocial maternal stress detrimentally affects prenatal processes in humans is less clear (Mansfield & Cohn, 1986; Molfese, Bricker, Manion, & Yaple, 1987). Furthermore, with the exception of fertility problems and premating drug exposure, the

Table 1.

BIRTH WEIGHTS BY GENERATION FOR CAPTIVE PIGTAILED MACAQUES

Generation	Females			Males		
	M	**SE**	**n**	**M**	**SE**	**n**
F_1	455	3.5	436	490	3.5	451
F_2	440	2.4	669	483	2.7	676
F_3	432	3.9	207	471	4.4	196

Note. All means are significantly different below the .01 level.

biological role of paternal influences on prenatal development has been ignored as a relevant factor (Gunderson & Sackett, 1982). In this chapter I present non-human primate data concerning prenatal stress and paternal influences on pregnancy outcome and postnatal development. These results are presented as a model of how prenatal factors might interact at different times in development to influence different dimensions of human growth and behavior.

INTERGENERATIONAL EFFECTS

Intergenerational changes in growth parameters were studied in a captive colony of 1,200 pigtailed macaques (*Macaca nemestrina*). The colony was in its third reproductive generation descending from wild captured animals. A computerized history contained reproductive, growth, health, and mortality information on over 5,000 animals covering a 20-year period. Measures from these records illustrate some simple but important changes in basic growth variables over colony generations.

Table 1 shows birth weights for males and females. F_1 animals were offspring of wildborn parents, F_2 animals had at least one F_1 parent, and F_3 monkeys had at least one F_2 parent. The average birth weight decreased in each succeeding generation for both sexes. This is a clear intergenerational change in an important index of fetal growth. A major question was whether this main effect of generation on the organismic variable of birth weight represents genetic change, increasingly poorer fetal growth in succeeding generations, or a change in the expression of normal fetal development.

Table 2 shows the average weight and age of females at the beginning of their first pregnancies. The F_1 offspring of wildborn parents were the heaviest and oldest. At their first pregnancy, each succeeding generation was lighter and younger than the last. Although this generational main effect could reflect genetic change, another possibility concerns fetal growth as a function of the mother's own fetal, infant, or juvenile development (Emanuel, 1986). Thus, improved colony nutrition, more certain climatic conditions, and lower stress due to lack

Table 2.

MEAN WEIGHT AND AGE AT FIRST CONCEPTION BY GENERATION FOR
CAPTIVE FEMALE PIGTAILED MACAQUES

Generation	Weight (kg)	Age (years)
F_1	4.65	4.3
F_2	4.05	3.8
F_3	3.61	3.5

Note. All means are significant below the .01 level.

of predation and no need to forage might facilitate developmental rates in some, but not all, systems. This could produce accelerated development of neural, glandular, and other systems, yielding earlier pregnancies without a concomitant increase in physical growth rate. The data in Table 3, showing correlations between parent and offspring birth weights, provide some evidence for this speculation.

F_1 paternal birth weights correlated about .30 with either F_2 sons or daughters. F_1 maternal correlations were significantly lower (both $p < .01$) and barely significantly different from zero for either sex of offspring. Thus, the F_1 paternal value provided a better estimate of genetic birth weight control than did the F_1 maternal value. This difference between the paternal and maternal correlations appears to reflect the effects of a captive environment on the pregnancy processes of wildborn mothers. The result seems to identify a grandmaternal (F_0) nongenetic intergenerational process. The effects of captivity on F_0 females appear to dilute the expression of F_1 female genetic factors on the control of F_2 fetal development. Such captivity effects might arise from psychological stress or disease. This nongenetic explanation is supported by the F_2 data in Table 3.

All F_2 maternal and paternal correlations were similar and significant and did not differ statistically. The F_2 maternal values also did not differ significantly from those of F_1 fathers. Of particular importance, these correlations were independent of colony parity. The same generational correlation patterns for F_1 and F_2 parents were found for their first, second, and third birth order offspring. Thus,

Table 3.

PEARSON CORRELATIONS FOR PARENT AND OFFSPRING BIRTH WEIGHTS
BY GENERATION FOR CAPTIVE PIGTAILED MACAQUES

| Offspring | F_1 parents | | F_2 parents | |
	Mother	Father	Mother	Father
Daughter	.142	.307**	.295**	.302**
Son	.179*	.296**	.263**	.271**

$*p < .05.$ $**p < .01.$

life experiences of the grandmothers appear to have affected the genetic expression of prenatal factors over the entire reproductive life of their female offspring.

Normative values of birth weight and age at menarche are important indexes of organismic processes determining maturation rate. Within a generation, extremes in these values often reflect high risk for developmental abnormalities and susceptibility to disease (Emanuel, 1986; Friedman & Sigman, 1980). The birth weight and menarche age data presented here suggest that intergenerational effects, probably of nongenetic origin, can influence these basic organismic processes. The birth weight correlation patterns provide more direct evidence that life experiences of a prior generation can influence the balance between genetic and environmental control of organismic processes in a subsequent generation.

In human developmental research, a lack of attention to real nongenetic intergenerational effects could appear in data as noise, inflating statistical error. This would greatly lower the statistical power to detect organism–environment interactions. More important, lack of attention to this source of temporal variation as an influence on organismic processes can have at least two other consequences. First, familial traits appearing across several generations might be accepted as evidence for genetic control, when in fact the transgenerational concordance could result from grandparental environmental experiences. It might be speculated that most, if not all, social class correlations with many aspects of human development are induced and maintained by such nongenetic sources. Second, as suggested by the birth weight correlations described here, nongenetic intergenerational effects can lower estimates of genetic variance, perhaps even to zero. This reduces the chances of detecting organism–environment interactions involving genetic differences in samples from a single generation.

PATERNAL EFFECTS AND PRENATAL STRESS

My interest in organism–environment interaction was stimulated by 15 years of work with macaque monkeys while I was studying the effects of varied rearing experiences on development. Researchers in this field had concluded that rhesus monkey infants reared without social experiences uniformly developed an isolation syndrome (e.g., Harlow & Harlow, 1965). This consists of self-directed and stereotyped behaviors, intense fear of novel objects, little or no species-typical social behavior, and abnormal sexual and maternal behavior. However, I found that the effects of social deprivation were not so straightforward (Sackett, 1982).

Rearing and follow-up studies showed that the quality and quantity of the rhesus isolation syndrome interacted with sex. Females were much less severely affected than males. Other work showed that different macaque species did not develop all aspects of the rhesus syndrome and recovered species-typical social and individual behavior later in life without any special therapy. Thus, the quality and persistence of rearing condition effects interacted with both sex and species.

These interactions showed that rearing effects varied by genotype. The sex effects also suggested prenatal involvement, as this is the period of primary sex differentiation in physiology and anatomy. To understand these interactions, an experimental model was required that would allow manipulation of genetic and prenatal factors along with rearing conditions.

In human studies, poor pregnancy outcomes involving low birth weight and prematurity are major risk factors for a number of developmental problems (Friedman & Sigman, 1980). Psychosocial stress during pregnancy is a risk factor believed to contribute to the incidence of poor pregnancy outcomes and to increase the chances of poor developmental outcomes (Field, Sostek, Goldberg, & Shuman, 1979). In our primate nursery we had observed that low birth weight monkeys exhibited a number of developmental problems similar to those found in humans (Sackett, 1984). These included poor development of sleep–wake diurnal cycles, retarded growth and social development, and poor performance on recognition memory and delayed response tests.

This background led to the idea that monkey breeders that produce excessive poor reproductive outcomes will have surviving offspring that are at risk for developmental problems. Furthermore, when coupled with prenatal stress, offspring of such parents might be particularly vulnerable to the effects of poor rearing environments. On the basis of these ideas, the studies described next were designed to develop a genetic–prenatal model for the future study of interactions with varied rearing environments. The work tested the hypotheses that (a) both maternal and paternal factors would contribute to poor pregnancy outcomes, (b) maternal and paternal factors would interact in affecting growth and behavioral development rates, and (c) prenatal stress would have its greatest effects on offspring of parents at high risk for poor pregnancy outcomes.

These hypotheses were studied in a 12-year selective breeding project. Colony computer records were used to identify female and male pigtailed macaque breeders at high and low risk for poor reproductive outcomes. These outcomes included fetal loss due to spontaneous abortion or stillbirth, an excess of low birth weight offspring, or both (Sackett, 1980). Colony norms for fetal loss were 21%. The 55 identified high-risk females averaged 5.5 prior pregnancies and as a group produced over 70% fetal losses. Forty-seven low-risk females had only 6% fetal losses in their reproductive histories. Five high-risk males, which averaged 35 prior conceptions with a random set of females, had a 65% fetal loss rate among their conceptuses. Seven low-risk males, chosen from those with the best reproductive records, had only 12% fetal losses.

These high- and low-risk monkeys were bred within and between risk groups (Sackett, 1990). Although their reproductive histories had been achieved while they bred in harem groups of 6–10 females and 1 male, on this project animals were singly caged and time-mated to produce offspring of known gestational ages.

Table 4.

FETAL LOSS BY SELECTIVELY BRED PIGTAIL MACAQUE DAMS: EFFECTS
OF SIRES AND PRENATAL STRESS

Stress level	Low-risk sires		High-risk sires	
	% Fetal loss	n	% Fetal loss	n
Low-risk dams[a]				
Low	10.3	62	37.5	24
High	25.8	31	74.0	25
High-risk dams[b]				
Low	20.5	39	51.5	64
High	21.7	23	44.4	33

Note. n = number of conceptions.
[a]n = 47; expected fetal loss = 6.2%.
[b]n = 55; expected fetal loss = 72.6%.

Timed mating was done by placing the female with a male for 24–48 hours on
the estimated day of ovulation.

About 40% of the 301 project pregnancies were conducted under a high
prenatal stress condition. Stressed females lived in a specific room during pregnancy. The stress procedure was begun at 30 gestational days and lasted until 130
days of the 170-day gestation period. Three times each day a handler entered the
room and captured a randomly selected female. The female was returned to her
living cage after brief confinement in a laboratory transport cage. Females became
highly excited when the handler entered and usually struggled during capture.
Few animals adapted to the procedure. Nonstressed pregnancies involved capture
only once for a blood draw at 110 gestational days.

Pregnancy Outcomes

Table 4 shows fetal losses during selective breeding. Low-risk females (those
under low stress with low-risk males), did not differ significantly from their prior
6.2% harem group rate. Fetal loss was more than doubled under high stress with
this mating combination ($p < .05$). When mated to high-risk males, low-risk
females tripled their loss rates over those with low-risk males under low stress
($p < .001$). When stress was coupled with mating to a high-risk male, low-risk
females experienced 74% fetal losses ($p < .01$). For high-risk females, fetal losses
were high when they were mated to high-risk males, although the rate was somewhat lower than that attained in harem groups ($p < .05$). When mated to low-
risk males, their loss rate was more than halved ($p < .001$). Surprisingly, high-

risk females were unaffected by stress when mated to either type of male (both $ps > .50$).

These results suggest two conclusions: (a) Prenatal stress had detrimental effects only on females with excellent reproductive histories, but these effects were strongest when low-risk females were mated with high-risk males. Thus, the effects of stress appeared only in interaction with maternal and paternal risk. This underscores the complexity of effects associated with these variables. Although it is not yet known why stress affected only low-risk females, one speculation is that factors producing poor outcomes in high-risk females are already so strong that stress cannot push this ceiling any higher. A second speculation is that high-risk males affect the low-risk females through a mechanism involving immune incompatibility. This incompatibility is then potentiated by prenatal stress, resulting in a very high rate of fetal loss. (b) The poor pregnancy outcomes of this study were primarily determined by paternal risk, which was the only statistically significant logistic regression main effect among the variables of maternal risk ($p > .15$), paternal risk ($p < .001$), and stress ($p > .45$).

Unfortunately, the actual mechanisms producing these paternal effects are not yet known. Sperm and gross chromosomal abnormalities have not been found, nor were bacterial or viral infection agents discovered in high-risk male semen. A possible genetic involvement for males and females is under study in an intergenerational project. This work is assessing reproductive outcomes among surviving offspring of these high- and low-risk males and measuring postnatal development of their grandchildren. Like the rat prenatal handling effect just described, in this study prenatal stress to grandmothers may also identify a nongenetic intergenerational effect in primates. It would be especially interesting in terms of organism–environment relationships if this stress effect interacts with the reproductive risk of the grandparents. In principle, such effects could be studied epidemiologically in humans. In fact, however, relevant data are available only for mothers and grandmothers because paternal pregnancy outcome data are rarely collected.

Unlike the case for males, biological differences between high- and low-risk females have been discovered. Rat embryos were cultured from Gestation Days 9.5–11.5 in media containing blood serum from high- and low-risk female monkeys (Klein et al., 1982). Over 85% of embryos cultured with low-risk female blood developed normally. Over 80% of embryos cultured with high-risk female blood developed poorly, with more than 50% exhibiting severe morphological abnormalities.

Subsequent studies have identified a number of molecular factors in the blood of individual high-risk females that produce these rat embryo effects (Carey et al., 1983). Some of these factors are immunological, whereas others involve deficits or excesses in nutritional elements. The most interesting result concerns high antibody titers to the protein laminin, which was found in the blood of 2 high-risk females. Laminin is essential for the development of liver and kidney basement membranes and also participates in neuronal migration during formation of the brain. Laminin antibodies are a known natural abortifacient in women and were shown experimentally to be an abortifacient in pigtailed monkeys (Weeks, Klein, Kleinman, Fredrickson, & Sackett, 1989). This work has led to the hypothesis that antibodies to basic proteins may be a factor producing variation in fetal development and subsequent individual differences in postnatal development. This idea is being pursued in current studies.

The data reviewed earlier lead to two conclusions. The first is that nongenetic intergenerational and paternal effects can be important sources of variation in the developmental organization of prenatal biological processes. Second, in terms of studying organism–environment interaction, these results also suggest that prenatal maternal stress affects fetuses only under complex interactions of maternal, paternal, and environmental factors. The questions addressed next concern main effect and interaction relationships of these variables to postnatal development.

Postnatal Development

Offspring in the selective breeding project were separated from their mothers at birth and reared in a nursery. A broad range of postnatal growth and behavior parameters were measured (Infant Primate Research Laboratory, 1987). Three of these—dental development, learning set formation, and perseverative behavior— are summarized here.

Dental Development

Figure 1 shows the tooth eruption ages for offspring having both parents at high or at low risk. This simple, single variable research design is common in many human developmental risk studies (e.g., Friedman & Sigman, 1980). Each of the five deciduous tooth types had a significantly delayed eruption date for high-risk offspring, which suggests a simple main effect for risk. However, the developmental complexity of this relatively simple dentition system is illustrated by the data from all breeding combinations shown in Figure 2.

For the central incisor, a significant Mating Type (within vs. between risk) × Dam's Risk interaction revealed delayed eruption only when both the mother and father were high risk. The lateral incisor was significantly delayed when the mother was high risk, regardless of paternal risk. The canine was unaffected by these variables, whereas the first molar showed a high-risk maternal delay that just failed to reach statistical significance. The latest appearing and most variable second molar was also affected by a Mating Type × Dam's Risk interaction. However, delayed eruption occurred only when the father was high risk, regardless of maternal risk. Prenatal stress main effects and interactions were not significant for any teeth.

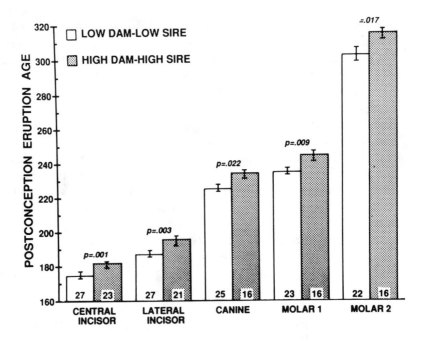

Figure 1.   Tooth eruption ages for offspring of within-risk mating. (Numbers in the bars give sample sizes.)

These results may serve as a model for ways in which one can expect many variables to interact temporally in their influence on development. With respect to the dental eruption measures studied here, it appears that maternal and paternal factors can operate both independently and in interaction. How they operate depends on the specific temporal state of the developing tooth system. More generally, as a model of potential developmental outcomes, these results suggest that at different times in the development of a system, the same variables may combine in different ways. Sometimes they exhibit only main effects; at other times they may interact. However, the direction of the interaction can be reversed at different periods of development. It seems clear that a simple two-group research design, such as the one shown in Figure 1, cannot identify such complex temporal interaction effects. As I discuss next, a similar degree of complexity can be identified for behavioral systems.

Learning Set Formation

A series of learning tests in the Wisconsin General Test Apparatus (Harlow, 1959) was begun at 5 months postnatal. The series ended with 240 six-trial discrimination learning set problems. Each problem involved two unique three-dimensional objects, with one randomly selected to indicate the location of food reward. The

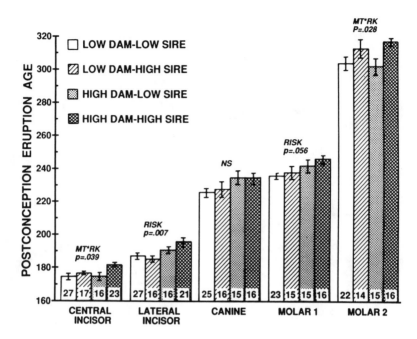

Figure 2.   Tooth eruption ages for offspring of within- and between-risk mating. (Numbers in the bars give sample sizes.)

subject received the reward by pushing the correct object away from a depression on the testing board. Displacing the incorrect object produced no reward and ended a trial. On Trial 1 of each problem, a subject has no clue to the correct object. In principle, a subject that displaces the correct object on Trial 1 should continue to choose that object on subsequent trials. A subject that displaces the incorrect object on Trial 1 should switch to the other object on subsequent trials. Acquiring this win–stay:lose–shift learning set concept can eventually lead to 100% correct responding on Trial 2.

Figure 3 shows the percentage of Trial 2 correct responses for each parental risk group, summarized in 30-problem blocks. Prenatal stress had no significant main or interaction effects on this task. The major finding was a significant Mating Type $\times$ Dam's Risk $\times$ Trial Block interaction ($p < .001$). Overall, infants with two high-risk parents were poorest in acquiring the learning set strategy. The other three groups performed similarly on the first 180 problems.

On the final 60 problems, infants with a low-risk mother and a high-risk father dropped to the low correct response level of those with two high-risk parents. Considering only these final problems, paternal risk was the sole determinant of poor performance, as offspring of low-risk fathers were clearly superior to those of high-risk fathers regardless of maternal risk. However, the pattern of poor

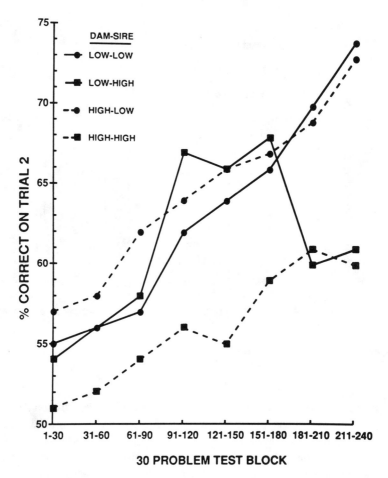

Figure 3.   Learning set formation by parental reproductive risk condition.

terminal responding after initial gradual improvement suggested that performance processes of infants with a low-risk mother and a high-risk father differed from that of the other groups. This was supported by analyses of response latencies and balks.

A pattern of increased latency and balks indicated a lack of motivation to perform on this task. Latencies to displace the stimulus object were measured for correct and incorrect trials. Balks, defined as trials terminated when a subject failed to displace an object within 60 seconds, were also measured. Balked trials were not included in analyzing latencies.

None of the groups differed in latency over the first 180 problems. On Block 6, the overall mean latencies were 1.1 and 1.5 seconds on correct and incorrect trials, respectively. On the last 2 blocks, the low-risk mother–high-risk father latencies were 7.4 and 7.1 seconds, respectively. These were both significantly longer than the 1.0- and 1.5-second overall mean latencies for the other groups on Blocks 7 and 8 ($p < .0001$), respectively. Similarly, the mean number of balks was less than 1 per block over the first 6 blocks for all four groups. On the last 2 blocks, offspring of low-risk mothers and high-risk fathers average 5.7 balks per 30 problems, values significantly greater than the overall average of 0.6 for the other groups ($p < .001$).

These patterns of correct responding, latencies, and balks suggest the following interpretations of the learning set results: (a) Having two high-risk parents produced offspring that were deficient in acquiring a discrimination learning set. However, as indicated by their short latencies and low balk level, they were not deficient in motivation to perform the task. (b) Having at least one low-risk parent of either sex offset this learning deficit. (c) The unique combination of a low-risk mother and a high-risk father yielded offspring that differed from the other groups in motivation to perform the task after initially adequate response acquisition.

Like the dental eruption system, maternal and paternal risk combined in a complex interaction to differentially affect a cognitive ability and the motivation to perform a partially acquired response strategy. These complex interactions were not expected. Rather, it was expected that any main effect or interaction would similarly affect all teeth and would operate uniformly over the course of a concept learning task. In both systems, complexity was introduced by effects apparent only at different temporal points in the acquisition process. Thus, having a high-risk father affected dental eruption and learning performance differently toward the end of the measurement period than it did earlier in the process. An implication of these results for methodology is that measures need to be taken across a sufficiently wide temporal range in order to test all possible ways in which specific variables may or may not interact.

Perseverative Behavior

The ability or willingness to change responses that are no longer appropriate for current environmental circumstances is an important behavioral attribute (e.g., Luchins, 1942). The Hamilton Search Test (Harlow, 1951) was used to study perseverative responding by 4-month-old project offspring. The apparatus consisted of a linear array of four small boxes with hinged lids. During adaptation, subjects learned to lift a box lid to retrieve a food reward after watching an experimenter bait the box.

The first 5 test days involved *set formation*. On each of 25 daily trials, a randomly chosen box was baited with a food reward out of the subject's sight. The boxes were then presented and the subject was allowed to open and reopen them until it discovered the reward. Any optimal strategy of opening a given box only once per trial will result in an average of 2.5 lid openings to find the reward. Over days, subjects developed search patterns that approached optimal strategies (see Figure 4, upper panel). Set formation was followed by 5 days of *set breaking*. The subject's least preferred first choice box was baited on every trial. The reward could now be obtained by opening only a single box if the previously developed search pattern was broken. Subjects were allowed to open and reopen all boxes during this phase. Testing ended with 5 days of *forced set breaking*. Again, the nonpreferred box was always baited. However, only a single choice was allowed on each trial.

Unlike dental eruption and learning set, which revealed complex interactions of maternal and paternal risk, prenatal maternal stress significantly affected perseveration (see Figure 4), whereas reproductive risk had neither main nor interactive effects. Although stress did not affect set formation (see Figure 4, upper panel), only low-stress offspring showed evidence of set breaking (see Figure 4, middle panel). On forced set breaking (see Figure 4, lower panel), low-stress subjects did not perseverate, making over 70% correct responses by Day 5. High-stress infants perseverated, showing no evidence of any set breaking behavior.

These results are important for several reasons. First, they suggest that different developmental systems may not be affected in the same way by parental and prenatal variables. Thus, stress did not influence dental eruption or concept learning, and parental factors did not affect perseverative responding. Such results also suggest that these systems may be relatively independent in their development. Second, these results reinforce the idea that studies may require multiple measures in order to assess the full extent of main effects and interactions on developmental processes.

CONCLUSIONS

The results summarized here suggest that understanding organism–environment effects on development involves more than obtaining a statistically significant interaction. Development involves temporal processes, some expressed in simple main effects (e.g., stress on perseveration), others in complex interactions (e.g., reproductive risk on dental eruption and learning set acquisition, colony generation on parent–offspring birthweight correlations). These processes produce an organization that *is* the biological organism *and* its modes of responding to the environment. Variables that influence aspects of this organization earlier in development may cease to do so later. Conversely, variables that do not have measurable early influences may reveal later delayed effects. This implies that methodology aimed at discovering how organismic effects interact with environments must span the full temporal developmental range of the organismic processes under study.

Results of this study show that organismic processes can be affected temporally even before the conception of the individual by nongenetic intergenerational factors. Subsequent prenatal influences can involve more than the mother, placenta, poisons, or psychosocial stressors. They can also involve active partic-

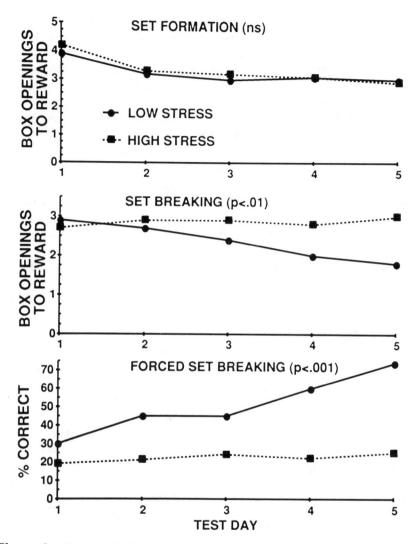

Figure 4. Perseverative behavior by maternal prenatal stress condition.

ipation by paternal biological factors of unknown genetic or nongenetic origin. As illustrated by these results, specific factors influencing development may do so at different times, with different directions of effect, and in different combinations depending on the temporal period under study.

Such changes in the main or interactive effects of organic and environmental variables at different maturational states are perhaps the most fundamental interactions in behavioral development. The study of these temporal interactions involving changed effect sizes and directions should be a major goal in developmental research. This goal involves describing the complete temporal organization of a developing behavioral system and its organismic bases, perhaps to the ultimate endpoint of death.

Human developmental psychology, with its contemporary interest in life span development, has worked toward this goal with respect to genetic and post-natal variables. Some animal research and research on human developmental risk factors has studied relationships among prenatal organismic processes, prenatal environmental effects, and postnatal behavior (e.g., Gottlieb, 1973; Smotherman & Robinson, 1988). However, nongenetic intergenerational variables have been almost completely neglected as potential temporal influences on human development. This may be due in part to having few human longitudinal studies measuring organismic variables influencing behavior. Another reason may be the lack of any influential developmental theory including this source of variation. Finally, a long generation time mitigates against attempting human transgenerational developmental studies. This suggests that animal model research may be required to develop theories about nongenetic intergenerational effects that can be tested in humans.

Gottlieb (1976, 1983) described a set of concepts and methods aimed at putting these temporal pieces together in experiments. His ideas concerned identifying the ways that experience and biology can interact to affect behavior during different temporal stages of a developmental process. As such, his views are one way of operationalizing the ideas concerning temporal effects expressed in this chapter.

Gottlieb proposed that developmental processes are under three sets of general influences: induction, facilitation, and maintenance. Induction concerns the organismic and experiential events that are necessary for a behavior to appear during development. These might involve main effects or interactions among variables determining the specific time at which a behavior is induced. Facilitation involves organismic and environmental factors regulating the rate of change in a behavior and achievement of typical or deviant endpoints. Maintenance concerns the factors necessary to preserve a developed behavior at its endpoint. Although it is not possible to go into the details of Gottlieb's ideas here, the implication of his approach for the ideas about temporal interactions presented in this chapter seems clear.

A temporal, and therefore developmental, analysis involves first specifying the organismic and environmental main effects and interactions responsible for induction. The next steps involve determining whether and how induction variables and new influences affect facilitation and maintenance. Clearly, with the exception of sexual differentiation (e.g., Hofer, 1981), induction processes in human behavior are essentially unknown. Thus, the primal source of potential organism–environment interaction, factors causing induction, is missing information for most human behavior development processes. Furthermore, studies of facilitation and maintenance in human development have involved mainly genetic and post-natal variables. The main conclusion of this chapter is that a more complete developmental analysis is needed that attends to potential nongenetic intergenerational and prenatal influences. Expanding a temporal view to include effects from these sources of variation on the induction, facilitation, and maintenance of developmental processes may open a new window for identifying important organism–environment interactions.

References

Bresler, D. E., Ellison, G., & Zamenhof, S. (1975). Learning deficits in rats with malnourished grandmothers. *Developmental Psychobiology*, *8*, 315–323.

Carey, S. W., Klein, N. W., Fredrickson, W. T., Sackett, G. P., Greenstein, R. M., & Sehgal, P. (1983). Analysis of sera from monkeys with histories of fetal wastage and the identification of teratogenicity in sera from human chronic spontaneous aborters using rat embryo cultures. *Trophoblast Research*, *1*, 347–360.

Cavalli-Sforza, L. L., Feldman, M. W., Chen, K. H., & Dornbusch, S. M. (1982). Theory and observation in cultural transmission. *Science*, *218*, 19–27.

Denenberg, V. H., & Rosenberg, K. M. (1967). Nongenetic transmission of information. *Nature*, *216*, 549–550.

Denenberg, V. H., & Whimbey, A. E. (1963). Behavior of adult rats is modified by the experiences their mothers had as infants. *Science*, *142*, 1192–1193.

Denenberg, V. H., & Zarrow, M. X. (1971). Effects of handling in infancy upon adult behavior and adrenocortical activity: Suggestions for a neurochemical mechanism. In D. H. Walcher & D. L. Peters (Eds.), *Development of self-regulatory mechanisms* (pp. 39–71). New York: Academic Press.

Emanuel, I. (1986). Maternal health during childhood and later reproductive performance. *Annals of the New York Academy of Science*, *477*, 27–39.

Field, T. M., Sostek, A., Goldberg, S., & Shuman, H. H. (Eds.). (1979). *Infants born at risk*. New York: Spectrum Publications.

Friedman, S., & Sigman, M. (Eds.). (1980). *Pre-term and post-term birth: Relevance to optimal psychological development*. San Diego, CA: Academic Press.

Gottlieb, G. (Ed.). (1973). *Studies on the development of behavior and the nervous system: Vol. 1. Behavioral embryology*. San Diego, CA: Academic Press.

Gottlieb, G. (1976). The role of experience in the development of behavior and the nervous system. In G. Gottlieb (Ed.), *Studies on the development of behavior and the nervous system: Vol. 3. Neural and behavioral specificity* (pp. 25–54). San Diego, CA: Academic Press.

Gottlieb, G. (1983). The psychobiological approach to developmental issues. In P. Mussen (Ed.), *Handbook of developmental psychology* (Vol. 2, pp. 1–26). New York: Wiley.

Gunderson, V., & Sackett, G. (1982). Paternal effects on reproductive outcome and developmental risk. In M. E. Lamb & A. L. Brown (Eds.), *Advances in developmental psychology* (pp. 85–124). Hillsdale, NJ: Erlbaum.

Harlow, H. F. (1951). Primate learning. In C. P. Stone (Ed.), *Comparative psychology* (3rd ed., pp. 101–128). New York: Prentice-Hall.

Harlow, H. F. (1959). The development of learning in the rhesus monkey. *American Scientist*, *47*, 459–479.

Harlow, H. F., & Harlow, M. K. (1965). The affectional systems. In A. M. Schrier, H. F. Harlow, & F. Stollnitz (Eds.), *The behavior of nonhuman primates* (Vol. 1, pp. 287–334). San Diego, CA: Academic Press.

Hofer, M. A. (1981). *The roots of human behavior.* New York: Freeman.

Infant Primate Research Laboratory. (1987). *Research protocols.* Seattle: University of Washington, Regional Primate Research Center.

Insel, P. (1972). The grandmother effect in personality. *New Science, 53,* 132–134.

Klein, N. W., Plenefisch, J. D., Carey, S. W., Fredrickson, W. T., Sackett, G. P., Burbacher, T. M., & Parker, R. M. (1982). Serum from monkeys with histories of fetal wastage causes abnormalities in cultured rat embryos. *Science, 215,* 66–69.

Luchins, A. S. (1942). Mechanization in problem solving: The effect of *Einstellung. Psychological Monographs, 54*(Whole No. 48).

Mansfield, P. K., & Cohn, M. D. (1986). Stress and later-life child bearing: Important implications for nursing. *Maternal-Child Nursing Journal, 15,* 139–151.

Molfese, V. J., Bricker, M. C., Manion, L., & Yaple, K. (1987). The influence of psychological and social mediators in perinatal experiences. *Journal of Psychosomatic Obstetrics and Gynaecology, 6,* 33–42.

Porter, I. H., & Hook, E. B. (Eds.). (1980). *Human embryonic and fetal death.* San Diego, CA: Academic Press.

Sackett, G. P. (1980). A nonhuman primate model for studying causes and effects of poor pregnancy outcome. In S. Friedman & M. Sigman (Eds.), *Pre-term and post-term birth: Relevance to optimal psychological development* (pp. 41–63). San Diego, CA: Academic Press.

Sackett, G. P. (1982). Can single processes explain effects of postnatal influences on primate development? In R. N. Emde & R. J. Harmon (Eds.), *The development of attachment and affiliative systems* (pp. 3–12). New York: Plenum Press.

Sackett, G. P. (1984). A nonhuman primate model of risk for deviant development. *American Journal of Mental Deficiency, 88,* 469–476.

Sackett, G. P. (1990). Sires influence fetal death in pigtailed macaques (*Macaca nemestrina*). *American Journal of Primatology, 20,* 13–22.

Smotherman, W. P., & Robinson, S. R. (Eds.). (1988). *Behavior of the fetus.* Caldwell, NJ: Telford Press.

Vorhees, C. V., & Mollnow, E. (1987). Behavioral teratogenesis: Long-term influences on behavior from early exposure to environmental agents. In J. D. Osofsky (Ed.), *Handbook of infant development* (2nd ed., pp. 913–971). New York: Wiley.

Weeks, B. S., Klein, N. W., Kleinman, H., Fredrickson, W. T., & Sackett, G. P. (1989). Laminin immunized monkeys develop sera toxic to cultured rat embryos and fail to reproduce. *Teratology, 40,* 47–57.

Wehmer, F., Porter, R. H., & Scales, B. (1970). Premating and pregnancy stress in rats affects behavior of grandpups. *Nature, 227,* 622.

Zamenhof, S., & van Marthens, E. (1978). Nutritional influences on prenatal brain development. In G. Gottlieb (Ed.), *Studies on the development of behavior and the nervous system: Vol. 4. Early influences* (pp. 149–186). San Diego, CA: Academic Press.

Zamenhof, S., van Marthens, E., & Grauel, L. (1971). DNA (cell number) in neonatal brain: Second generation (F_2) alteration by maternal (F_0) dietary protein restriction. *Science, 172,* 850–851.

CHAPTER 3

GENOTYPE–ENVIRONMENT INTERACTION

ROBERT PLOMIN AND SCOTT HERSHBERGER

Behavioral geneticists have traditionally been interested in documenting the contribution of genetics to individual differences—in animal behavior through the use of inbred strains and selection studies and in human behavior through the use of twin and adoption studies (Plomin, DeFries, & McClearn, 1990). Such studies have made a case, increasingly accepted in the social and behavioral sciences, for nearly ubiquitous genetic main effects on behavioral variability. Indeed, the tide has shifted so dramatically during the past decade that it is now becoming important to emphasize that these same studies indicate that behavioral variability is by no means entirely genetic in origin, that is, genetic influence seldom accounts for as much as half of the variance.

As the field of behavioral genetics matures, it will move beyond such "main effects" questions to consider the interface between nature and nurture, especially

Support for the Colorado Adoption Project (J. C. DeFries, D. W. Fulker, and R. Plomin, co-investigators) was provided by the National Institutes of Health (grants HD10333, HD18426, and MH43899) and the National Science Foundation (grant BNS8806589). Research support for the Swedish Adoption/Twin Study of Aging (G. E. McClearn, J. R. Nesselroade, N. Pedersen, and R. Plomin, co-investigators) was provided by the National Institutes of Health (grant AG04563) and the MacArthur Foundation Research Network on Successful Aging. Preparation of this chapter was supported by the Non-Shared Environment Project (D. Reiss, E. M. Hetherington, and R. Plomin, co-investigators; grant MH87513).

We gratefully acknowledge the helpful suggestions of Ted Wachs and Lee Cronbach, as well as discussions with other participants at the American Psychological Association's workshop on the conceptualization and measurement of organism–environment interaction.

as they transact during development. In quantitative genetics, the theory of multiple genetic and environmental influences that has been applied to the study of behavior, two concepts are especially relevant to this interface: genotype–environment (G × E) interaction and genotype–environment correlation. These concepts are analogous to the distinction between interaction and correlations in the study of organism–environment interaction (see chap. 1). As is the case for other quantitative genetic parameters, G × E and genotype–environment correlation refer to "anonymous" components of variance of measured outcomes in the population rather than to interactions and correlations between specific genes and environmental factors or to the processes by which genetic influence emerges for an outcome measure. G × E denotes phenotypic (observed) variance that is attributable to the statistical interaction between genotypes and environments. Genotype–environment correlation, which literally refers to covariance between genetic and environmental deviations, is often confused with G × E. Genotype–environment correlation occurs when individuals are exposed to environments on the basis of their genetic propensities (e.g., musically gifted children might be selected as gifted and given special opportunities that foster their talent). In contrast, G × E occurs when the effects of environment depend on genetic differences among individuals (e.g., the effect of musical training might be greater for musically gifted children). More progress has been made conceptually and empirically in understanding genotype–environment correlation than G × E (Hershberger, 1991; Plomin, 1986). For example, three heuristically useful categories of processes leading to genotype–environment correlation have been identified: passive, reactive, and active (Plomin, DeFries, & Loehlin, 1977). However, no such categorization of G × E mechanisms has yet been proposed. Empirically, genotype–environment correlation, at least the passive variety, can be easily encompassed by standard model-fitting enterprises; G × E does not fit so neatly. Despite the greater understanding of genotype–environment correlation, the topic of this book and length restrictions dictate that our chapter be limited to G × E.

There are many ways to construe coaction of predictor variables as they relate to an outcome variable, only some of which can be detected as statistical interactions (Rutter, 1983). Rather than attempting to address all forms of coaction between genotypes and environments, we focus on the limited but testable type of interaction that describes a conditional relationship in which the behavioral effect of environment depends on genotype. Although other concepts of interaction are interesting and important, a focus restricted to such statistical interactions by no means reduces G × E to an easily solved problem, as this chapter attests. We describe quantitative genetic concepts and methods used to assess G × E, difficulties in finding G × E, and ways in which the search for G × E might be improved.

CONCEPTS OF G × E AND METHODS TO DETECT IT

An initial clarification concerning "interactionism" may still be necessary. A frequently cited discussion of the interface between heredity and environment asserted that the "organism is a product of its genes and its past environment" (Anastasi, 1958, p. 197). The point was that there could be no behavior without both environment and genes. Although no one would deny this truism, it does not mean that researchers cannot study the effects of environment or of heredity. Quantitative genetics does not apply to *an* organism or to *the* organism; rather, its focus is on variance, differences among individual organisms in a population. Even though there can be no behavior without both genes and environment, researchers can study the relative contributions of genes or environment to individual differences in a population for a particular behavior. Environmental differences can occur when genetic differences do not exist (e.g., differences observed between members of an identical twin pair). In addition, genetic differences can be expressed in the absence of environmental differences (e.g., differences observed between inbred strains of mice reared in the same controlled laboratory environment). Heritability is a statistic that describes the proportion of phenotypic variance in a particular population that can be ascribed to genetic variance among individuals in the population. If genetic or environmental sources of variance differ across populations or change in a population across time, the relative magnitude of genetic influence can change, as can other descriptive statistics such as means or variances. Although quantitative genetic parameter estimates are specific to a particular sample and by no means refer to all possible combinations of genotypes and environments, it is a reasonable first step toward understanding the origins of individual differences to study the combinations of genotypes and environments that exist in a representative sample. As discussed later, one way of viewing G × E is in terms of changes in heritability as a function of environment.

Since its inception in the early part of this century, quantitative genetic theory has considered interactions between genes in addition to additive effects of genes (Falconer, 1981; Fisher, 1918). G × E has not been given nearly as much attention as has interactions among genes. The goal of quantitative genetics is to decompose phenotypic (observed) variance into genetic and environmental components of variance, and G × E is important in this context because it adds to phenotypic variance beyond the variance contributed by the main effects of genotype and environment. This added variance cannot be attributed either to genetics or to environment because it is due to joint effects of genes and environment, although G × E has traditionally been viewed in the field of quantitative genetics as environmental variance (Falconer, 1981). However, the effect of G × E on heritability estimates depends on the design. For example, in the classical twin design that compares identical and fraternal twins, G × E could be read as genetic variance in certain circumstances (Lathrop, Lalouel, & Jacquard, 1984; Plomin et al., 1977). Another issue is that variance due to G × E has often been removed by transformation of the data (Mather & Jinks, 1982), although the counterargument is that "a change of scale is a change of trait" (Eaves, Last, Martin, & Jinks, 1977, p. 4).

The relative lack of interest in G × E might in part be due to difficulties in estimating the overall contribution of G × E to total variance in a population (see Plomin, 1986). Nonetheless, it is possible to investigate specific interactions between genotypes and environments, and this is more interesting to students of organism–environment interaction. For example, the classic design in research on nonhuman animals studies different genotypes—inbred strains or selected lines—reared in different environments. Rearing different strains in different environments permits direct tests of genetic effects, environmental effects, and G × E. The best known example is the study by Cooper and Zubek (1958), in which rats selectively bred for good or poor maze performance were reared in normal, impoverished, or enriched conditions. This approach was used with greater rigor in a series of studies by Henderson (1967, 1970, 1972), who systematically explored G × E interaction by rearing mice from six inbred strains and their hybrid crosses in impoverished or enriched conditions.

The search for G × E interaction can be conceptualized schematically as a 2 × 2 factorial arrangement in which one variable is the genotype and the other is the environment. For any dependent variable, the design can be used to investigate the effect of genotype independent of the environment, the effect of the environment independent of genotype, and G × E. Using the Cooper and Zubek (1958) study as an example, main effects as well as interactions were reported. The "maze-bright" rats performed much better than the "maze-dull" rats in the normal laboratory environment, which is not surprising because this is the environment in which the rats were reared during the course of the 21-generation selective breeding study. Similarly, it is not surprising that rearing in a deprived environment resulted in poorer maze performance on average. The interesting finding is that the deprivation condition had no effect on the already poorly performing maze-dull rats, but deprivation was extremely detrimental to the performance of the maze-bright rats. Conversely, an enriched rearing condition did not enhance the performance of the maze-bright rats, but it substantially improved the performance of the maze-dull animals. What, then, is the effect of deprivation on maze-running ability in rats? It depends on genetic factors. Because interactions are joint effects, it is equally appropriate to think about such interactions as showing that the effect of genetic factors depends on the environment.

Another way of thinking about G × E is that the magnitude of genetic effects (heritability) differs as a function of environment. For example, the Cooper and Zubek (1958) interaction indicates that genetic effects for maze-running performance are substantial in the normal laboratory environment, that is, maze-bright animals perform much better than maze-dull animals. However, genetic effects are negligible in the deprived and enriched environments in the sense that the performances of maze-bright and maze-dull animals do not differ. (It should be kept in mind that these rats were selected for maze performance in a normal environment.)

In this way, differences in heritability as a function of environment indicate the presence of G × E. However, important information is overlooked if the magnitude of genetic effects alone is considered rather than the specifics of interaction. For example, heritabilities can be the same in two environments, but G × E interaction may be important. In the Cooper and Zubek (1958) example, heritability is negligible for both the enriched and deprived conditions, but there is an important interaction: The deprived environment is detrimental to the performance of the maze-bright rats but does not affect the maze-dull rats, whereas the converse is true for the enriched rearing environment. Moreover, even when heritabilities are found to differ for two environments, the nature of the interaction is not illuminated if all ones knows is that heritability differs. For example, heritability of maze-running performance is high in the normal environments and low in both the deprived and enriched rearing conditions. This suggests G × E for both deprived and enriched rearing as compared with normal rearing; however, from this conclusion one would not know that the nature of the G × E is very different for the two conditions. This distinction between G × E and heritabilities that differ in different environments is useful because the few attempts to introduce G × E in model-fitting analyses of human behavior have been limited to attempts to show that heritability differs in different environments. For example, a recent study has suggested that the heritability of alcohol consumption is greater for unmarried women than for married women (Heath, Jardine, & Martin, 1989).

In research with the human species, it is not possible to select genotypes as different as inbred strains of mice, nor is it possible to subject them to environments as extreme as those used in laboratory research on nonhuman animals. Human behavioral genetic researchers have the mixed blessing of working with naturally occurring genetic and environmental variation. The cost is a loss of experimental control; the benefit is an increased likelihood that the results of the research will generalize. A method for identifying G × E using the adoption design has been proposed by Plomin et al. (1977). The test is analogous to the method used in Strain × Treatment animal research. The genotype of adopted children can be estimated from phenotypic measures of their biological parents. Unlike selected lines or inbred strains known to differ genetically, in human research an indirect index of genotype must be used, a limitation to which we return later. The environment of the adopted children can be assessed using any measure of the adoptive home environment or any characteristic of their adoptive parents, although as emphasized in chapter 4 by Wachs, there are good reasons not to use just any measure of the environment. The first analysis of this sort was a reanalysis of data from the classic adoption study by Skodak and Skeels (1949) using education levels of the biological and adoptive parents as measures of genotype and environment, respectively, and IQ of the adopted children as the dependent variable (Plomin et al., 1977). The goal of the analysis was to look beyond the main effects of genotype (as indexed by biological parents' educational attainment as an indirect index of IQ) and environment (as indexed by adoptive parents' education) to ask whether these indexes of genotype and environment interact in their effect on children's IQ. For example, although it is pure speculation, if Cooper and Zubek's (1958) study of maze-bright and maze-dull rats were to generalize to human IQ, children whose biological parents have low IQ scores might be expected to profit from the enriched environment of highly educated adoptive parents to a greater extent than would children whose biological parents have high IQ scores.

Rather than dichotomizing continuous variables such as IQ or education of parents to conform to a 2×2 analysis of variance, continuous variables can be analyzed in a similar manner using stepwise multiple regression, which removes main effects of genotype and environment and then assesses their interaction. The interaction term is typically a variable created by the product of the main variables of genotype and environment, although other models of interaction could be used. References for additional discussion of $G \times E$ in human analyses include Eaves (1984); Eaves, Eysenck, and Martin (1989); Eaves et al. (1977); Jinks and Fulker (1970); Kendler and Eaves (1986); Lathrop et al. (1984); Vale (1980) and Wahlsten (1990).

PROBLEMS IN DETECTING G × E

The basic problem is that $G \times E$ is difficult to document using the quantitative genetic concepts and methods described in the previous section. Even Cooper and Zubek's (1958) results are questionable; for example, it is worrisome that "ceiling" and "floor" artifacts of measurement could have produced the same results. This would be an important study to replicate. Henderson's (1967, 1970, 1972) thorough series of investigations in this area using inbred strains of mice rather than selectively bred rats showed little evidence of $G \times E$ that replicated within or across studies. Nonetheless, some animal research suggests that environmental effects on behavior differ as a function of genotype (Erlenmeyer-Kimling, 1972; Fuller & Thompson, 1978; Mather & Jinks, 1982; Sackett, chap. 2 of this book).

It has been especially difficult to document $G \times E$ for human behavior. For example, the reanalysis of Skodak and Skeels's (1949) adoption data mentioned earlier yielded a strong main effect for education of biological parent, no significant effect for education of adoptive parent, and no $G \times E$ interaction between these variables as they affect adopted children's IQ scores. Systematic analyses of this type have been undertaken in the Colorado Adaption Project (CAP), a study of over 200 adoptive families and 200 matched nonadoptive families in which the parents (biological and adoptive parents of adopted children) were tested once and the adopted and nonadopted children and their home environments were assessed when the children were 1, 2, 3, and 4 years of age (Plomin, DeFries, & Fulker, 1988). However, hundreds of analyses involving various combinations of environmental measures and behavior measures yielded about as many statistically significant interactions as expected on the basis of chance alone. Analyses based on reared-apart identical twins in the Swedish Adoption/Twin Study of Aging (SATSA; Bergeman, Plomin, McClearn, Pedersen, & Friberg, 1988) have suggested more evidence for G × E than the CAP. In terms of G × E analyses, the CAP is limited in the power of its genetic estimates (first-degree relatives rather than identical twins) and in its use of children rather than adults. Other approaches, such as correlating pair sums and differences for identical twin pairs (Jinks & Fulker, 1970), have shown no greater success in identifying G × E. This approach is conceptually meaningful because it assesses the differential sensitivity of genotypes (indexed by pair sums for identical twins) to environmental differences (differences within pairs of identical twins); however, its reliance on difference scores within pairs of identical twins who are substantially correlated is likely to attenuate the correlation between pair sums and pair differences.

POSSIBILITIES FOR DETECTING G × E INTERACTION

Difficulties in finding interactions are not unique to quantitative genetic research. Indeed, the major impetus for the conference on organism–environment interaction, the forerunner of this book, was the difficulties experienced by researchers in many fields in identifying interactions. Many suggestions for improving the odds of finding interactions that emerged during the course of the conference will be useful in investigating G × E, as we discuss later. In this section, however, we emphasize those possibilities for improving the detection of interaction that are relatively more specific to the search for G × E. These include improving the conceptualization, measurement, and analysis of (a) organismic variables; (b) environmental variables; (c) moderator interaction variables; (d) outcome variables; and (e) combinations of environmental, organismic, outcome variables, and developmental stages most likely to show interactions.

The Organismic Variable: Genotypic Indexes

General issues concerning organismic variables most suited for interaction analyses are discussed elsewhere in this book (see, e.g., chapters 2 and 5). Obviously, organismic variables that do not show genetic influence cannot show G × E, but this scarcely narrows the field because most variables show genetic influence.

An issue specific to G × E is the adequacy of the indicator of genotype. Quantitative genetic analyses of G × E for insect and rodent behavior have the advantage of using inbred strains and selected strains as manipulations to produce contrasting genotypes. Even so, as mentioned earlier, consistent G × E has not been easy to demonstrate. One possibility is that more extreme differences in genotype might yield greater evidence for G × E (see also chapters 4, 5, and 6 in this book). Cooper and Zubek (1958), for example, studied rats selectively bred for maze-running performance, and these two lines appeared to show a marked differential effect of early rearing environment. In contrast, the careful series of studies by Henderson (1967, 1970, 1972) that yielded little evidence for G × E used inbred strains of mice to investigate the differential effect of early environment on learning. Inbred strains differ genetically but not nearly as much as lines selectively bred to be as different as possible for a particular measure.

Analyses of G × E in the human species are much more limited by their index of genotype, which is indirect. For example, the CAP analyses mentioned earlier relied on first-degree relatives as an index of the genotype variable. This was a major limitation because, even for a completely heritable trait with additive genetic variance, this index of genotype would at best correlate .50 with the genotypes of adoptees. Use of identical (monozygotic [MZ]) twins adopted apart early in life provides a better index of genotype, and this may be the reason that the SATSA analyses mentioned earlier yielded more evidence for G × E (Bergeman et al., 1988). Nonetheless, even though the genotypes of MZ cotwins are identical, behavioral measures are rarely more than 50% heritable, which means that the phenotype of one MZ twin is still only a weak index of the genotype of the cotwin, although it is twice as good as first-degree relatives. Of course, MZ twins reared apart are extremely rare, which attenuates the practical usefulness of this approach in identifying G × E. Although the genotype index is weak in human analyses, it should be emphasized that if G × E is found using this relatively blunt instrument, the G × E is all the more impressive.

In the short run, two other approaches should be explored. First, heritability differences as a function of environment should be assessed more systematically. This approach has the advantage that it fits easily within model-fitting analyses because it merely requires testing whether a model fits better when heritability is allowed to differ for two or more groups defined, in this case, in terms of the environment. The phrase "different environments" could imply micro- or macroenvironmental differences. G × E would be interesting regardless of the level of environment for which an interaction was found. As mentioned in chapter 4, the best strategy is to assess multiple levels of the environment in order to maximize the chances of finding salient environmental influences. An example of a macroenvironmental G × E of this type was mentioned earlier: Heritability of alcohol consumption was found to be greater for unmarried women than for married women (Heath et al., 1989). However, the same study showed little evidence for G × E for many other variables using this approach (Heath & Martin, 1986), which suggests caution in relying on the interaction between alcohol consumption and marital status in women until that finding is replicated. One problem is that large sample sizes are needed to detect differences in heritability, as we discuss later.

A second short-term suggestion may be more controversial. For human investigations, researchers have much greater power to detect organism–environment (O × E) interaction than G × E because they can assess organismic variables directly, whereas genotype is indexed indirectly. Given that many and much of the "O" shows genetic influence, the most efficient approach to G × E may be to follow up findings of O × E by assessing the genetic contribution to the particular organismic variable. In lieu of a theory as to where to find G × E, findings of strong O × E can serve as a beacon to guide analyses of G × E.

In the longer run, the most exciting approach to improving genotypic estimates is the use of DNA probes that directly assess genotypic variability among individuals as indexes of genotype. Rapid advances in the field of molecular genetics make this a real possibility as early as the turn of the century (Plomin, 1990). Although genetic variance for behavioral traits involves many genes, a set of DNA probes that accounts for a portion of the genetic variance for a particular trait can be used in G × E studies to estimate trait-relevant genetic factors for an individual without relying on familial resemblance as an indirect index of genotype (Plomin, Rende, & Rutter, 1991).

Another issue relevant to the "G" part of G × E is the likelihood that genes involved in G × E might differ from genes that affect the trait (Eaves et al., 1977). For example, recent research in molecular genetics has begun to consider genes that respond to environmental events such as stress. The response of these so-called "jumping genes" is to create copies of themselves that are inserted elsewhere in the genome, often producing dramatic changes in gene function (Wills, 1989). An interesting way to think about G × E in this vein in relation to quantitative genetics is to consider the genetic correlation between a trait in different environmental conditions, which requires that the same individuals be exposed to the various environmental conditions (Falconer, 1981). The concept of genetic correlation is key in multivariate genetic analyses of the covariance between traits rather than the traditional univariate analysis of the variance of a single trait. The genetic correlation refers to the extent to which genetic deviations that affect one trait correlate with genetic deviations that affect another trait. In the present instance, the genetic correlation refers to the "same" trait in different settings. A high genetic correlation indicates that genetic effects are very similar in the two situations. A low genetic correlation suggests that genetic effects differ across situations, which is a type of G × E.

Environmental Variables

Obviously, measures of the environment must be included in investigations of
G × E. For example, a recent review of genetic research on personality concluded
the following:

> The weakest area in behavioral genetics today is the treatment of genotype-
> environmental interaction. It will stay this way as long as genetic studies
> fail to measure the environmental factors that may contribute to G × E.
> (Eaves et al., 1989, p. 414)

In the previous section, we suggested that G × E might profit from an initial
focus on extreme genotypes; a similar emphasis on extreme environments might
also facilitate the search for G × E.

Two recent findings from quantitative genetic research have far-reaching
implication for the "E" part of G × E. The first finding is that measures of the
environment show genetic influence (Plomin & Bergeman, in press). Genetic
influence has been found for adolescents' and adults' perceptions of their family
environment, for observation measures of the home environment, and for measures
of life events and social support. Genetic involvement in ostensible measures of
the environment complicates the identification of G × E and its interpretation.
An obvious suggestion is to use measures of the environment that are less influenced by genetics. For example, a finding replicated in three twin studies is that
measures of parental affection show substantial genetic influence, whereas parental
control does not. Also, controllable life events (e.g., serious conflicts with family
members) show greater genetic influence than uncontrollable events (e.g., serious
illness of family members). For additional discussion relevant to this issue, see
chapter 4.

A second suggestion for improving the "E" part of G × E is to develop
measures of *nonshared environment*. Nonshared environment refers to environmental factors that are experienced no more similarly by children growing up in
the same family than by children reared in different families. It has been argued
that such nonshared factors, rather than factors shared by children in the same
family, are primarily responsible for environmental influences in behavioral development (Dunn & Plomin, 1990; Plomin & Daniels, 1987). For this reason,
nonshared factors may be useful in searching for G × E. The goal is to find
environmental factors that are responsible for making children in the same family
so different; such measures of nonshared environment must be specific to an
individual child and they must be experienced differently by children in the same
family. Nonshared environment has begun to be investigated as a possible main
effect of the environment, but it has not yet been studied as a possible source of
interaction with organismic variables. Although nonshared environmental variables could well involve interaction, they do not assess interaction per se because

they do not necessarily entail the same environmental factor experienced differently by children. Also, nonshared environment is not equivalent to G × E because nonshared environmental factors also create differences within pairs of identical twins. Measures of nonshared environment have just begun to be developed (Chipuer, Plomin, DeFries, & Fulker, in press; Daniels & Plomin, 1985).

Moderator Interaction Variables

A statistical issue that is not specific to G × E should be mentioned, although it is discussed at length in chapter 6. Analyses of statistical interaction rely on a multiplicative interaction term; for example, G × E analyses use a multiplicative term to determine whether there is a nonadditive relationship between an outcome measure and indexes of genotype and environment. However, such multiplicative terms are unlikely to identify interactions if, as is most likely, G × E is attributable to only a small portion of the interface between genotype and environment. That is, if G × E occurs only for "high G" children, a model that tests a multiplicative interaction term across the entire sample is unlikely to detect interaction. G × E is more likely to be found if extreme groups of subjects are contrasted.

A useful strategy is to calculate a residualized outcome measure in which variance attributable to the main effects of genotype and environment have been removed, as described by Rosnow and Rosenthal (1989), and then to attempt to explain this variance by contrasting specific "G" and "E" groups such as the extremes. Preliminary simulation studies as well as empirical analyses in our laboratory suggest that this approach is more likely to identify G × E, although caution must be exercised in relation to Type I errors.

Outcome Variables

Are certain outcome measures more likely than others to yield G × E? Although suggestions on this topic can be found elsewhere in this book, quantitative genetic research has little to offer in this regard. As indicated earlier, organismic variables that do not show genetic influence cannot show G × E, but this does not aid the search for G × E because most organismic variables show moderate genetic influence. The same consideration applies to outcome variables in G × E.

Combinations of G, E, and Outcome Variables

The possible combinations of G, E, and outcome variables that can be analyzed for G × E are overwhelming. For example, in the longitudinal CAP with multiple environmental and behavioral measures, millions of possible two- and three-way interactions could be assessed (Plomin et al., 1988). It would be most helpful if there were a theory to guide the search for G × E in general or at least for specific combinations of G, E, and outcome variables. One hypothesis is that heritability is greater when environments are less controlling, perhaps permitting genetic differences to be expressed to a greater extent (Bergeman & Plomin, 1989). In Henderson's (1967, 1970, 1972) studies of mice, heritability was much greater in the enriched environment. Some support for this hypothesis can be gleaned from human G × E analyses as well (Bergeman & Plomin, 1989). Thus, in lieu of other research guideposts, research might consider G × E of this type in which environmental control inhibits the expression of genetic variability. Nonetheless, it is likely that different forms of G × E will apply to different combinations of environmental, organismic, and outcome variables, as discussed in chapter 4.

CONCLUSIONS

In this chapter, we used G × E as a case study of the problems and possibilities for detecting organism–environment interaction. Despite its potential for providing a more refined approach to the environment, little progress has been made in identifying specific G × E, especially in human analyses. The lack of progress might merely be due to lack of effort: Only recently have environmental measures begun to be incorporated into behavioral genetic research.

As discussed in chapters 4 and 6, power considerations are important in the analysis of organism–environment; power is even more demanding in the search for G × E if, as seems likely, such interactions account for only small amounts of variance. For example, the sample size of the CAP provided approximately 80% power to detect interactions that accounted for 5% or more of the total variance, assuming a variance accounted for of 10% for the full stepwise model described earlier. However, if interaction effects accounted for as little as 1% of the variance, a sample size three times larger would be needed to detect a significant interaction with 80% power given a variance accounted for of 10%. Similarly, the approach to G × E that compares heritabilities in different environments requires very large sample sizes because differences in heritabilities entail huge standard errors of estimate. For example, in a twin study, over 500 pairs of each type of twin are needed to demonstrate a significant difference between a heritability of .40 (based on an identical twin correlation of .40 and a fraternal twin correlation of .20) and a heritability of .60 (based on an identical twin correlation of .60 and a fraternal twin correlation of .30). Given the current exploratory stage of research on G × E, it is unlikely that an effort of this magnitude will be mounted specifically to identify G × E. However, many large-scale behavioral genetic studies are underway because large samples are needed to estimate all quantitative genetic parameters with reasonable precision. The most urgent recommendation, then, is that environmental measures be included in these studies so that analyses of G × E will be made possible.

We considered other possibilities for sharpening our search for G × E. Three that seem most promising are the use of genetic markers to provide direct measures of genotypic variation rather than relying on indirect indexes of genotype based on family members, the development and application of nonshared environmental measures, and contrasts between groups that are extreme on genetic and environmental indexes. Many other suggestions generally valuable for the analysis of interaction may also find specific application in the study of G × E. For example, the search for G × E will surely profit from consideration of multiple levels of environment assessment, multiple time periods, and longitudinal analyses.

However, these are promissory notes for finding G × E interaction, and at some point promissory notes are cashed. Despite our shared belief that G × E must be important, we must keep our minds open to other possibilities: that interactions might entail such specific combinations of genotypes and environments that they are essentially idiosyncratic or that additive effects of genes and environment might account for most of the variance.

References

Anastasi, A. (1958). Heredity, environment, and the question "How?" *Psychological Review, 65*, 197–208.

Bergeman, C. S., & Plomin, R. (1989). Genotype-environment interaction. In M. H. Bornstein & J. S. Bruner (Eds.), *Interaction in human development* (pp. 157–171). Hillsdale, NJ: Erlbaum.

Bergeman, C. S., Plomin R., McClearn, G. E., Pedersen, N. L., & Friberg, L. T. (1988). Genotype-environment interaction in personality development: Identical twins reared apart. *Psychology and Aging, 3*, 399–406.

Chipuer, H. M., Plomin, R., DeFries, J. C., & Fulker, D. W. (in press). Using siblings to identify nonshared and shared HOME items. *British Journal of Developmental Psychology*.

Cooper, R. M., & Zubek, J. P. (1958). Effects of enriched and restricted early environments on the learning ability of bright and dull rats. *Canadian Journal of Psychology, 12*, 159–164.

Daniels, D., & Plomin, R. (1985). Differential experience of siblings in the same family. *Developmental Psychology, 21*, 747–760.

Dunn, J., & Plomin, R. (1990). *Separate lives: Why siblings are so different*. New York: Basic Books.

Eaves, L. J. (1984). The resolution of genotype × environment interaction in segregation analysis of nuclear families. *Genetic Epidemiology, 1*, 215–228.

Eaves, L. J., Eysenck, H. J., & Martin, N. G. (1989). *Genes, culture and personality: An empirical approach*. San Diego, CA: Academic Press.

Eaves, L. J., Last, K. A., Martin, N. G., & Jinks, J. L. (1977). A progressive approach to non-additivity and genotype-environmental covariance in the analysis of human differences. *British Journal of Mathematical and Statistical Psychology, 30*, 1–42.

Erlenmeyer-Kimling, L. (1972). Gene-environment interactions and the variability of behavior. In L. Ehrman, G. S. Omenn, & E. Caspari (Eds.), *Genetics, environment and behavior* (pp. 181–208). San Diego, CA: Academic Press.

Falconer, D. S. (1981). *Introduction to quantitative genetics* (2nd ed). London: Longman.

Fisher, R. A. (1918). The correlation between relatives on the supposition of Mendelian inheritance. *Transactions of the Royal Society of Edinburgh, 52*, 399–433.

Fuller, J. L., & Thompson, W. R. (1978). *Foundations of behavior genetics*. St. Louis, MO: Mosby.

Heath, A. C., Jardine, R., & Martin, N. G. (1989). Interactive effects of genotype and social environment on alcohol consumption in female twins. *Journal of Studies on Alcohol, 50*, 38–48.

Heath, A. C., & Martin, N. G. (1986). Detecting the effects of genotype × environment interaction on personality and symptoms of anxiety and depression. *Behavior Genetics, 16*, 622.

Henderson, N. D. (1967). Prior treatment effects on open field behaviour of mice: A genetic analysis. *Animal Behaviour, 15*, 364–376.

Henderson, N. D. (1970). Genetic influences on the behavior of mice can be obscured by laboratory rearing. *Journal of Comparative and Physiological Psychology, 79*, 243–253.

Henderson, N. D. (1972). Relative effects of early rearing environment on discrimination learning in house-mice. *Journal of Comparative and Physiological Psychology, 79*, 243–253.

Hershberger, S. L. (1991). *The measurement of passive, evocative, and active genotype-environment effects*. Manuscript submitted for publication.

Jinks, J. L., & Fulker, D. W. (1970). Comparison of the biometrical, genetical, MAVA, and classical approaches to the analysis of human behavior. *Psychological Bulletin, 73*, 311–349.

Kendler, K. S., & Eaves, L. J. (1986). Models for the joint effects of genotype and environment on liability to psychiatric illness. *American Journal of Psychiatry, 143*, 279–289.

Lathrop, G. M., Lalouel, J. M., & Jacquard, A. (1984). Path analysis of family resemblance and gene-environment interaction. *Biometrics, 40*, 611–625.

Mather, K., & Jinks, J. L. (1982). *Biometrical genetics* (3rd ed). London: Chapman & Hall.

Plomin, R. (1986). *Development, genetics, and psychology*. Hillsdale, NJ: Erlbaum.

Plomin, R. (1990). The role of inheritance in behavior. *Science, 248*, 183–188.

Plomin, R., & Bergeman, C. S. (in press). The nature of nurture: Genetic influence on "environmental" measures. *Behavioral and Brain Sciences*.

Plomin, R., & Daniels, D. (1987). Why are children in the same family so different from each other? *Behavioral and Brain Sciences, 10*, 1–16.

Plomin, R., DeFries, J. C., & Fulker, D. W. (1988). *Nature and nurture in infancy and early childhood*. Cambridge, England: Cambridge University Press.

Plomin, R., DeFries, J. C., & Loehlin, J. C. (1977). Genotype–environment interaction and correlation in the analysis of human behavior. *Psychological Bulletin, 84*, 309–322.

Plomin, R., DeFries, J. C., & McClearn, G. E. (1990). *Behavioral genetics: A primer* (2nd ed.). New York: Freeman.

Plomin, R., Rende, R., & Rutter, M. (1991). Quantitative genetics and developmental psychopathology. In D. Cicchetti & S. Toth (Eds.), *Rochester Symposium on Developmental Psychopathology* (Vol. 2, 155–202). Hillsdale, NJ: Erlbaum.

Rosnow, R. L., & Rosenthal, R. (1989). Definition and interpretation of interaction effects. *Psychological Bulletin, 105*, 143–146.

Rutter, M. (1983). Statistical and personal interactions: Facets and perspectives. In D. Magnusson & V. L. Allen (Eds.), *Human development: An interactional perspective* (pp. 295–319). San Diego, CA: Academic Press.

Skodak, M., & Skeels, H. M. (1949). A final follow-up of one hundred adopted children. *Journal of Genetic Psychology, 75*, 85–125.

Vale, R. (1980). *Genes, environment, and behavior: An interactionist approach.* New York: Harper & Row.

Wahlstein, D. (1990). Insensitivity of the analysis of variance to heredity-environment interaction. *Behavioral and Brain Sciences, 13*, 109–120.

Wills, C. (1989). *The wisdom of the genes: New pathways in evolution.* New York: Basic Books.

CHAPTER 4

ENVIRONMENTAL CONSIDERATIONS IN STUDIES WITH NONEXTREME GROUPS

THEODORE D. WACHS

Traditional definitions of the psychosocial environment typically refer to conditions, forces, or external stimuli that are directly or indirectly encountered by the individual (Wachs & Gruen, 1982). Although traditional definitions of environment have proved to be operationally satisfactory, on theoretical grounds a distinction must be made between the objective situation encountered by the individual (environment) versus those aspects of the objective environment that actually influence development (experience; Thomas & Chess, 1976). Although the focus of this chapter is on the environment of the child, it must be remembered that environment and experience are not necessarily synonymous.

The history of the study of environmental influences on development has gone through a series of discrete stages (Bronfenbrenner & Crouter, 1983; Wachs, 1986a). The first stage was characterized by attempts to determine whether variability in environment was predictive of variability in development. Much of the research done in this stage was based on what Bronfenbrenner (Bronfenbrenner & Crouter, 1983) has described as "social address" measures of the environment (e.g., parent socioeconomic status, institutional rearing of the child). The second stage in the evolution of environmental research was characterized by questions about the nature of specific environmental dimensions that related to variability

Thanks are due to Lee Cronbach and Robert Plomin for their comments on a preliminary version of this chapter.

in development. This stage was characterized by identification of a variety of salient environmental parameters, including parental responsivity, parental punitiveness, parental scaffolding, authoritative rearing styles, and variety of stimulation (Wachs & Gruen, 1982). The third and current stage in the evolution of the study of environmental influences on development is characterized by a series of more complex questions related to what Bronfenbrenner (Bronfenbrenner & Crouter, 1983) has called "person–process–context models." One prime example of a person–process–context question would be the following: Across different contexts, how are specific aspects of the macro- and microenvironment related to specific aspects of development for specific individuals? The relevance of the study of organism–environment interaction for understanding person–process context questions of this type seems obvious.

One critical point that emerges from an understanding of the changes in the questions asked by environmentally oriented researchers over the past 50 years is that the different questions asked at each stage require different approaches for assessing the environment (Wachs, 1986a). What are the criteria that influence choice of environmental assessment procedures? Obviously, a primary consideration is the nature of the research question being asked. For example, a social address measure such as institutional rearing may be quite appropriate for answering Stage 1 questions about whether the environment influences development; however, the same social address measure would be of little value when attempting to answer Stage 2 questions about which specific aspects of the environment are related to development.

Second, there are practical (cost) considerations, which typically involve factors such as the amount of effort (research time) required to collect the necessary data for a single subject. The more time per subject needed, the less likely it is that large numbers of subjects can be tested. For certain questions, or with unlimited resources, practical considerations may not be critical. With limited resources, or for other questions such as the detection of organism–environment interaction (Plomin & Daniels, 1984), practical considerations such as sample size may be essential when choosing an environmental assessment measure.

Finally, there are validity considerations. Validity considerations typically include questions such as how well the obtained score reflects the construct under study, as opposed to assessing random or nonenvironmental variance. Validity considerations may also involve representativeness: how much of the total range of environmental influences encountered by the child are actually captured by the researcher's measure. Validity considerations are particularly critical when one attempts to study organism–environment interaction. The term *organism–environment interaction* implies differential reactivity of individuals to specific aspects of the environment. What this means in practice is that the ability to detect existing organism–environment interactions will depend on the ability to adequately measure the environment (see chap. 8 in this book). Unreliable, inadequate, or inappropriate measures of the environment may mean that *organism–error interaction* rather than organism–environment interaction is being assessed. To the extent that error is random, the findings in studies of organism–error interaction will also be random. Thus, if one wishes to obtain replicable findings in studies of organism–environment interaction, it would be desirable if the environmental measures were as precise as possible.

Ideally, practical and validity considerations would not be in conflict, allowing researchers to use the most valid instruments available. All too often they are, however. A highly precise environmental measure that is very time consuming may mean that only a small sample of subjects can be studied, leading to a loss of statistical power (Cohen, 1988). Depending on the research question being asked, or the characteristics of the research design, a less precise but also less costly environmental assessment procedure may be more appropriate. Selecting an appropriate environmental assessment procedure thus becomes an exercise in balancing the precision of measures that are appropriate to the question being asked with the availability of resources. The prime focus of this chapter is the selection on environmental assessment procedures for one type of research question: the study of organism–environment interaction with nonextreme populations.

THE MEASUREMENT OF ENVIRONMENT

Before making recommendations about which methods of environmental assessment are appropriate for studying organism–environment interaction in nonextreme groups, it would seem appropriate to briefly review existing environmental assessment methods. An understanding of the strengths and weaknesses of each method becomes important when attempting to determine what method is most appropriate for a specific research design. A summarization of the points made are shown in Table 1. Many of the points briefly noted are based on my earlier reviews of available approaches to assessing the environment (Wachs, 1988a; Wachs & Gruen, 1982). In this brief review I assume some degree of psychometric adequacy for each of the measures (i.e., adequate internal consistency for questionnaires or adequate interobserver reliability for observational measures).

Parent Report Measures

For both parental interviews or parental questionnaires, parents are asked about the characteristics of the environment they provide their children. Both approaches have good representativeness, in that parents can be questioned about the environment provided for their children across a number of content domains and contexts. Report measures may be particularly useful in situations in which it is necessary to document rarely occurring events, such as family trips, which may

Table 1.

ENVIRONMENTAL MEASURES THAT COULD BE USED IN STUDIES OF
ORGANISM–ENVIRONMENT INTERACTION

Environmental measure	Strengths and weaknesses
Parental report: Interview	Strengths include good representativeness and the ability to assess rarely occurring events. Cost is moderate. The prime limitation is accuracy of measurement.
Questionnaire	Strengths include good representativeness, low cost and the ability to assess rarely occurring events. The prime limitation is accuracy of measurement.

Social address
  Demographic measures
  Epidemiological measures
	For both types of measures primary strength is low cost, allowing large sample sizes. The primary limitation is accuracy of measurement.

Individual treatment	Although the cost tends to be high, accuracy of measurement also is likely to be high.
Group	Depending on whether the unit of measurement is the group or the individual, cost may or may not be high. In terms of accuracy, caution is warranted in assuming that differently labelled treatments mean functionally different environments.
Structured observation	Although accurate measurement can be made of ongoing transactions, cost is high and there are questions about whether what is observed is representative of normally occurring caregiver–child transactions.
Naturalistic observation	If repeated measurements are taken across time and context, highly accurate and representative environmental assessments can be obtained. There is a major cost trade off, however, in that sample sizes will, of necessity, be small.
Child perception	Cost is low and the child's perception may be a more accurate reflection of the effective environment than more objective measures. However, the method cannot be recommended for children below 10 years of age because of reliability problems.

not be accessible by other means.[1] Parental questionnaires are also low cost because they can be easily and quickly administered to large numbers of parents. Parental interviews are potentially more costly in that interviews take more time to do, which may limit sample size.

---

[1] Parental reports may also be critical when it is necessary to assess parental perception of the environment, as in macroenvironmental studies on the availability of parental support networks. Although invaluable when these types of parental perceptions are desired, my focus is on the microenvironment of the child rather than on macroenvironmental factors such as support.

The major limitation of both methods involves accuracy of measurement. The accuracy problems associated with retrospective parental reports have been well documented in the literature (e.g., Yarrow, Campbell, & Burton, 1970). In terms of parent report measures assessing parental attitudes about child rearing, Holden and Edwards (1989) basically concluded that currently used parent attitude report measures "have outlived their usefulness and should be retired from the repertoire of standard methodological tools" (p. 50). Both major psychometric and conceptual problems with existing attitude report measures underlie this pessimistic conclusion. When concurrent parental reports of child-rearing *procedures* are used, for the most part correlations between parental report and actual parent–child transactions are modest. For example, in a recently reported study by Kochanska, Kuczynski, and Radke-Yarrow (1989), only about one third of the correlations between parental report and parent–child transactions were significant; for those that were significant, the range was .21–.45, with the median correlation being .28 and the mean being .29.

Social Address Measures

Bronfenbrenner (Bronfenbrenner & Crouter, 1983) has defined social address measures as those in which environment is not actually measured but inferred. Two types of social address measures have been reported in the literature. One is based on composite demographic characteristics, such as social class or parental educational level. The other class of measures is found in experiments of nature, or "epidemiological studies" (Rutter, in press), which involve relating outcomes to specific ecological contexts encountered by children at various points in their development. Ecological contexts may include prolonged institutionalization or hospitalization at specific ages, being reared apart (in the case of twins), residing in urban versus rural areas, or changes in family structure.

The strengths and weaknesses of social address procedures as a measure of environment have been repeatedly documented in the literature (Bronfenbrenner & Crouter, 1983; Wachs, 1983). To the extent that various types of environments covary with social addresses (i.e., greater risk of abuse or inadequate schools can covary with low socioeconomic status), social address procedures do allow for reasonably representative measures of what the *modal* child at a *typical* social address may encounter. Social address information is relatively easy to come by, which also means large sample sizes and hence greater power. On the negative side, the tremendous variability in actual environments encountered within a given social address have been repeatedly noted in the literature (Bronfenbrenner & Crouter, 1983; Wachs, 1983). For example, in their review of institutionally reared children in Czechoslovakia, Langmeier and Matejcek (1975) noted that although there was central state control over orphanages, covering such factors as standards of staff training, available materials, and the nature of buildings, there was tremendous heterogeneity in the nature of specific environments encountered by individual children in different orphanages or even in different wards in the same orphanage.[2]

Treatment Studies

In treatment studies either individual children or groups of children are treated in different ways, with the different treatment forming the measure of environment. By virtue of the time involved, individual treatment studies often have relatively small sample sizes, particularly if the treatment has to be administered over several sessions, and thus tend to be costly. Group treatment studies, such as educational intervention studies, typically involve larger samples and thus have potentially lower cost and greater power (although, as Cronbach & Snow, 1977, have noted, if the correct unit of analysis in group treatment studies is the group rather than the individual, this may severely limit actual "sample" size).

If the investigator has clearly specified what situations or rewards children in each treatment will encounter, then, ideally, only a minimal check should be needed to determine whether the treatment plans are being carried out as designed. However, in practice there is always some degree of departure, even from the most elaborate research protocol; in less well-specified designs, it is often difficult to determine exactly the composition of the environment provided. For example, in group treatment studies, researchers often make the dual assumption that children given treatments with different labels are in functionally different environments, whereas children given treatments with similar labels are in functionally equivalent environments. The potential problems with this dual assumption in Aptitude × Treatment interaction (ATI) studies have been reviewed by Cronbach and Snow (1977), who urged caution in accepting this assumption: "Contrast labels gloss over potentially important variations within and between treatments, making treatments appear to be the same though they are not. . . . One cannot rely on labels; interpretation must be based on the more detailed (though still limited) treatment descriptions in individual reports" (p. 222). More recent reviews (Carbo, 1983; Keogh, 1986) have expressed similar concerns.

---

[2] The same point can also be made when looking at "organism address models," which refer to the use of supposedly homogeneous *groups* as the measure of *individual* characteristics (i.e., mentally retarded children, schizophrenic children, autistic children). Available evidence suggests that even when groups have similar labels, there still may be a good deal of heterogeneity in critical process dimensions within groups (Belmont, Ferretti, & Mitchell, 1982; Erlenmeyer-Kimling & Cornblatt, 1984; Gersten, 1983; Nuechterlein, 1983; Rutschmann, Cornblatt, & Erlenmeyer-Kimling, 1986). The same point can also be made in regard to "task address studies," wherein it is assumed that different measures of a specific outcome variable are fundamentally equivalent. In many cases, this assumption also may not be justified (Harvey, Weintraub, & Neale, 1984).

Observation of Caregiver–Child Transactions in Structured Situations

This approach typically involves short-term observations of parent and child trans-actions in a laboratory setting. Either the parent is told to behave as he or she normally would toward the child, or the parent is asked to play a game or teach something to the child. Parent transactions are either coded on-line or from vid-eotape, and these transactions are assumed to reflect characteristic parent behav-iors.

Because children need to be seen individually, there are limitations on the number of children who can be reasonably assessed by this approach; hence, the cost of this method is high. In addition, this method is not likely to capture environmental influences provided by caregivers other than the parents (i.e., sitters or teachers). In terms of validity, there usually is no problem in accurately mea-suring what goes on in a structured situation. However, as defined, validity can also involve the question of whether what is being measured is an accurate re-flection of what the child normally encounters in transactions with his or her caregivers (i.e., representativeness). In terms of comparisons of parent behaviors in structured and naturalistic situations, available research suggests that measures of caregiver behaviors made in structured laboratory situations often do not reflect what occurs when similar measures are made at home (Belsky, 1980; Novak, Olley, & Kearney, 1980). The degree of correspondence between home and laboratory typically is lower when highly overt laboratory observations are used (Field & Ignatoff, 1981), or when mothers are given little guidance as to how to structure their behavior at home (O'Brien, Anderson-Goetz, & Johnson, 1988).[3]

Naturalistic Observation

Naturalistic observation encompasses direct assessment of ongoing caregiver–child transactions in real time, in environments the child commonly encounters. By directly measuring caregiver–child transactions in the child's natural habitat, the chances of obtaining accurate measures of the child's environment are max-imized, as long as certain conditions are met. These include the following: (a) Given that an increasing number of infants and toddlers are spending at least some time out of home care (Clarke-Stewart, 1989), to say nothing of school-age children, to ensure representativeness observers must be prepared to go into other settings besides the home. (b) Available evidence suggests that the pattern of

---

[3] It may be possible to overcome the representativeness problem by use of repeated measurement of caregiver–child transactions in structured laboratory situations. Stewart and Burgess (1980) have reported no differences in laboratory and home observation results when repeated measurements across time were taken in both situations. However, the validity of their conclusion of no differences is seriously compromised by the very small sample used in their study.

mother–child transactions may be different either when the father (Clarke-Stewart, 1978) or siblings or other children are present (Wachs, 1986b, 1989). This suggests the need to do observations at various times of the day rather than just at a single point in time. (c) Although the presence of an observer often will cause initial distortions in caregiver behaviors (Zegiob, Arnold, & Forehand, 1975), with repeated exposure to the observer, caregiver behaviors tend to return to their own natural baseline (Wachs & Gruen, 1982). For example, data from one of my studies (Wachs, 1987a), using multiple observations with 12-month-old infants, indicated that there were significant shifts in parental behavior across observations for 40% of the environmental codes used. However, with one exception, all of the shifts in parental behavior occurred between the first and second observations. After the second observation, there were no more significant changes in observed parental behavior. (In the one exception there was a change from the first to the third observation, but none thereafter.) This emphasizes the importance of using repeated observations to maximize parent acclimatization to the presence of an observer.

Although highly representative and accurate environmental data can be obtained using naturalistic observations, there is a major price to pay. Specifically, maximizing the probability of obtaining representative environmental assessments requires repeated direct observations of caregiver–child transactions across multiple contexts and times. Obviously, this type of design is extremely time consuming and thus extremely costly. The major cost consequence is that the time-consuming nature of direct observation severely reduces the number of subjects that realistically can be studied. The problem with small sample sizes is, of course, a potentially serious loss of power (Cohen, 1988), which means a loss in the ability to detect existing organism–environment interactions with this type of procedure.

Child Report Measures

A final approach would involve the use of child reports about their perceptions of the environment. Kagan (1967) has argued that caregiver behaviors, scored in a particular way by observers or rated a specific way by parents, may be construed quite differently by the child. Thus, in terms of the impact of the environment, it may be the child's perception of the environmental event, not the parents' interpretation or the observers' coding, that may be particularly salient. The use of child perceptions as an index for assessing the environment has several advantages. First, children can be asked about their experiences across a wide range of areas, such as experiences with parents, peers, and school, thus maximizing representativeness. To the extent that the child's perceptions meet psychometric standards for reliability, questions of accuracy may well be unimportant, given that the child's perception of the environment rather than objective reality may be critical in influencing developmental outcomes. Because child perceptions can be obtained from questionnaires, large sample sizes can be used at a relatively low cost.

However, before concluding that children's perception of their environment is the "gold standard" of environmental measures, several caveats must be noted. First, in contrast to other measurement approaches, there are only a few child perception questionnaires available (e.g., Daniels & Plomin, 1985; Schaefer, 1965), and information on the psychometric qualities of these measures is limited. More critically, available evidence suggests that reports of children below 10 years of age tend not to be reliable (Edelbrook, Costello, Dulcan, Kales, & Conover, 1985). One consequence of this is that the ability to accurately measure child perceptions of the environment will be restricted primarily to later childhood and adolescence.

Are Precise Measures the Most Appropriate Measures?

Purely on the basis of validity considerations, a choice of environmental measures to use seems fairly simple. For infants and toddlers, even given the high cost, unstructured naturalistic observations would seem to be the measure of choice. For preschoolers and young schoolchildren, either group or individual treatment manipulations may be the most appropriate. For older school-age children, child perception measures would seem to have the greatest utility. However, as noted earlier, practical considerations and the nature of the question being asked must also be considered when selecting a measure of the environment. Depending on the goals and design of the study, a less representative, less accurate but lower cost measure may be as, if not more appropriate, than a highly accurate, highly representative, high-cost measure. Put another way, under certain conditions, to precisely assess the presence or nature of organism–environment interaction, one may need highly accurate and highly representative measures, regardless of cost. Under other conditions less costly measures may be more appropriate. I now discuss what design conditions allow judgments to be made about the most appropriate environmental measures to use.

THE STUDY OF ORGANISM–ENVIRONMENT INTERACTIONS IN CATEGORICAL VERSUS CONTINUOUS GROUPS

Although behavioral researchers have primarily been interested in studying traits that have a continuous, quantitative distribution (Kagan, 1989), for the most part the study of organism–environment interactions in human developmental studies has been based on comparison of environment outcome relations across two or more highly distinctive, qualitatively different (extreme) groups. Thus, one traditional test of organism–environment interaction typically involves comparison of environment development relations for males versus females (e.g., Bergman, 1981; Block, Block, & Morrison, 1981; Compas, 1987; Wachs, 1979). Other examples of this type of design include tests for differential reactivity for developmentally disabled versus normal children (e.g., Brice, 1985; Casto, 1987; Smith & Hagan, 1984); hyperactive versus normal children (e.g., Brimer & Levine, 1983; Magnusson, 1988); preterm versus normal children (Field, 1981); normal children versus children at risk for schizophrenia (e.g., Brodsky & Brodsky, 1981; Emery, Weintraub, & Neale, 1982) or antisocial behavior (e.g., Cadoret, Cain, & Crowe, 1983); securely versus insecurely attached children (e.g., Donovan & Levitt, 1985; also see chap. 5 in this book); reflective versus impulsive children (e.g., Kogan, 1983; Trickett, 1983); temperamentally easy versus temperamentally difficult children (e.g., Gordon, 1981; Maziade et al., 1985; Wachs & Gandour, 1983); introverted versus extraverted children (e.g., McCord & Wakefield, 1981); and highly reactive versus low reactive children (Strelau, 1983).

In contrast, studies of organism–environment interaction comparing nonextreme groups of quantitatively different children (i.e., children who do not fall into distinctive groups but are closer to the middle range of individual characteristics) are much rarer. Perhaps the largest literature in this area involve ATI studies that have investigated differential reactivity to educational treatments for nonextreme groups of children who differed either in ability or anxiety level (e.g., Corno, 1980; Cronbach & Snow, 1977; Freebody & Tirre, 1985; Wade, 1981), stimulus preferences (e.g., Carbo, 1983), or classroom attitudes (e.g., Fraser & Fisher, 1983). Outside of the ATI literature, few studies have examined organism–environment interaction in nonextreme, continuous groups, although some evidence indicates differential reactivity to the environment as a function of children's affective response to stimuli (e.g., Hammen & Zupan, 1984; Slife & Rychlak, 1982); children's activity level, excluding abnormal populations such as hyperactive children (e.g., Escalona, 1968; Gandour, 1989; Wachs, 1987b); temperament (e.g., Keogh, 1986); or the use of moderate risk in addition to high- and low-risk groups (e.g., Finkelstein, Gallagher, & Farran, 1980).

There are good reasons why most research studies on organism–environment interaction have involved the use of extreme groups. For the most part, the evidence suggests that more clear-cut results occur when distinctive, qualitatively different groups are used in studying organism–environment interaction (see chap. 8 in this book). There are a variety of reasons why existing interactions are more likely to be identified when highly contrasting, qualitatively distinct groups are studied. As noted by Vale and Vale (1969), smaller group differences may be less meaningful in terms of reflecting basic individual characteristics. Put another way, with less distinct groups there may be more noise, that is, error in the design (Myers, 1979). One consequence is that when more heterogeneous, nondistinctive subject populations are compared, there is increased subject misclassification resulting in a reduction in power (Dance & Neufeld, 1988; also see chap. 6 in this book).

Because the use of qualitatively distinct contrast groups may reduce subject misclassification and thus increase power, there are certain implications for the choice of environmental measures in studies of organism–environment interaction. As noted earlier, more precise environmental measures typically involve higher cost, both in terms of subject involvement time and lower power. Because of the increased precision and power found when qualitatively distinct groups are used, more costly environmental measures may not be necessary for qualitative contrast extreme group designs. In terms of a cost:benefit ratio, when qualitatively distinct groups are used, less precise but also less costly environmental measures (e.g., the use of epidemiological data, parental reports on concurrent child-rearing practices, group treatments) may provide a sufficiently accurate picture of environmental influences to allow a satisfactory test of the presence or nature of organism–environment interaction. These types of measures may also be appropriate for large-scale behavior genetic studies, which are investigating whether different heritabilities can be found in different environments. (For details on this type of design, see chap. 3 in this book.)

Does this mean that future studies of organism–environment interaction should focus on extreme groups, using the types of lower cost environmental measures described earlier? What must be kept in mind is that when attempting to study the process of organism–environment interaction, there are certain problems associated with the use of qualitatively distinct groups that may require the use of noncontrasting, quantitatively different groups. Part of the problem involves the assumptions made when qualitatively distinct groups are studied. For example, studies using qualitatively distinct groups often assume a linear relation between predictor and outcome variables. However, if the pattern of relations is nonlinear, then highly misleading conclusions can emerge from these types of studies (Myers, 1979). Over and above this problem, there is also the question of generalizability. Not only may obtained results differ when less distinct groups are studied, but the very processes underlying developmental change may be distinctively different in intermediate versus extreme groups (Cloninger, Bohman, & Sigvardson, 1981; Kidd & Matthysee, 1978). Thus, to test both the generalizability of interactions and the nature of the processes underlying interactions may require the use of intermediate, nonextreme, quantitative groups.

When qualitatively distinct groups are used, less precise environmental measures may be highly satisfactory. However, as one moves toward the middle range of organismic characteristics, it is doubtful if the less precise, less accurate environmental measures, appropriate for the study of organism–environment interaction with qualitatively distinct groups, will be sufficient. Rather, given the greater noise—error in the middle range—it would seem especially critical to use the most precise, most accurate environmental measures (e.g., individual treatments, unstructured naturalistic observation, child perceptions) when attempting to document the existence or nature of organism–environment interaction in nonextreme, quantitatively different groups. However, even the use of these more precise measures may be insufficient unless certain other conditions are met, given the increased cost and (and lower power) associated with these more precise measures. When studying organism–environment interaction in nonextreme quantitatively different groups, adjustments in research design and conceptual models may be necessary. It is to this point that I now turn. Specifically, I consider both theoretical and empirical considerations relevant to studying organism–environment interaction in the middle ranges of organismic characteristics.

The Role of Theory

Anderson (1972) has cogently argued that the processes governing higher order levels of functioning cannot violate laws or principles associated with lower levels of functioning. For my purposes, what this suggests is that the nature of higher order organism–environment interactions cannot violate what is known about the nature of lower order environment–development relations. Existing theories of environmental action suggest two principles that are especially critical in understanding the role of environment on development. Although these principles do not allow investigators to delineate which specific environmental characteristics are most likely to interact with individual characteristics, they do offer a guide to research strategies that may be particularly promising in illustrating the process of organism–environment interaction.

The Principle of Environmental Specificity

The principle of environmental specificity states that different aspects of the environment influence different aspects of development (Wachs, 1986a; Wachs & Gruen, 1982). Using a specificity framework means that one should not expect that all aspects of the environment will enter into organism–environment interactions. Some aspects of the environment may act primarily in a main effects fashion, whereas other aspects of the environment may be more sensitive to the interactive influences of individual characteristics.[4] This suggests the necessity for measuring multiple dimensions of the environment rather than relying only on a small subset of environmental codes.

Similarly, the specificity model also suggests the possibility that different aspects of the environment may be more likely to enter into specific types of

---

[4] The same point can also be made for other aspects of organism–environment interaction. It may well be that only certain individual characteristics are sensitive to the interactive aspects of the environment (Vale & Vale, 1969). Similarly, it may well be that only certain outcome variables are sensitive to interactions, as opposed to being sensitive to main effects of the organism or of the environment (Dance & Neufeld, 1988). As with environment, the critical question is which individual characteristics or which outcome variables are most sensitive to interactions.

interactions. Thus, some aspects of the environment may interact in a synergistic manner, whereas others are more likely to function as buffers; some aspects of the environment may primarily interact in ordinal fashion, whereas other aspects may primarily interact in disordinal fashion. If different environmental dimensions are more likely to enter into different types of interactions, extrapolating from both Rutter (1983) and Barron and Kenny (1986), different analytical procedures may be called for when analyzing organism–environment interactions rather than assuming that the same analytical technique will be appropriate for all types of situations.

Ecological Theory: The Multidimensional Nature of the Environment

For many developmental researchers, the term *environment* is commonly used as a global summary term. However, as elegantly described by ecological theorists such as Bronfenbrenner (Bronfenbrenner & Crouter, 1983), the environment is multidimensional in nature and can be differentiated not only into hierarchically organized levels but also into subdimensions within a given level of the hierarchy. Most developmental studies on organism–environment interaction have been conducted at the lowest level of the hierarchy of environmental influences: the microenvironmental level. Furthermore, at the microenvironmental level, virtually all studies have considered only one aspect of the microenvironment: the social environment (child–caregiver transactions). However, there is another major dimension of the microenvironment: the physical environment which is the stage or setting on which social transactions take place (Wohlwill & Heft, 1987). Few studies have investigated whether environmental contributions to organism–environment interaction may involve physical as well as social aspects of the microenvironment. It is thus noteworthy that of the few studies that have examined *both* physical and social aspects of the microenvironment, across all of these studies, physical aspects of the microenvironment were more likely to enter into significant interactions with individual characteristics than were social aspects of the environment (Wachs, 1987b; Wachs & Gandour, 1983; Yarrow, Rubenstein, & Pedersen, 1975). One conclusion investigators may wish to ponder is that when looking for microenvironmental contributions to organism–environment interaction, an unduly restrictive concept of the microenvironment might have been used. Specifically, in looking for organism–environment interactions, it may be equally important to consider physical aspects of the environment as well as social transactions.

A second aspect of ecological theory is the concept that microenvironmental relations can be influenced by contextual factors (e.g., social support, paternal work pressures, or prevailing economic conditions) that the child may not directly experience (Belsky, Hertzog, & Rovine, 1986; Cotterell, 1986; Crockenberg & McCluskey, 1986; Elder, Van Nguyen, & Caspi, 1985). The critical question is not whether contextual factors can influence the microenvironment encountered by the child but whether contextual factors can also influence the process of organism–microenvironmental interactions.

Some of the most consistent examples supporting this possibility are found in ATI research. Because individual students learn in classroom groups, it would be a logical step to consider classroom contexts, as well as individual characteristics, when looking for ATI (Corno, 1979). Indeed, available evidence suggests that dimensions such as classroom ability level (Corno, 1980), classroom anxiety level, or classroom attitudes (Corno, Mitman, & Hedges, 1981) may have as much salience for illustrating ATI as do individual aptitude characteristics. (Examples of classroom context effects are also seen in the 1977 book by Cronbach & Snow, pp. 301–302). Ecological evidence outside of the ATI literature is sparse, but what evidence there is also suggests the importance of considering environmental context when looking for organism–environment interactions. For example, ecological characteristics may magnify existing organism–environment interactions, as seen in data suggesting that the greater male vulnerability to biological stress is increased when stressed males also come from poverty backgrounds (Birns, 1976). The relevance of culture as a higher order mediator is supported by evidence indicating that the interactive relation between sex of child and exposure to television on cognitive performance will, in turn, be mediated by the characteristics of the cultures involved (Conner, Thorndike, Forbes, & Ashworth, 1985). The relevance of ecological factors for understanding the processes governing organism–environment interaction is also seen in the Lebanese data of Day and Ghandour (1984), which indicates that exposure to real-life violence overcomes socially conditioned sex differences in reaction to modeled aggression.

What this suggests is not that researchers need to declare a moratorium on traditional organism–microenvironmental interaction studies. Rather, what is suggested is that adequate measurement of the environment may need to include both contextual as well as physical microenvironmental parameters. Inclusion of these aspects of the environment in studies of organism–environment interaction may be particularly important given the point raised by Plomin and Hershberger (see chap. 3) that environmental factors that are uncorrelated with parental genotype may be particularly salient in studies of organism–environment interaction. Although there is virtually no data on this question, at least logically, physical microenvironment or contextual parameters should be less influenced by parental genotype than are environmental measures that assess parent–offspring transactions.

Empirical Considerations

The Use of Aggregated Data

Unless environmental assessments are relatively stable within a given time period, the environmental contribution to the interaction term will essentially encompass random variability. Thus, to the extent that one has stable measures of the environment, one is more likely to be assessing true environmental variance and not random error. Under these conditions existing interactions are more likely to be identified. Under what conditions can the stability of environmental assessments be maximized? One approach comes from the area of personality theory, as seen in the comparison of results from studies using aggregated versus nonaggregated measures. *Aggregated measures* refer to data based on multiple measurements obtained across occasions, observers, or related measures. Combining measurements tends to average out errors associated with a single measurement and thus should lead to more accurate and stable measurement of specific traits or behaviors (Rushton, Brainerd, & Pressley, 1983). A substantial data base, including studies of personality (Epstein, 1980) and aggressive behavior (Rushton, 1988), supports the proposition that single measurements of either personality traits or specific behaviors show little stability across time, whereas aggregated measurements do show significant stability. Generalization of this pattern of results to developmental areas, such as judgments of children's behavior patterns, stages of cognitive development, and the relation of cognition to behavior, has been reported by Rushton et al. (1983).

Although the advantages of data aggregation seem clear, relatively few studies in the area of environmental influences have used this approach (Wachs, 1987a). The studies that have used aggregated data have reported increases in stability, particularly when observational data are used. Specifically, in the infancy area, research involving dimensions of the social environment (Wachs, 1987a) and the physical environment (Wachs, 1988b) has demonstrated that by using repeated observations and by aggregating across observations, substantially more stable measures of the environment can be obtained than if single, nonaggregated observations are used. The importance of aggregation for obtaining stable measures of the environment has been noted not only in infancy but also for school-age children (Patterson, 1983) and adults (Conger, Moisan-Thomas, & Conger, 1989).[5] The implications of this line of research for assessing environmental contributions to organism–environment interactions with quantitatively distinct populations seem clear. To maximize precision of environmental assessments, the use of aggregated data seems essential. In the case of unstructured naturalistic observations, aggregation across occasions would seem to be the most appropriate strategy. For individual treatment studies, use of repeated treatment sessions would be recommended. For child perception scales, either aggregation across occasions or measures would seem to be equally appropriate. Child report measures taken in

---

[5] The importance of aggregation as a methodological tool goes well beyond assessment of the environment and also encompasses outcome measures (Rushton, 1988; Rushton, Brainerd, & Pressley, 1983) as well as individual characteristics (Kenrick & Funder, 1988). Thus, to the extent that researchers wish to avoid random error in either their outcome data or measures of individual characteristics, the importance of aggregation seems obvious for these domains as well when attempting to test for organism–environment interactions.

the classroom may be particularly useful, not only because these scores are derived from the reports of multiple observers but also because classes can be split, with alternate forms being given to each half of the class (Cronbach, personal communication, 1990).

The virtues of aggregation as a design feature go beyond just stability, however. As was noted earlier, the more precise environmental assessments tend to be costly, leading to smaller sample sizes and reduced power. Besides increasing stability, a second *potential* benefit of aggregation may also be to increase power.

Theoretically, reducing measurement error increases power through reducing variability in sources that are unrelated to the phenomena under study (Cohen, 1988). As demonstrated by both Sutcliffe (1980) and Zimmerman and Williams (1986), by reducing errors of measurement power can, in fact, be increased. Thus, aggregation across observations or measures may help to compensate, at least to some degree, for one of the major potential deficits in highly precise environmental studies: lower power associated with small sample sizes. How much compensation there is remains unknown. When reliability is low, increases in power can be obtained both by increasing test length (which is somewhat akin to increasing the number of observations) and by increasing sample size, although the benefits from increasing test length are never, in practice, as great as that for increasing sample size (Maxwell, 1980). Given that the reliability of a single environmental assessment tends to be modest at best (Wachs, 1987a) suggests that at least some degree of increased power could result when aggregated measurements are used with small samples. This may be particularly true if one also follows the suggestion by Cohen (1988) and sets a less stringent alpha level when testing for interactions (also see chap. 6 in this book).

The Use of Marker Variables

A second design strategy derives from suggestions by Cronbach and Snow (1977) and Finney, Mitchell, Cronkite, and Moos (1984), who noted the possibility that in a small sample size study, statistically nonsignificant interaction terms do not necessarily mean the absence of interaction. If a group of small sample size studies yields nonsignificant interactions and the interactions are in the same direction, this may mean that organism–environment interaction actually exists but is not detectable in any given study because of low power. A potentially viable research strategy for this type of situation would be for researchers to use a common set of environmental markers across studies. (Ideally, there could also be agreement to use a common set of organismic markers and a common set of outcome variables as well.) Under these conditions it might be possible to still investigate interactions, even if the results of individual studies are not significant. This could be done through aggregating across common variables across studies to increase sample size. Alternatively, the researcher could use techniques such as meta-analysis to determine if significant effect sizes occur when the results from a group of studies are treated collectively rather than singly.

The critical question, of course, is, What environmental measures would be the best markers? As noted earlier in this chapter, current theory is of little help in identifying specific environmental parameters that would be appropriate markers. In the absence of theoretical guidance, an empirical approach to this question may be useful as a starting point. To this end I surveyed the environmental influences literature in the infancy period (0–2 years), looking for studies that (a) yielded evidence for significant organism–environment interaction and (b) had a detailed description of the environmental measures that were used. I further restricted myself to studies in which there was at least some evidence that what was found was organism–environment interaction (differential reactivity of different individuals to similar environmental stimulation) and not organism–environment covariance (different environments being provided to different individuals). With these restrictions, I identified 12 studies (Beckwith & Cohen, 1984; Bradley & Caldwell, 1984; Crockenberg, 1987; Gandour, 1989; Gunnar & Donahue, 1980; Smith & Hagen, 1984; Wachs, 1978, 1979, 1984, 1987b; Wachs & Gandour, 1983; Yarrow et al., 1975). For each of the studies, I listed the environmental variables that had been shown to interact with individual characteristics. In a number of cases, when different labels were used but the same environmental process seemed to be assessed, I combined environmental measures into a single category (i.e., caregivers' responses to child distress and caregivers' responses to child vocalization were combined into a response contingencies category). I ended up with a list of 22 environmental variables, which interacted with one or more organismic characteristics in terms of relating to developmental outcome.

To further reduce the list to those environmental variables that seemed to most consistently interact with individual characteristics, I then applied the cutting score technique, which I have used in my previous environmental research (e.g., Wachs, 1979) to the listing. Specifically, I took the number of times each environmental parameter had entered into an interaction and obtained the mean and standard deviation for the total distribution of 22 variables. I then added the mean and standard deviation together, rounded them to the nearest whole number, and obtained a cutting score. Thus, the mean number of times a specific environmental variable interacted with organismic characteristics across the 12 studies was 2.32; the standard deviation was 1.28. The raw cutoff score was 3.60, which I rounded to 4. This meant that a consistent environmental variable was defined as any one that had yielded evidence for an interaction as defined earlier: 4 or more times across the 12 studies. Five environmental variables met this criterion and are now described.

Three of the variables come from the physical environment side (probably reflecting the heavy representation of my own research). These are physical restriction on exploration, home "traffic pattern" (number of people coming and going in the home),[6] and degree of stimulus variety in the home. The remaining two measures involve aspects of the social environment. These are adult mediation of the environment for the child and environmental contingencies. I would argue that in terms of delineating environmental marker variables to be used in studies of organism–environment interaction in quantitatively different populations, at least in infancy all or some subset of these variables are the ones that should receive first consideration.

This list of environmental variables is relevant not only for identifying potential environmental markers but also in terms of beginning to develop theory-driven studies defining the process of organism–environment interaction. As noted earlier in this chapter, from the viewpoint of environmental specificity, one should not expect all environmental variables to interact with organismic characteristics in influencing development. From a specificity viewpoint, the critical question is which environmental variables are most likely to be involved in interactions. Inspection of the list suggests that at least for the infancy period, a potentially testable hypothesis emerges. Specifically, the two identified social parameters involve measures of the child's transactions with significant others in the environment. Of the three physical environment parameters identified, one of these—home traffic pattern—has been repeatedly identified as *interfering* with the infant's transactions with caregivers (Wachs, 1986b, 1989). Although the empirical data for physical restrictions are less clear (Wachs, 1989), at least conceptually, physical restrictions (i.e., use of playpens) can also be viewed as a physical environment parameter that may influence the child's transactions with individuals in the environment.

This suggests that in terms of future research on organism–environment interaction with nondiscrete populations, environmental variables that either directly or indirectly influence the child's *transactions* with his or her environment, particularly those transactions that involve adult–child relations, should be a major focus of study.

CONCLUSIONS

It seems clear that if the prime research goal is to identify existing organism–environment interactions, then qualitatively different extreme group studies are the most profitable avenue at present. For this type of study, as noted earlier in this chapter, less precise but more cost-effective environmental measures would seem to be quite adequate. However, a detailed understanding of the processes involved in organism–environment interaction will, at some point, require the use of nonextreme, quantitatively different group studies. For this type of study, a

---

[6] The empirical and conceptual rationale for including home traffic pattern as a dimension of the physical environment is detailed in a recent article by Wachs (1989).

less cost-effective but highly precise environmental assessment is required. Examples of these types of measures are detailed in the chapter. To maximize the probability of detecting and illustrating organism–environment interactions in non-extreme groups, it will be necessary to go beyond just using more precise environmental measures. Specifically,

1. Researchers should not expect all aspects of the environment to enter into interactions or to interact with organismic variables in the same way. This interactional specificity may well require different analytical techniques for different aspects of the environment.
2. Researchers need to focus on the physical microenvironment and on contextual features of the environment, as well as on the traditional measures of parent–child relations, when investigating the process of organism–environment interaction in nonextreme groups.
3. Whenever possible, aggregated environmental measurement is to be preferred over single environmental measurements.
4. Given that the more precise measures of the environment are quite costly in terms of research time, especially if aggregated measurements are taken, studies of this type will typically involve small sample sizes. This may necessitate the use of environmental marker variables across a series of small sample studies so that results across studies can be combined to compensate for the reduced power inherent in a single, small sample study. An example of marker variables that would be useful for studies in the infancy period was detailed earlier in this chapter.

These conclusions suggest that the current generation of studies of organism–environment interaction with nonextreme groups will be empirically rather than theory driven. However, if researchers can identify a replicable set of organism–environment interactions in nonextreme groups, it may then be possible to develop inductive or prototheories, which illustrate the process whereby organism–environment interactions are relevant for the normal range of development. These inductive or prototheories could then be used to guide the selection of environmental variables for the next generation of research studies on the nature and process of organism–environment interaction.

References

Anderson, P. (1972). More is different. *Science, 177*, 393–396.
Barron, R., & Kenny, D. (1986). The moderator–mediator variable distinction in social psychological research. *Journal of Personality and Social Psychology, 51*, 1173–1182.

Beckwith, L., & Cohen, S. (1984). Home environment and cognitive competence in preterm children during the first five years. In A. Gottfried (Ed.), *Home environment and early cognitive development* (pp. 235–272). San Diego, CA: Academic Press.

Belmont, J., Ferretti, R., & Mitchell, D. (1982). Memorizing: A test of untrained mildly mentally retarded children's problem solving. *American Journal of Mental Deficiency*, *87*, 197–210.

Belsky, J. (1980). Mother-infant interaction at home and in the laboratory: A comparative study. *Journal of Genetic Psychology*, *137*, 37–47.

Belsky, J., Hertzog, C., & Rovine, M. (1986). Causal analysis of multiple determinants of parenting. *Advances in Developmental Psychology*, *4*, 153–202.

Bergman, L. (1981). Is intellectual development more vulnerable in boys than in girls? *Journal of Genetic Psychology*, *138*, 175–181.

Birns, B. (1976). The emergence and socialization of sex differences in the earliest years. *Merrill-Palmer Quarterly*, *22*, 229–254.

Block, J., Block, J., & Morrison, A. (1981). Parental agreement–disagreement on child rearing orientations and gender related personality correlates in children. *Child Development*, *52*, 965–974.

Bradley, R., & Caldwell, B. (1984). One hundred seventy-four children: A study of the relationship between home environment and cognitive development during the first five years. In A. Gottfried (Ed.), *Home environment and early cognitive development* (pp. 5–56). San Diego, CA: Academic Press.

Brice, P. (1985). A comparison of levels of tolerance for ambiguity in deaf and hearing school children. *American Annals of the Deaf*, *130*, 226–230.

Brimer, E., & Levine, F. (1983). Stimulus seeking in hyperactive and non-hyperactive children. *Journal of Abnormal Child Psychology*, *11*, 131–140.

Brodsky, P., & Brodsky, M. (1981). A model integrating risk variables in the development of the schizophrenia spectrum. *Journal of Nervous and Mental Disease*, *169*, 741–750.

Bronfenbrenner, U., & Crouter, A. (1983). The evolution of environmental models in developmental research. In W. Kessen (Ed.), *History, theory and methods: Handbook of child psychology* (Vol. 14, pp. 357–414). New York: Wiley.

Cadoret, R., Cain, C., & Crowe, R. (1983). Evidence for gene-environment interaction in the development of adolescent antisocial behavior. *Behavior Genetics*, *13*, 301–310.

Carbo, M. (1983). Research in reading and learning style. *Exceptional Children*, *49*, 486–494.

Casto, G. (1987). Plasticity and the handicapped child. In J. Gallagher & C. Ramey (Eds.), *The malleability of children* (pp. 103–114). Baltimore: Brooks Publishing.

Clarke-Stewart, K. (1978). And Daddy makes three: The father's impact on mother and young child. *Child Development*, *49*, 446–478.

Clarke-Stewart, K. (1989). Infant daycare: Maligned or malignant? *American Psychologist*, *44*, 266–273.

Cloninger, R., Bohman, N., & Sigvardson, S. (1981). Inheritance of alcohol abuse. *Archives of General Psychiatry*, *38*, 861–868.

Cohen, J. (1988). *Statistical power analysis for the behavioral sciences* (2nd ed.). Hillsdale, NJ: Erlbaum.

Compas, B. (1987). Stress in life events during childhood and adolescence. *Clinical Psychology Review*, *7*, 275–302.

Conger, J., Moisan-Thomas, P., & Conger, A. (1989). Cross situational generalizability of social competence. *Behavioral Assessment*, *11*, 411–432.

Conner, W., Thorndike, R., Forbes, N., & Ashworth, C. (1985). The influence of television on measured cognitive abilities. *Journal of Cross Cultural Psychology*, *16*, 355–380.

Corno, L. (1979). A hierarchical analysis of selective naturally occurring aptitude treatment interactions in the third grade. *American Educational Research Journal, 16,* 391–409.

Corno, L. (1980). Individual and class-level effects of parent-assisted instruction in classroom memory support strategies. *Journal of Educational Psychology, 72,* 278–292.

Corno, L., Mitman, A., & Hedges, L. (1981). The influence of direct instruction on students' self appraisal: A hierarchical analysis of treatment and aptitude treatment interaction effects. *American Educational Research Journal, 18,* 39–61.

Cotterell, J. (1986). Work and community influences and the quality of child rearing. *Child Development, 57,* 362–374.

Crockenberg, S. (1987). Predictors and correlates of anger toward and punitive control of toddlers by adolescent mothers. *Child Development, 58,* 964–975.

Crockenberg, S., & McCluskey, K. (1986). Change in maternal behavior during the babies' first year of life. *Child Development, 57,* 746–753.

Cronbach, L., & Snow, R. (1977). *Aptitudes and instructional methods.* New York: Halstead Press.

Dance, K., & Neufeld, R. (1988). Aptitude–treatment interaction in the clinical setting. *Psychological Bulletin, 104,* 192–213.

Daniels, D., & Plomin, R. (1985). Differential experiences of siblings in the same family. *Developmental Psychology, 21,* 747–760.

Day, R., & Ghandour, M. (1984). The effects of television mediated aggression and real life aggression on the behavior of Lebanese children. *Journal of Experimental Child Psychology, 38,* 7–18.

Donovan, W., & Levitt, L. (1985). Physiologic assessment of mother-infant attachment. *Journal of the American Academy of Child Psychiatry, 24,* 64–70.

Edelbrook, C., Costello, A., Dulcan, M., Kalas, R., & Conover, N. (1985). Age differences in the reliability of the psychiatric interview of the child. *Child Development, 56,* 265–275.

Elder, G., Van Nguyen, T., & Caspi, A. (1985). Linking family hardship to children's lives. *Child Development, 56,* 361–375.

Emery, R., Weintraub, S. & Neale, J. (1982). Effect of marital discord on the school behavior of children of schizophrenic, affectively disordered and normal parents. *Journal of Abnormal Child Psychology, 10,* 215–228.

Epstein, S. (1980). The stability of behavior: II. Implications for psychological research. *American Psychologist, 35,* 790–806.

Erlenmeyer-Kimling, L., & Cornblatt, B. (1984). Biobehavior risk factors in children of schizophrenic parents. *Journal of Autism and Developmental Disabilities, 14,* 357–374.

Escalona, S. (1968). *The roots of individuality.* Chicago: Aldine.

Field, T. (1981). Infant arousal, attention and affect during early interactions. In L. Lipsitt (Ed.), *Advances in infant behavior and development* (pp. 58–100). Hillsdale, NJ: Erlbaum.

Field, T., & Ignatoff, T. (1981). Videotaping effects on the behaviors of low income mothers and their infants during floor play interaction. *Journal of Applied Developmental Psychology, 2,* 227–236.

Finkelstein, N., Gallagher, J., & Farran, D. (1980). Attentiveness and responsiveness to auditory stimuli of children at risk for mental retardation. *American Journal of Mental Deficiency, 85,* 135–144.

Finney, J., Mitchell, R., Cronkite, R., & Moos, R. (1984). Methodological issues in estimating main and interactive effects. *Journal of Health and Social Behavior, 25,* 85–98.

Fraser, B., & Fisher, D. (1983). Student achievement as a function of person-environment fit. *British Journal of Educational Psychology*, *55*, 89–99.

Freebody, P., & Tirre, W. (1985). Achievement outcomes of two reading programs. *British Journal of Educational Psychology*, *55*, 53–60.

Gandour, M. (1989). Activity level as a dimension of temperament and toddlers: Its relevance for the organismic specificity hypothesis. *Child Development*, *60*, 1092–1098.

Gersten, R. (1983). Stimulus overselectivity in autistic, trainable mentally retarded and nonhandicapped children. *Journal of Abnormal Child Psychology*, *11*, 61–76.

Gordon, B. (1981). Child temperament and adult behavior. *Child Psychology and Human Development*, *11*, 167–178.

Gunnar, M., & Donahue, M. (1980). Sex differences in social responsiveness between 6 and 12 months. *Child Development*, *51*, 262–265.

Hammen, C., & Zupan, B. (1984). Self schema, depression and the processing of personal information in children. *Journal of Experimental Child Psychology*, *37*, 598–608.

Harvey, P., Weintraub, S., & Neale, J. (1984). Distractability in learning disabled children: The role of measurement artifact. *Journal of Learning Disabilities*, *17*, 234–236.

Holden, G., & Edwards, L. (1989). Parental attitudes toward child rearing: Instruments, issues and implications. *Psychological Bulletin*, *106*, 29–58.

Kagan, J. (1967). On the need for relativism. *American Psychologist*, *22*, 131–141.

Kagan, J. (1989). Temperamental contributions to social behavior. *American Psychologist*, *44*, 668–674.

Kenrick, D., & Funder, D. (1988). Profiting from controversy: Lessons from the person-situation debate. *American Psychologist*, *43*, 23–34.

Keogh, B. (1986). Future of the learning disability field. *Journal of Learning Disabilities*, *19*, 455–460.

Kidd, K., & Matthysee, S. (1978). Research designs for the study of gene–environment interaction in psychiatric disorders. *Archives of General Psychiatry*, *35*, 925–932.

Kochanska, G., Kuczynski, L., & Radke-Yarrow, M. (1989). Correspondence between mothers' self-reported and observed child rearing practices. *Child Development*, *60*, 56–63.

Kogan, N. (1983). Stylistic variation in childhood and adolescence. In J. Flavell & E. Markman (Eds.), *Magnusson's handbook of child psychology* (4th ed., pp. 630–706). New York: Wiley.

Langmeier, J., & Matejcek, Z. (1975). *Psychological deprivation in childhood*. New York: Wiley.

Magnusson, D. (1988). *Individual development from an interactional perspective*. Hillsdale, NJ: Erlbaum.

Maxwell, S. (1980). Dependent variable reliability determinants of sample size. *Applied Psychological Measurement*, *4*, 253–260.

Mazaide, M., Caperra, P., Laplante, B., Boudrealt, M., Thivirge J., Cote, R., & Boutin, P. (1985). Value of difficult temperament among seven year olds in the general population for predicting psychiatric diagnosis at age 12. *American Journal of Psychiatry*, *142*, 943–946.

McCord, R., & Wakefield, J. (1981). Arithmetic achievement as a function of introversion-extroversion and teacher presented reward and punishment. *Personality and Individual Differences*, *2*, 145–152.

Myers, J. (1989). *Fundamentals of experimental design* (3rd ed.) Boston: Allyn & Bacon.

Novak, M., Olley, J., & Kearney, D. (1980). Social skills of children with special needs in integrated and separate preschools. In T. Field, S. Goldberg, D. Stern, & A. Sostek (Eds.), *High risk infants and children* (pp. 327–346). San Diego, CA: Academic Press.

Nuechterlein, K. (1983). Signal detection in vigilance tasks and behavioral attribution among offspring of schizophrenic mothers and among hyperactive children. *Journal of Abnormal Psychology, 92*, 4–28.

O'Brien, M., Anderson-Goetz, D., & Johnson, J. (1988, April). *Mother-infant interaction: Effects of task and context*. Paper presented at the International Conferences on Infant Studies, Washington, DC.

Patterson, G. (1983). Stress: A change agent for family processes. In N. Garmezy & M. Rutter (Eds.), *Stress, coping and development in children* (pp. 235–264). New York: McGraw-Hill.

Plomin, R., & Daniels, D. (1984). The interaction between temperament and environment: Methodological considerations. *Merrill-Palmer Quarterly, 30*, 149–161.

Rushton, J. (1988). Epigenetic rules in moral development. *Aggressive Behavior, 14*, 35–50.

Rushton, P., Brainerd, C., & Pressley, M. (1983). Behavioral development and construct validity: The principle of aggregation. *Psychological Bulletin, 94*, 18–38.

Rutschmann, J., Cornblatt, B., & Erlenmeyer-Kimling, L. (1986). Sustained attention in children at risk for schizophrenia. *Journal of Abnormal Child Psychology 14*, 360–368.

Rutter, M. (1983). Statistical and personal interactions. In D. Magnusson & V. Allen (Eds.), *Human development: An interactional perspective* (pp. 295–320). New York: Academic Press.

Rutter, M. (in press). Epidemiological approaches to developmental psychopathology. *Archives of General Psychiatry*.

Schaefer, E. (1965). Children's reports of parental behavior: An inventory. *Child Development, 36*, 413–423.

Slife, B., & Rychlak, J. (1982). Role of affect assessment in modeling aggressive behavior. *Journal of Personality and Social Psychology, 43*, 861–868.

Smith, L., & Hagen, V. (1984). Relationships between the home environment and sensory motor development of Down Syndrome and non-retarded infants. *American Journal of Mental Deficiency, 89*, 124–132.

Stewart, R., & Burgess, R. (1980, April). *Parent–child interaction in home and laboratory settings*. Paper presented at the Second International Conference on Infant Studies, New Haven, CT.

Strelau, J. (1983). *Temperament-personality-activity*. San Diego, CA: Academic Press.

Sutcliffe, J. (1980). On the relationship of reliability to statistical power. *Psychological Bulletin, 88*, 509–515.

Thomas, A., & Chess, S. (1976). Behavioral individuality in childhood. In L. Aronson, E. Tobach, D. Lehrman, & J. Rosenblatt (Eds.), *Development and evolution of behavior* (pp. 529–543). San Francisco: Freeman.

Trickett, P. (1983). The interaction of cognitive style and classroom environment in determining first grade behavior. *Journal of Applied Developmental Psychology, 4*, 43–65.

Vale, J., & Vale, C. (1969). Individual differences and general laws in psychology. *American Psychologist, 24*, 1093–1108.

Wachs, T. D. (1978). The relationship of infants' physical environment to their Binet performance at 2½ years. *International Journal of Behavioral Development, 1*, 51–65.

Wachs, T. D. (1979). Proximal experience and early cognitive-intellectual development: The physical environment. *Merrill-Palmer Quarterly, 25*, 3–41.

Wachs, T. D. (1983). The use and abuse of environment in behavior genetic research. *Child Development, 54*, 396–407.

Wachs, T. D. (1984). Proximal experiences and early cognitive intellectual development: The social environment. In A. Gottfried (Ed.), *Home environment and early mental development* (pp. 273–328). San Diego, CA: Academic Press.

Wachs, T. D. (1986a). Understanding early experience and development: The relevance of stages of inquiry. *Journal of Applied Developmental Psychology, 7,* 153–165.

Wachs, T. D. (1986b). Models of physical environmental action. In A. Gottfried (Ed.), *Play interactions: The contribution of play material and parent involvement to child development* (pp. 273–298). Lexington, MA: Lexington Books.

Wachs, T. D. (1987a). Short term stability of aggregated and nonaggregated measures of parent behavior. *Child Development, 58,* 796–797.

Wachs, T. D. (1987b). Specificity of environmental action as manifest in environmental correlates of infant's mastery motivation. *Developmental Psychology, 23,* 782–790.

Wachs, T. D. (1988a). Environmental assessment of developmentally disabled infants and preschoolers. In T. D. Wachs & R. Sheehan (Eds.), *Assessment of young developmentally disabled children* (pp. 321–346). New York: Plenum Press.

Wachs, T. D. (1988b). Validity of observers' rating of ambient background noise in the home. In U. Berglund, J. Berglund, J. Karlsson, & T. Landvall (Eds.), *Noise as a pubic health problem* (Vol. 3, pp. 301–306). Stockholm: Swedish Council.

Wachs, T. D. (1989). The nature of the physical microenvironment: An expanded classification system. *Merrill-Palmer Quarterly, 35,* 339–420.

Wachs, T. D., & Gandour, M. (1983). Temperament, environment and six month cognitive intellectual development: A test of the organismic specificity hypothesis. *International Journal of Behavioral Development, 6,* 135–152.

Wachs, T. D., & Gruen, G. (1982). *Early experience and human development.* New York: Plenum Press.

Wade, B. (1981). Highly anxious pupils in formal and informal primary classrooms. *British Journal of Educational Psychology, 51,* 39–41.

Wohlwill, J., & Heft, H. (1987). The physical environment and the development of the child. In I. Altman & D. Stokols (Eds.), *Handbook of environmental psychology* (pp. 281–328). New York: Wiley.

Yarrow, M., Campbell, J., & Burton, R. (1970). Recollections of childhood: A study of the retrospective method. *Monographs of the Society for Research in Child Development, 35* (5, Serial No. 138).

Yarrow, L., Rubenstein, J. & Pedersen, F. (1975). *Infant and environment.* New York: Wiley.

Zegiob, L., Arnold, S., & Forehand, R. (1975). An examination of observer effects in parent-child interactions. *Child Development, 46,* 509–512.

Zimmerman, D., & Williams, R. (1986). Note on the reliability of experimental measures and the power of significance tests. *Psychological Bulletin, 100,* 123–124.

CHAPTER 5

ILLUSTRATIONS OF PERSON– ENVIRONMENT INTERACTION FROM A LONGITUDINAL STUDY

L. ALAN SROUFE AND BYRON EGELAND

For the last 15 years we have been conducting a longitudinal study of the development of children in poverty. Comprehensive and detailed observations over time and in several contexts have provided numerous opportunities to document organism–environment interactions, covariations, and transactions.

Two aspects of our approach have influenced our research on interaction. First, as we elaborate later, we define *organism* as the person at a given point in time. This definition of organism is broader than genetic endowment. It also includes previous experiences and the previous history of development. Therefore, given our longitudinal format and the comprehensiveness of our measures, person–environment interactions may be assessed repeatedly at each phase of development. Second, we have had available ways of grouping subjects. Although some of these, such as gender, are obvious and more in keeping with usual ways of defining organismic variables, others refer more to patterns of adaptation evolved by children over time. A prime example here is infant–caregiver attachment classification, which is presumed to be a product of the total developmental history through the infancy period.

We have found this capacity to group individuals to be a powerful means of uncovering organism–environment interaction. For example, we can ask questions such as, Do different aspects of experience influence outcome for one gender more than the other? or Does the same environmental variable influence boys and girls differently? Likewise, we may examine whether children with different at-

68

tachment histories react differently to similar environmental opportunities or stresses, whether strengths and weaknesses of such groups will show up in different circumstances, and whether different attachment groups will elicit different reactions from the social environment. All of these are examples of interaction between organism or person and environment, broadly defined, although the latter example is specifically referred to as covariation.

Our work and the work of others have also shown that the strength of many environmental variables is at times best revealed in terms of interaction with organism variables, often based on extreme groups. For example, social support available to caregivers shows only modest overall relation to child adaptation in our work, yet improving social support is a powerful predictor of improved adaptation in kindergarten for children showing poor adaptation in the first 2 years (Erickson, Egeland, & Sroufe, 1985). In a similar vein, Musick et al. (1987) found that a number of babies recovered from the effects of having been raised in a high-stress home by a mentally ill parent. The most competent of these preschool children were those whose grandparents or well parent were able to provide nurturance for the child and also cooperated with the nursey school staff.

Likewise, Crockenberg (1981) found a strong interaction between newborn irritability (on the Brazelton Neonatal Assessment Scale) and social support in predicting attachment outcome. Irritability by itself did not show a significant relation to attachment in this middle-class sample, and social support showed only a modest relation. However, irritable infants, reared by caregivers with low social support, were highly likely to show anxious attachment by 1 year of age. Moreover, although Brazelton status did not relate by itself to attachment outcome in Crockenberg's middle-class sample, it did in our poverty sample (Vaughn, Egeland, Waters, & Sroufe, 1979). Again, all of these findings may be viewed in terms of organism–environment interaction.

In the remainder of this chapter, we provide illustrations of such interactions from our research, but first we briefly present a perspective on organism and organism–environment interaction and transaction.

A DEVELOPMENTAL PERSPECTIVE ON ORGANISM AND ENVIRONMENT

A major focus of our current work is on what may be called the third determinant of behavior and development. The first two determinants are genes and current environment (and their interaction). Our research project has in the past examined environmental influences and, to some extent, organismic factors presumed to be at least partly under genetic control (e.g., IQ, temperament). The third determinant—prior developmental history—has captured our attention in recent years. Prior developmental history is not simply past environmental influence but the cumulated organism–environment transaction.

The power of this third determinant of development is best illustrated by work in embryology, especially that concerned with "induction." This work illustrates not only that the genetic code and the cellular context influence the development of a given segment of tissue but also that the contextual influences themselves are influenced by the development of the tissues prior to that point (Arms & Camp, 1987). For example, a small square of tissue is transplanted from the developing "thigh" of a chick embryo to the tip of a bud that will form a wing. Remarkably, this tissue may develop into normal wing tissue, anomalous tissue, or even claw tissue depending on the precise timing of the transplant. The fate of the transplanted tissue, of course, depends on its genetic code (it will never become a fin) and the new context or environment in which it is placed (it will never become upper wing tissue). However, whether it becomes normal wing tip tissue (early), anomalous thigh tissue (late), or, amazingly, claw (intermediate) depends on the prior development of the tissue. That is, if the tissue is already "committed" (the embryologists term) prior to the transplant to becoming thigh tissue, the transplant will not take. If it is committed to becoming leg but not yet thigh tissue, the surrounding tissues may still induce it to be a tip, but only the tip of a leg. Thus a claw! Developmental history constrains the influence of the environment and even the action of genes (i.e., which genes are turned on or off).

In the case of human psychological development, new complexities are added, but, if anything, past history attains even greater importance. Developing humans behave in terms of motives or goals, which include expectations and desires based on past experience. People may actively attempt to influence their environments, at times with awareness and at other times likely without awareness. It becomes clearer that environment is never independent of organism. The two are mutually influencing (covary; see chap. 1 in this book) in ongoing transaction. Children select, interpret, distort, and in countless ways create their own environment. Furthermore, the child's role in creating the environment apparently increases with each phase of development.

In the terms of Bowlby (1973), development is always the product of current circumstances *and* development up to that time. In this position organism is defined more broadly than the individual's constitutional endowment; rather, organism is all genetic, environmental, and developmental influences that have occurred to that point. Currently emerging genetic influences might even be better considered as part of the current circumstances rather than as identical to organism.

Interaction, in the broad sense, comes to the fore in such a perspective. Behavior is rarely, if ever, attributable to genetic inheritance or environmental context alone, but always to the transaction between person and environment. The person is a product of interactive, covarying, and transactive influences. Change is a product of both person and circumstances, and even circumstances are increasingly influenced by the person. Not only are circumstances partly a matter of selective interpretation and exclusion (Bowlby, 1980), but they are actively sought and molded by individual children. Interaction in this broad sense is ubiquitous. Demonstrating interaction in the specific sense of different children reacting differently to the "same" environment has proved difficult, possibly because child and environment are inextricably intertwined. Even the "same" environment (the "effective environment") is different for different children.

On the surface this position has some overlap to Scarr and McCartney's (1983) idea of "niche-picking." However, the present idea of organism actively engaging in the environment (creating and being shaped by it) is broader than Scarr and McCartney's gene-driven system, and it has a larger developmental component, including the idea of increasing influence with development.

To date, much of our research has been aimed at illustrating that from knowledge of the child's developmental history (i.e., person assessments at an earlier point in time), one can predict differential environments created by different children (covariation) and different reactions of social environments to them (transaction), as well as different reactions of children to the same environments (interaction). We are at a beginning stage, but we can provide empirical evidence that organism influences environment, even when that environment represents a very new (even nonoverlapping) social context. Also, we can show that different groups of children are differentially influenced by various environmental circumstances or factors.

ATTACHMENT STATUS–ENVIRONMENT TRANSACTION

A primary organism or person variable in our work is infant–caregiver attachment classification at 12 and 18 months of age. These assessments are based on a series of observations of separations and reunions with the caregiver (Ainsworth, Blehar, Waters, & Wall, 1978). The way the infant adjusts behavior across episodes of cumulating stress, the active nature of the contact- and interaction-seeking behaviors, and the way involvement with the caregiver promotes exploration and affect modulation are assessed. Infants readily able to use the caregiver as a source of support and whose reunions are unimpaired by anger or ambivalence are viewed as having secure attachment relationships with that caregiver. Those who mix contact seeking with anger, withhold contact, or otherwise are unable to draw reassurance from the caregiver under stress are classified as anxiously attached (either "avoidant" or "resistant").

Although such classifications are actually characterizations of the relationship between infant and a particular caregiver (Sroufe, 1985), infant–primary caregiver attachment strongly predicts subsequent adaptation of the child, even apart from the caregiver, during toddler, preschool, and middle childhood periods (i.e., personality formation; see Sroufe, 1988). Therefore, they may serve as organism or person variables in our research on interaction effects.

In many ways attachment assessments are well suited for this task because they are specifically aimed at capturing cumulative developmental influences. We believe that they predict future adaptation so well because they do summarize developmental influences throughout the infancy period. They are presumed to reflect the history of caregiver–infant transaction, which, in turn, is at each point influenced by the three determinants of development. Attachment assessments are predicted by endogenous infant factors, such as extreme prematurity and ill health (Plunkett, Meisels, Stiefel, Pasicke, & Roloff, 1986). Both initial attachment classification and change in classification also are predicted by environmental variables such as social support and life stress (Crockenberg, 1981; Erickson et al., 1985; Vaughn et al., 1979). Finally, the strongest and most consistent predictors of attachment classification are, in fact, assessments of quality of caregiver behavior with the infant (responsiveness, sensitivity) throughout the first year of life (Ainsworth et al., 1978; Belsky & Isabella, 1988; Egeland & Farber, 1984; Grossmann, Grossmann, Spangler, Suess, & Unzer, 1985). In the following sections we describe how this organism variable both interacts and covaries with subsequent environmental influences.

Different Attachment Groupings in the "Same" Environment

Some of our observations of the behavior and adaptation of children with different attachment histories have occurred in naturalistic settings that we controlled. These included two nursery school classes and a series of three summer camps at age 10–11 years. These settings were well suited to examining differences in individual adaptation and changing adaptation across time in a (relatively) constant environment. When one examines individual children in countless different classrooms, it is difficult to know how child, teacher, and other context effects combine to produce behavior. However, when children are all observed in what is at least to some extent a "standard" environment, one may observe not only how children react differently to the same environmental opportunities and challenges (interaction as defined in chap. 1 of this book), but also differential reactions of adults and children in that environment to target children (covariation). Because particular adults and other children are a constant in these contexts, their differential reactions to a target child may be presumed to be due to differences in the children.

Using groups of children assembled on the basis of attachment history allowed a statistical test of these ideas. At least one third of the children in each preschool class or summer camp had histories of secure attachment as infants, that is, they were effective in using the caregiver as a secure base for exploration, were active in seeking interaction or contact following separation, and were readily reassured by contact with the caregiver when distressed. Another group had manifest anxious–avoidant attachments. These children separated readily in the Strange Situation procedure, but on reunions with the caregiver they turned away from, moved away from, ignored, or otherwise actively avoided the caregiver, even when distressed. Moreover, such avoidance interfered with a return to active exploration of the environment. Such behavior has been interpreted as conflict between desire for contact and underlying feelings of anger (Main, 1977). The final group manifested anxious–resistant attachment. These children show poverty of exploration, wariness, great separation anxiety, and great difficulty settling following brief separation. They often manifest explicit ambivalence by strongly seeking contact with the caregiver, yet pushing away, continually shifting the body, stiffening, batting away toys, or struggling against being held during contact.

We found that children grouped on the basis of attachment history did indeed react very differently within these controlled environments. In both the nursery school (aged 4½) and in our summer camps 6 years later, children with histories of anxious attachment more often were socially isolated, were more often involved with adults and less often with peers, and, generally, were more dependent (Elicker, Englund, & Sroufe, in press; Sroufe, 1983). In the nursery school, they more often sought physical contact with teachers and were either shown to be rejected (more for those with avoidant histories) or neglected in peer sociometrics. In the summer camp, those with secure histories more likely formed a friendship, more frequently associated with and formed friendships with other secure children, and were more accepted by and involved with the same gender peer group, which is normative during late middle childhood. In addition, in both settings those with secure histories were judged by teachers–counselors and observers to better take advantage of opportunities afforded (more engaged in activities, more confident in approaching new experiences, more flexible in self-management).

Thus, in this specific sense, person–environment interaction was amply demonstrated in these studies. As a function of variables assessed historically to account for differential histories (our person variables in infancy), children reacted very differently even in putatively constant environments. Specifically, these environments were designed to promote social engagement, development of interactive skills, and formation of friendships. Teachers and counselors explicitly provided such opportunities and promoted such behavior, but only some children responded to these opportunities. Some isolated themselves, some alienated others, and some focused largely on interactions with adults to the relative exclusion of peer relationships. The environment provided opportunities to develop relationships with peers, but only some children responded positively to this environmental opportunity.

The fact that these different groups of children also elicited different reactions from adults and other children in these settings (covariation as described in this book) is also noteworthy. We discuss this in a later section.

Finally, changes in children's behavior over time in these settings (transaction) also was observed. On the first day or first few days of nursery school or camp, those with secure histories held back somewhat. They surveyed the environment and closely attended other children and adults. They were responsive and friendly but not forward. Those with avoidant histories were very outgoing and superficially friendly. Had assessments terminated at this initial phase, they often would have been judged to be very sociable. However, over time they became increasingly isolated and often failed to form a close friendship, even at camp age. We also have more to say about these differences in a later section.

Different Attachment Groups in Varying Environments

Another definition of organism–environment interaction involves differentiation between types of people across varying environments or contexts. This too has been documented in our research.

The Three Summer Camps
Despite our intention, the three summer camps (16 children each) were not identical. The first camp especially was less well organized, there were fewer full-time counselors (three vs. six), and the schedules of the part-time counselors were less well coordinated. There also was less smooth coordination among the counselors and less unified expectations concerning the children. By the third camp, the whole operation was remarkably smooth and well functioning.

These naturally occurring differences in camp structure allowed us to see how children with different histories would react to different types of environments. The differences in isolation, dependency, and social competence outlined earlier held for all three camps, but certain differences between attachment groups held only for the first camp. Those with anxious histories were more often disciplined, more frequently engaged in hostile encounters and, especially, showed less appropriate responses to conflict only in the first camp. By Camp 3 these differences were null. Remarkably, there was virtually no aggression and no disciplining required for any child. Even children known through observations and teacher reports to be chronic bullies at school were not bullies in this context. We assumed that these different findings across camps resulted from the lessened stress, better structure, and more available adult support in the later camps. Regardless, the findings indicate another kind of person–environment interaction: Group differences emerge only in certain environments. People do not behave in a constant fashion regardless of environment.

Different Social Partners
In our nursery school, we were able to carry out an experimental manipulation of the social environment. We assigned children play partners, systematically varying all six combinations of attachment history (secure–secure, secure–avoidant, avoidant–resistant, etc.). These partners spent 14 or more sessions together in a playroom, and we assessed the nature of the resulting relationships (Pancake,

1988; Troy & Sroufe, 1987). This strategy allowed us to investigate how children with different histories would react to exposure to different types of peers. The major result was that the behavior of children from each attachment group depended on the history of the partner. For example, children with avoidant histories systematically "victimized" (demeaned, aggressed against, etc.) partners with resistant histories. However, the latter children were not victimized if they were paired with partners with secure histories. In fact, secure children were quite nurturant and supportive of the less able resistant partner. In addition, those with avoidant histories did not exploit partners from the secure group. These relationships were characterized by mutual distance or a power "standoff." Where both partners had secure histories, relationships were mutually responsive and sensitive.

Stated in terms of interaction, the kind of playmate a given child is and the way he or she treats the partner depends on the nature of the partner he or she is given. A "bully" does not victimize a self-confident, assertive partner, only a vulnerable one. A secure child does not victimize even a vulnerable partner. Different children react to the same social partner and to different partners in different ways.

Varying Task Situations

It is not simply the case that children with anxious attachments always as a group show maladaptation in every context. In many situations both those with avoidant attachment histories and those with histories of resistant attachment do manifest developmental problems. Both groups, for example, are less enthusiastic in solving problems (Matas, Arend, & Sroufe, 1978) and rated as more dependent by preschool teachers (Sroufe, Fox, & Pancake, 1983). However, there are certain contexts or measures that reveal no differences between secure and anxious groups and many more in which only one group of anxiously attached children shows maladaptation, whereas the other is equivalent to those with secure histories. By now, we may specify such varying circumstances. This, again, is a form of interaction between a person variable and environment.

Those with anxious–resistant attachment will, as a group, appear at a disadvantage in any situation involving novelty, challenging environmental problems, or the need for autonomous functioning. Thus, they were very stressed by an initial encounter with a peer as toddlers (Pastor, Vaughn, & Dodds, 1981). They had great difficulty with our tool problems at age 24 months (Gove, 1983) and our barrier box situation at age 3½ years, wherein they faced the challenge of opening a locked box while alone (Arend, 1984). For those with secure histories, such environmental challenges represented intriguing opportunities, which were approached with enthusiasm and positive affect. However, for those with resistant histories, these problems were viewed as overtaxing and threatening, even prior to beginning the task. They also were markedly impaired in Banta's (1970) curiosity box situation at age 4½ (Nezworski, 1983). This was especially striking because the only challenge here was novelty per se. There were no difficult problems to solve. (Those with avoidant histories showed absolutely no limitations in this situation.) Children with resistant histories had great difficulty with the first few days of nursery school and the first day of kindergarten; that is, when the situation was new. These beginning days were precisely those in which those with avoidant histories looked competent.

Those with avoidant histories show few difficulties in situations involving challenges in the inanimate environment. Moreover, in social situations, their difficulties become more apparent over time. Intimacy and interpersonal closeness pose special challenges for these children, as do environmental contexts that call for the sharing or even expression of personal feelings (Elicker, 1990; Sroufe, Schork, Motti, Lawroski, & LaFrenier, 1984). They often appeared worse in early childhood in assessments in which their mothers were present. Those with resistant histories had difficulties with their mothers, but they completely deteriorated when they left to solve problems on their own (Gove, 1983). Those with avoidant histories have special difficulty maintaining personal relationships over time. When placed in ongoing relationships with play partners in the nursery school, relationships formed by these children were judged to be less deep (Pancake, 1988).

These findings are put forward as examples of interaction, that is, different groups of children responding to given environmental challenges in different ways. They also may be discussed in terms of transaction. Doubts about the emotional availability of others and self-isolation or hostility will feed each other in an ongoing way for those with avoidant histories. Likewise, the lack of confidence shown by those with resistant histories in problem situations is partly responsible for and attributable to failures in problem situations. In our theoretical work, we emphasize the early lack of support by the caregiver as underlying the initial incompetence. However the process started, expectation of failure and failure experiences will feed each other. Doubt leads to failure, and problem-solving failure leads to doubt. It is only at a given point in time that this takes the form of simple interaction, with hesitant children faring poorly in novel or challenging situations and confident children faring well. We discuss this more later.

Differential Environmental Reactions to Attachment Groups

One topic that has been of great interest to us concerns differential reactions of new adults and peers to children with different attachment histories. This is conceptually related to the ''niche-picking'' ideas discussed earlier in that it refers to the *nonindependence or covariation* between organism and environment. We are referring not to the child's manner of engaging the environment (e.g., self-isolation) but to the differential reaction of others such that different experiences are created in the same standard environment. Earlier we mentioned that children with avoidant histories were more often "rejected" by peers, whereas those with resistant histories were more often "neglected" and those with secure histories more often sought out and were attributed leadership status. Here we focus on relationships with teachers.

On the basis of many hours of videotape made in our nursery school classes, we assembled 50 randomly selected segments of each principal teacher interacting with each child. Raters without any prior knowledge of the children then viewed the tapes and rated the teachers on salient aspects of their treatment of the child. For a subset of teacher–child dyads, alternative samples of interactive sequences rated by two different coders were compared (analogous to split-half reliability). This preliminary analysis revealed remarkable consistency across collections of sequences, that is, a given teacher was quite consistent in relating to a particular child. We then examined the influence of attachment history on teacher behavior.

Teachers behaved quite differently toward children with different histories (Motti, 1986; Sroufe & Fleeson, 1988). Ratings revealed that in relating to children who had been securely attached, teachers were in general warm, matter of fact, and age appropriate. They held up high standards of behavior for these children and expected them to comply with classroom rules and with their directives. (Children with secure histories were, in fact, more compliant with teacher directives.) With those having anxious or resistant histories teachers were controlling, yet warm and nurturant. They tolerated minor rule infractions by these children and had low expectations for compliance. They treated them much like one would treat a considerably younger child (infantilizing), at times, we believe, to the detriment of the child. (Years later, our camp observations showed that counselors initiated far more contacts with resistant children, even compared with those with avoidant histories that they rated as being equally high on dependency.) Teachers also were controlling of those with avoidant attachment histories and did not expect them to comply with directives. In contrast to those with resistant histories, however, teachers were not nurturant toward these children and, uniquely with this group, at times showed anger toward them. Such a pattern of angry control was reminiscent of the histories of these children. More generally, we believe that environments created by children often reproduce central aspects of prior experience and consolidate preexisting patterns of adaptation.

A unique form of organism–environment interaction observed in this study involved teacher gender. The differences described for nurturance primarily held for the female teacher, whereas the group differences on control held more for the male teacher. This could suggest differential reactivity by male and female teachers to specific child characteristics. Because there was only one of each sex, we could not determine whether these finding would generalize to other male and female teachers or whether they were attributable to other personal qualities of the individuals.

Continuity and Change in Adaptation

Some of the findings outlined earlier (e.g., the prediction of self-isolation and friendship patterns at 10–11 years from assessments in infancy) imply great continuity in individual development. In part, this continuity is explained by the transactional nature of development and the covariation of person and environmental variables. Different children engage the environment differently and elicit different environmental reactions. Moreover, the resulting environmental input often is congruent with the prior pattern of adaptation, encouraging further differential reactions. Children who are hostile and aggressive, behavior that is associated with a history of rejection, expect hostility from others (Dodge & Frame, 1982) and often behave in a contentious manner, leading new social partners to express anger toward or rejection of them, and so forth.

Fundamental change, of course, also occurs, which we have amply documented in our project. Sufficiently powerful changes in the environment lead to changes in adaptation (Erickson et al., 1985; Egeland, Kalkoske, Gottesman, & Erickson, 1990). An important research question, not adequately resolved, concerns whether the nature of change in the face of particular environmental inputs differs for children with different patterns of prior adaptation. That is, is adaptational change also a result of interactive effects of person and environment? For example, consider a group of children, functioning poorly but now encountering new environmental opportunities. Can subgroups be defined that will and will not respond positively to these opportunities?

We have started to explore this by investigating whether different subgroups of children showing poor adaptation are more or less likely to improve in functioning on the basis of differences in earlier history. In brief, those 3½–4½-year-olds who had shown healthy patterns of adaptation as infants and toddlers but who were now functioning poorly were more likely to show positive adjustment in the elementary school environment than those children who had shown poor adaptation both during the preschool years and earlier. We interpreted this as revealing an ongoing impact of early experience (Sroufe, Egeland, & Kreutzer, 1990), but it also could be interpreted as a form of interaction effect. Some poorly functioning preschoolers, predictably, were able to take advantage of opportunities in the elementary school environment; others were not. To confirm this interpretation one would need to know that both groups also experienced comparable reductions in family life stress.

GENDER–ENVIRONMENT INTERACTION

Gender differences have been amply demonstrated in research on personality and social development. Interestingly, such differences are not commonly found in terms of mean differences on variables of interest (Maccoby & Jacklin, 1974) but in correlations among variables (Block, 1979). This has been interpreted to mean that the same status on a particular variable may mean different things for boys and girls; that is, it has different implications in terms of status on other variables.

We have followed up this lead in our longitudinal research by asking whether different aspects of environment or experience have different developmental implications for boys and girls. Gender may even be viewed as an organismic variable in the classic sense, although it certainly is not purely so. If certain environmental features or events influence developmental outcome for one gender but not the other, or influence the two genders differently, this would provide another important example of person–environment interaction.

Routinely in our research we have found that different types of variables predicted developmental outcomes for boys and girls. These differences occurred across a large set of variables and outcome measures in numerous domains: normative developmental-level assessments, school adjustment, emotional disturbance, and so forth. In general, we found that personality or attitudinal assessments of the primary parent (single mothers in the majority of our families), and her capacity to maintain a harmonious relationship with a partner, predicted individual differences in girls but not boys. For boys, parent–child involvement, quality of interaction, organization of the home environment, and the degree of stress prevalent in the home predicted developmental outcomes (Egeland & Farber, 1984; Pianta, Egeland, & Sroufe, 1990).

For example, although observations of caregiver sensitivity and responsiveness at 3 and 6 months of age predicted attachment security for both boys and girls at 12 and 18 months, the predictions were far stronger for boys. In contrast, measures of the mother's confidence and autonomy predicted far better for girls (Egeland & Farber, 1984). Moreover, personal qualities of mothers also accounted for improving adaptation from infancy to age 42 months for girls, but not boys, whereas the reverse was true using an assessment of the organization of the home environment (Egeland & Rahe, 1983).

In another domain, one of our students (Miller, 1989) examined the longitudinal antecedents of gender concept stability (the degree to which the child understands that gender is a permanent characteristic). She found that maternal anger and depression from the Profile of Mood States (McNair, Loor, & Droppleman, 1971) distinguished girls who had not achieved this level of gender constancy from those who had but that these variables did not predict for boys. In contrast, mothers' support for their 2-year-olds in a tool problem task, parental responsiveness to 2½-year-olds (and general quality of the environment) rated in the home, and guidance and limit setting for 3½-year-olds in another laboratory task all differentiated boys with and without gender stability status, but not girls.

We have also examined stress and protective factors as these vary depending on gender (Pianta et al., 1990). Although general assessments of stress were found to predict behavioral and emotional problems at school for both boys and girls, the relation was stronger for boys. Moreover, specific stressors had varying impacts. Family violence predicted strongly for boys, but not girls, whereas change in mother's relationship status predicted differentially for girls. Moreover, family stress had more impact on achievement for boys, whereas it affected expression of emotional problems for girls but had no measureable affect on achievement.

Likewise, different factors served as protectors for boys and girls in high-stress families (Pianta et al., 1990). Protective factors for boys (i.e., those predicting boys who are competent within the high-stress group) included a well-organized and appropriately stimulating home environment, maternal warmth, and quality of maternal support and instruction in problem-solving situations. None of those were predictive for girls. However, assessment of maternal characteristics such as maturity, self-confidence, and self-sufficiency served as protective factors for girls, but not for boys.

Such gender–predictor differences were pervasive in our mostly single-parent sample. This considerable body of data may be summarized in the following way: Boys' development seems to be influenced by the way their mothers treat them and the degree of stressfulness or support in the environments provided for them. On the other hand, girls seem to be influenced primarily by the person their mother is, perhaps through the process of identification. Whether the reverse would be true in studies focusing on fathers and children is not yet known. Nonetheless, this represents a major example of organism–environment interaction.

CONCLUSION

In their introduction to this book, Wachs and Plomin outlined three basic meanings of the term *interaction*. The first is *transaction*, which refers to the ongoing process of adaptation between organism or person and environment. Genetic influences, existing circumstances, and prior development underlie the emergence of a particular pattern of adaptation. The child, thus adapted and in the face of continuing genetic influences and new challenges and opportunities in the environment, forges a new adaptation, and so on, in an ongoing way. This transactional process, illustrated in our work by early emerging differences in attachment and subsequent continuity and change in adaptation, is one major approach to understanding the process of development.

The second usage refers to interaction, or *differential reactivity*. The transactional process just described implies an active role for the child. Children are not simply changed by additional environmental inputs because different children react differently to specific environmental influences. Children with different attachment histories reacted differently to the nursery school and camp environments in terms of self-isolation, preoccupation with adults, and seeking and building friendships or peer group ties. Moreover, only some children were overtaxed by the least well structured of our three camps. Also, when paired with a vulnerable nursery school play partner, some (mostly those with avoidant histories) became exploitative; others gained experience in nurturing or "teaching." Similarly, some children (primarily those with resistant histories) became disorganized in the face of modest increases in stress observed in naturalistic settings or imposed by our procedures. Likewise, we consistently found boys to be more reactive to environmental stress than girls. In brief, environmental influence interacted with person variables.

The final usage of interaction, implied earlier, is captured by the term *covariation*. Environment or circumstances and person are not independent. Not only do people selectively engage (and interpret) the environment, but environments, in the form of social interactants, respond differently to different children. Those with avoidant attachment histories often are rejected by peers and responded to with anger, suspicion, distance, or control by adults. Those with resistant attachment histories often are neglected by peers and infantalized by adults.

These various processes that shape development are *interrelated* and in large measure account for positive patterns of adaptation, on the one hand, and spirals of negative adaptation, on the other. The way different children engage their social environment influences the reactions of others to them, which often further consolidates the prior patterns of adaptation. Secure children, having received responsive care, engage others positively and empathically, are liked and held in esteem in return, and further develop their expectations that they are valued and that relationships are worthwhile. Those with histories of resistant attachment, having experienced chaotic, neglectful, or inconsistent care, behave in passive and immature ways, are neglected by other children and infantalized by adults, deepening their social incompetence and doubts about their personal agency. Those with avoidant histories, who experienced early emotional unavailability or rejection, become involved in cycles of aggression, peer rejection, and negative expectations. Maladaptation may be defined as relating to the environment such that what is needed to promote healthy development is not obtained, and what is received supports continuance of the nonoptimal pattern. Positive adaptation, or competence, refers to engaging the environment in such a way as to encounter experiences that promote both growth and flexibility. This view of transaction underlies the proposition in our model that over time, the role of the child in adaptation increases.

References

Ainsworth, M., Blehar, M., Waters, E., & Wall, S. (1978). *Patterns of attachment*. Hillsdale, NJ: Erlbaum.

Arend, R. (1984). *Infant attachment and patterns of adaptation in a barrier situation at age 3½ years.* Unpublished doctoral dissertation, University of Minnesota, Minneapolis.

Arms, K., & Camp, P. (1987). *Biology* (3rd ed.). Philadelphia: W. B. Saunders.

Banta, T. (1970). Tests for the evaluation of early childhood education: The Cincinnati Autonomy Test Battery (CATB). In J. Helmuth (Ed.), *Cognitive studies* (pp. 424–490). New York: Brunner/Mazel.

Belsky, J., & Isabella, R. A. (1988). Maternal, infant, and social-contextual determinants of attachment security: A process analysis. In J. Belsky & T. Nezworski (Eds.), *Clinical implications of attachment* (pp. 41–94). Hillsdale, NJ: Erlbaum.

Block, J. H. (1979, August). *Personality development in males and females: The influence of different socialization.* Paper presented at the 87th Annual Convention of the American Psychological Association, New York.

Bowlby, J. (1973). *Separation.* New York: Basic Books.

Bowlby, J. (1980). *Attachment and loss* (Vol. 3). New York: Basic Books.

Crockenberg, S. (1981). Infant irritability, mother responsiveness and social support influences on the security of infant-mother attachment. *Child Development, 52,* 857–865.

Dodge, K. A., & Frame, C. L. (1982). Social cognitive biases and deficits in aggressive boys. *Child Development, 53,* 620–635.

Egeland, B., & Farber, E. (1984). Infant-mother attachment: Factors related to its development and changes over time. *Child Development, 55,* 753–771.

Egeland, B., Kalkoske, M., Gottesman, N., & Erickson, M. F. (1990). Preschool behavior problems: Stability and factors accounting for change. *Journal of Child Psychology and Psychiatry, 31,* 891–909.

Egeland, B., & Rahe, D. (1983, April). *Factors accounting for change in the quality of mother-child relationships between infancy and 42 months.* Paper presented at the meeting of the Society for Research in Child Development, Detroit, MI.

Elicker, J. (1990). *Individual differences in thinking about self and peers in preadolescence: The influence of attachment history.* Unpublished doctoral dissertation, University of Minnesota, Minneapolis.

Elicker, J., Englund, M., & Sroufe, L. A. (in press). Predicting peer competence and peer relationships in childhood from early parent-child relationships. In R. Parke & G. Ladd (Eds.), *Family-peer relationships: Modes of linkage.* Hillsdale, NJ: Erlbaum.

Erickson, M., Egeland, B., & Sroufe, L. A. (1985). The relationship between quality of attachment and behavior problems in preschool in a high risk sample. *Monographs of the Society for Research in Child Development, 50*(1–2, Series No. 209).

Gove, F. (1983). *Patterns and organizations of behavior and affective expression during the second year of life.* Unpublished doctoral dissertation, University of Minnesota, Minneapolis.

Grossmann, K., Grossmann, K. E., Spangler, G., Suess, G., & Unzer, L. (1985). Maternal sensitivity and newborn orienting responses as related to quality of attachment in Northern Germany. *Monographs of the Society for Research in Child Development, 50*(1–2, Series No. 209).

Maccoby, E. E., & Jacklin (1974). *The psychology of sex differences.* Stanford, CT: Stanford University Press.

Main, M. (1977). Analysis of a peculiar form of reunion behavior seen in some daycare children: Its history and sequaelae in children who are home reared. In R. Webb (Ed.), *Social development in daycare* (pp. 33–78). Baltimore: Johns Hopkins University Press.

Matas, L., Arend, R., & Sroufe, L. A. (1978). Discontinuity of adaptation in the second year: The relationship between quality of attachment and later competence. *Child Development, 49,* 547–556.

McNair, D., Loor, M., & Droppleman, L. (1971). *Profile of Mood States manual.* San Diego, CA: Educational and Industrial Testing Service.

Miller, G. (1989). *A longitudinal perspective on the antecedents of gender constancy.* Unpublished Master's thesis, University of Minnesota, Minneapolis.

Motti, E. (1986). *Patterns of behaviors of preschool teachers with children of varying developmental history.* Unpublished doctoral dissertation, University of Minnesota, Minneapolis.

Musick, J., Stott, F., Spencer, C., Goldman, J., & Cohler, B. (1987). Maternal factors related to vulnerability and resiliency in young children at risk. In E. J. Anthony & B. Cohler (Eds.), *The invulnerable child* (pp. 229–252). New York: Guilford Press.

Nezworski, M. T. (1983). *Continuity in adaptation into the fourth year: Individual differences in curiosity and exploratory behavior of preschool children.* Unpublished doctoral dissertation, University of Minnesota, Minneapolis.

Pancake, V. (1988). *Quality of attachment in infancy as a predictor of hostility and emotional distance in preschool peer relationships.* Unpublished doctoral dissertation, University of Minnesota.

Pastor, D., Vaughn, B., & Dodds, M. (1981, April). *The effects of different family patterns on the quality of the mother-infant attachment.* Paper presented at the meeting of the Society for Research in Child Development, Boston.

Pianta, R., Egeland, B., & Sroufe, L. A. (1990). Maternal stress in children's development: Predictions of school outcomes and identification of protective factors. In J. Rolf, A. Masten, D. Cicchetti, K. Nuechterlein, & S. Weintraub (Eds.), *Risk and protective factors in the development of psychopathology* (pp. 215–235). Cambridge, England: Cambridge University Press.

Plunkett, J., Meisels, S., Stiefel, G., Pasicke, P., & Roloff, D. (1986). Patterns of attachment among preterm infants of varying biological risk. *Journal of the American Academy of Child Psychiatry, 25,* 794–800.

Scarr, S., & McCartney, K. (1983). How people make their own environments: A theory of genotype-environment effects. *Child Development, 54,* 425–435.

Sroufe, L. A. (1983). Infant-caregiving attachment and patterns of adaptation and competence. In M. Perlmutter (Ed.), *Minnesota Symposium in Child Psychology* (Vol. 16, pp. 41–83). Hillsdale, NJ: Erlbaum.

Sroufe, L. A. (1985). Attachment classification from the perspective of infant-caregiver relationships and infant temperament. *Child Development, 56,* 1–14.

Sroufe, L. A. (1988). The role of infant-caregiver attachment in development. In J. Belsky & T. Nezworski (Eds.), *Clinical implications of attachment* (pp. 18–38). Hillsdale, NJ: Erlbaum.

Sroufe, L. A., Egeland, B., & Kreutzer, B. (1990). The fate of early experience following developmental change: Longitudinal approaches to individual adaptation in childhood. *Child Development, 61,* 1363–1373.

Sroufe, L. A., & Fleeson, J. (1988). The coherence of family relationships. In R. Hinde & J. Stevenson-Hinde (Eds.), *Towards understanding families* (pp. 27–47). Oxford, England: Oxford University Press.

Sroufe, L. A., Fox, N., & Pancake, V. (1983). Attachment and dependency in developmental perspective. *Child Development, 54,* 1615–1627.

Sroufe, L., Schork, E., Motti, F., Lawroski, N., & LaFrenier, P. (1984). The role of affect in social competence. In C. Izard, J. Kagan, & R. Zajonc (Eds.), *Emotions, cognition, and behavior* (pp. 289–319). Oxford, England: Oxford University Press.

Troy, M., & Sroufe, L. A. (1987). Victimization among preschoolers: Role of attachment relationship history. *Journal of the American Academy of Child and Adolescent Psychiatry, 26,* 166–172.

Vaughn, B., Egeland, B., Waters, E., & Sroufe, L. A. (1979). Individual differences in infant-mother attachment at 12 and 18 months: Stability and change in families under stress. *Child Development, 50,* 971–975.

PART TWO

DESIGN AND STATISTICAL CONSIDERATIONS

CHAPTER 6

EMERGING VIEWS ON METHODOLOGY

LEE J. CRONBACH

Because the joint actions of multiple variables are the concern of scientists studying any system, research methods relevant for investigators evolve in many subcommunities. This evolution appears to be especially rapid just now; there have been advances in statistics, and low-cost computing encourages analyses that were impractical a decade ago.

This chapter can only note briefly a fraction of the options that have come to my attention. An important supplement is the reference list for this chapter, which is a bibliography of methodological sources: each was nominated by me or by another chapter author. (A few nonmethodological sources are also cited.) An investigator who inspects this list of possibilities will find that some seem likely to fit his or her kind of investigation. Most often, the investigator will find several relevant methods that serve different functions. Only gaining familiarity with each particular method in the context of a particular investigation will permit the investigator to apply and blend the methods appropriately.

NEED FOR A LONG-RUN, STRATEGIC VIEW

Methodology has both tactical and strategic aspects. Analyzing a data set in a certain way is a tactical choice. However, the most elegant analysis can impede progress if strategic perspective is lacking. Serious interaction research ought to be a program of several years' duration, although there are few examples in behavioral science. A single study displaying a pair of regressions is often the first and last report from its author on that subject; readers can understand such occurrences while lamenting them. Only an evolving, repeatedly revised research plan will establish the reasons for a relation and the limits of its generality.

A substantive program ought to concentrate on one topic for an extended period; from some fraction of such efforts, investigators can expect a payoff. I could have said "concentrate on one variable," but that suggests an inappropriate operationalism. Rather, the concern is with a phenomenon that might be evidenced in many ways. Or one's topic might be broadly defined conditions thought to have powerful effects, as in Wachs's work on the physical environment of a young child (see Wachs, this volume).

I apologize for the bluntness of recommendations such as the one that opened the preceding paragraph; the style reflects my distaste for flaccid prose. In truth, doing science is an art; there are occasions for violating almost any rule. Thus, despite what I have said, concentrating effort is not always best. An omnium gatherum naturalistic approach can sometimes be productive, Darwin providing the notable example. Darwin's phenomenon-to-be-explained emerged from his observations after he had made them.

Generally, the style of investigation should change over time (Srivastava, 1984). For a person not bound by the artificialities of dissertation research, the best first approach is likely to be little structured. It may be quantitatively assisted naturalistic observation, or a string of interventions in which possibly interesting situational variables are altered after each few observations. Limiting the number of focal variables and standardizing treatment protocols to shape a publishable study is rarely a good investment until experience has identified a promising corner of the field.

The austerity of formal hypothesis testing is suited to late-stage checks on a theoretical formulation. It enables researchers to learn only one thing from a study: was a sound prediction made about one prespecified effect? (Well, about a few effects at most.) Throughout a program of inquiry, one should be mindful of the many alternative models consistent with experience to date. As more information comes in, some models become less plausible, or the plausible range of parameters within a viable model is narrowed. Keeping the null hypothesis alive when the data have not rejected it is sound; going forward as if it were the only plausible hypothesis is unintelligent (see Meehl, 1991, pp. 41–47).

In the 1970s, psychologists who believed in the prevalence of interactions were bowed down if not crushed by the pileup of nonsignificant findings. Gradually, thanks especially to Jacob Cohen, they came to recognize that the disappointments were often attributable to lack of statistical power (for a recent presentation, see Cohen, 1988). The current literature is saying over and over that studies of the usual size are likely to accept the null hypothesis in the presence of a meaningful interaction (see, e.g., Wahlsten, 1990). The time has come to depose the null hypothesis from its seat as censor. A research question that can be given a yes–no answer has not been well stated. Data are limited; hence, many alternative conclusions are tenable. A kinder, gentler evaluation will enable more of these seedling hypotheses to reach mature, sustainable form. Researchers can make better use of sparse data than they have so far.

Another general point will be developed as I proceed. When someone who accumulates extensive data achieves great precision and yet finds no interaction, the conclusion that the variables do not interact could be wrong. Decisions of the investigator or circumstances beyond his control can cause a lawlike interaction to vanish in the data. Sometimes, per contra, they will generate an apparent interaction that is artifactual.

BEYOND THE NULL HYPOTHESIS: A BAYESIAN EXAMPLE

In aptitude testing, Person $\times$ Situation interactions are often at issue. Traditionally, industrial psychologists have thought that a particular kind of job had different aptitude requirements in different firms. It followed that, for a given selection test, the within-firm validity coefficient ρ^* (a population parameter freed of sampling error, effects of range restriction, and criterion measurement error) would differ from firm to firm.[1] If the strength of the relationship varies, test scores and firms interact. The recent literature, however, is dominated by Schmidt and Hunter's concept of validity generalization (Schmidt, Pearlman, Hunter, & Hirsh, 1985). Their analysis of accumulated data has established that $\sigma(\rho^*)$ is not so large as observed variation among sample validity coefficients had suggested. They go further, however, proclaiming the truth of a null or near-null hypothesis; $\sigma(\rho^*)$ over firms, they say, is negligible. The issue is pertinent to developmental psychologists, who have occasion to examine "aptitude" data, for example, in checking how outcomes from early intervention relate to characteristics measured at intake. The relation may vary across types of program or across sites within a type. The logic extends broadly to any problem where similar data have been collected in a number of local studies or settings.

Hedges (1987) gets a better fix on variation over sites by applying a Bayesian method. Conventional statistical inference treats each new sample in isolation, as experience written on a blank slate; Bayesian analysis uses external information in determining a range for plausible conclusions. Hedges analyzed in terms of Fisher's z, but I report approximate equivalents on the correlation scale. Because he aimed only to demonstrate a method, Hedges worked with data that came readily to hand, on prediction of algebra achievement in 14 schools. The corrected validity coefficients ρ^* had an estimated central value of .65. Hedges checked the likelihood of the data's arising when $\sigma(z)$ takes on various values; the maximum likelihood came at $\sigma(z)$ near .2. This implies that ρ^* values spread at least from

---

[1] One would prefer to compare regression coefficients, but the absence of a common criterion scale across firms forces reliance on correlations.

.45 to .85—distinctly nonnegligible variation. Hedges could also estimate ρ^* in each setting. My reading of his summary chart indicates that, in the range of σ that has moderate or high likelihood, the estimated ρ^* for one outlier school is .54–.62, midway between .65 and its "flat prior" face value of .51.

Hedges's study was a meta-analysis; having many studies of the same variables permitted Hedges's Bayesian estimates to be wholly data-based. An alternative is to use subjective priors, that is, a judgment about the plausible range for a parameter that is derived informally from tangentially related experience (Fornell & Rust, 1989). Either way, one gains more from samples of modest size and is left with a statement of posterior uncertainties instead of an overly firm "conclusion."

THE PLACE OF NARRATIVE INFORMATION

Improved estimates are all to the good, but science seeks understanding. Technical discussions of design and analysis tend to divert attention from the value of descriptive information about backgrounds, settings, and the course of events. With regard to the preceding example, someone concerned with the meaning of the variation in validity coefficients would have to ask what is exceptional about each outlier school or firm. Such information would be mostly qualitative. Suggested explanations would be woven into a best-for-now understanding of the interaction.

Virtually all research is or should be exploratory. Even a study designed to test quantitatively a prespecified hypothesis ought to collect much side information, to enrich thinking about within-cell variation in processes and results. The investigator ought to keep as full a record as possible of supplementary variables and of transactions during the course of the study (Cronbach, 1982).

My next example shows how qualitative inquiry can change "error variance" to "interaction." The classic Brownell and Moser (1949) study contrasted meaningful with rote instruction in third grade. In half of the 41 classes, teachers explained the moves in double-digit subtraction; in the other, teachers just laid out steps to be practiced. Although explanation had a positive effect on average, effects varied with the school. An examination of school practices showed that explanation helped only where arithmetic had been taught meaningfully in the first 2 grades. Children in schools in which previous learning had been by rote could make little use of the explanations. There was interaction, then, between educational history and treatment.[2]

---

[2] An additional interaction from a planned contrast deserves passing mention. Each class was taught one of two algorithms. The benefit from explanation was substantial only for the algorithm that was easy to explicate.

Narrative information became the center of interest in the research program of Noreen Webb. To study learning in small working groups, she started out (with encouragement from Snow and me) to contrast pupil groups having wide-ranging ability with homogeneous groups. The outcome means in Ability × Treatment cells looked highly irregular, and statistical interpretation seemed hopeless. Fortunately, Webb had taped the sessions; in sorting out the behavior, she observed, among other things, that those who gave help and those who got help were the beneficiaries of mixed-group work. Proneness to help (when associated with high ability) thus emerged as an organismic variable interacting with heterogeneity of ability. Similarly, help-seeking came mostly from a subset of the low-ability members, and they benefited more than average pupils from the mixed group— another interaction. In the original work and that of the next decade (Webb, 1978, 1989), many such qualitative hypotheses were elaborated. Evidently, the character of the explanation affects what is learned by the helper and by the person helped.

OPEN-MINDEDNESS VERSUS TOUGH-MINDEDNESS: AN ETERNAL CONFLICT

Interaction research is caught in a double bind. The bounty of nature, the sheer abundance of interaction effects, implies an infinitude of hypotheses worthy of attention. Yet the constraining traditions of tough-mindedness—quantification, statistical inference, and parsimony—press researchers to amass excellent data on a narrow set of variables and circumstances. Narrowing the field of inquiry increases the power of the study, setting sharper bounds on the few parameters investigated, but one can narrow the field prematurely.

The tradeoff between generality and simplicity has been much discussed as it applies to the distinction between internal and external validity (Cook & Campbel, 1979; Cronbach, 1982). A tightly controlled study describes one or more effect sizes and can bound the population estimate for each. The finding applies to the particular circumstances of the study: the local setting, the local population, the way the treatments were delivered, and so on. In policy research, one wants to generalize over communities and over the realistic variation in service delivery. One therefore comes closer to answering the policy question by drawing samples from many communities and constraining deliverers by broad guidelines only. The more varied the initial sources of data, the better the interpreter knows what can go wrong with delivery and what can impede the working of the treatment. Whatever the design, policymakers generalize to unexamined settings, some of which will develop after the policy is in place. This extrapolation is intuitive and qualitative; it cannot be reduced to statistics. To be sure, one can sometimes select a representative national sample and form a generalization describing the national-average effect. Even that is a time-bound truth, and generalizing to another day requires the same nonformal inference as before.

Scientific studies of interaction encounter the same problem, inasmuch as we want to generalize over families, communities, or even cultures. A quantitative relation found in one locality has little value if it is not transportable, and a description of an aggregate of localities has limited value unless it fits most localities individually. Again, the best resolution is probably to accumulate local studies, with sufficient information on the localities to gain insight into factors associated with variation (see the later section on distinguishing relationships at multiple levels).

SADDLE SURFACES

Most studies of interaction have used either a 2×2 design or a comparison of two regression slopes. Because only a few variables (e.g., sex) are truly binary, it is best to regard these designs as taking test borings or cross-sections from a continuous surface. If variables X and Y interact to affect dependent variable D, the relationship can logically correspond to the saddle surface. (A response surface could take other forms: for example, $D = Ye^X$. Most comments that apply to the saddle surface apply to other surfaces.)

The saddle model is a generalization over the X,Y domain:

$$E(D|X,Y) = b_0 + b_1X + b_2Y + b_{12}XY$$

The equation can readily accommodate additional variables and higher order products, and there is an argument for adding X^2, . . .terms. A saddle surface can be fitted to categorical data—from strains, for example. (The seminal paper was Tukey's (1949) on "one degree of freedom for interaction"; for an overview of the initial developments, see Freeman, 1973.) Here I neglect the several extensions.

Figure 1 shows one such surface. Diagonal slices across the surface are parabolas; left-to-right and front-to-back slices are straight lines. The figure depicts the trend in depression of adult women as a function of stress and coping effort. The possible ranges of the variables are as follows: stressors, 0–15; coping, 0–4; and depression, 0–4. The underlying values of b_0, . . ., b_{12} are .540, .311, .182, and $-.120$, respectively. Note the "saddle point" at stress = 1.5, coping = 2.6. Imagine a bowlegged cowboy astraddle the surface there, facing toward the pommel of the saddle at front and right. The cantle rises up behind him when the surface is extended. As can be seen, depression goes up rapidly with increasing stress for the people low on coping. When coping is between 2 and 3, however— in the neighborhood of the saddle point—depression is at the same rather low level no matter what the pressure of events. For a person at the extreme of 4 on coping, by extension, depression peaks when stress is minimal. Such a person appears to gain mental health from challenge.

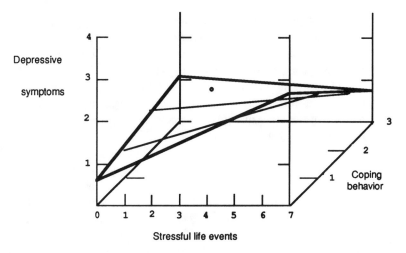

Figure 1.   Saddle surface describing an interaction. (Adapted from Finney, Mitchell, Cronkite, & Moos, 1984, p. 87. The small circle indicates the saddle point where the right-to-left and front-to-back slopes are horizontal.)

The most common statistical analysis is stepwise regression, which (properly handled; see Cronbach, 1987) obtains coefficients for the following sample-specific variant of the preceding equation (where x and y are deviations from the sample means):

$$E(D|X,Y) = b_{0s} + b_{1s}x + b_{2s}y + b_{12s}xy \quad .$$

The conventional analysis concludes that interaction is present if including the last term increases the multiple correlation significantly. Interaction is thus defined as the trend remaining after main effects are removed. Analysis of variance works the same way and is interpreted similarly.

Traditional analyses generally underrate the importance of interactions.

Significance tests, and descriptions of effects in terms of percentage of variance, are misleading. On these points see Abelson (1986), Anderson (1982), Levins and Lewontin (1985), Wahlsten (1990), and the remainder of this chapter.

INSIGHTS FROM THE GAS LAWS

One of the most famous saddle surfaces is the law describing how pressure and volume of an ideal gas interact: $PV = cT$. (The saddle point is at 0, and 0 and only positive numbers are meaningful.) Psychologists expect multiplier effects from many variables, particularly in the motivational domain (stress, drive strength, and interests, for example), although the theoretical models usually include additive effects as well. Because the classic gas law is part of the history of a matured program of research, thought about it can illuminate our investigative path.

1. No one would dispute that best present theory should guide data collection, but there is a lesson in the fact that the P–V–T relations stood as molar empirical findings for 200 years before the pertinent molecular-level theory became available to explain them.

2. The choice of dependent variable is arbitrary, determined by one's interest rather than by the data. Any one of P, V, and T moderates the relation of the other two. (The choice is not arbitrary for developmental variables having a time sequence.)

3. A scientific law is stated so as to cover the conceivable domain of the variables, subject to the discovery of boundary conditions. The continuous function is a powerful heuristic. Identifying boundaries where the relation breaks down, or where the fit of observations is poor, brings amendments. Thus, physicists were led to recognize the limit of temperature as $0°$ K. Also, the poor fit for certain gases at low temperatures implied stickiness of molecules as an additional interacting variable and led to a more complicated law that serves in that range.

4. Conventional wisdom minimizes findings of interaction that can be made linear by monotone transformation of scales. One should not dismiss nonlinearity just because a relation can be transformed to linearity. To write $\log T + \log c = \log P + \log V$ does seem to "get rid of" the interaction, but it does not change physical nature. Physical scientists do not linearize this relation because, in the network of theory, the P, V, and T scales produce a generally simpler set of laws than do their log equivalents. (Making a similar comment about the law for attraction, Wahlsten, 1990, stresses that a conceptual revolution was embodied in Newton's multiplying two masses rather than adding their logarithms.)[3]

5. Finally, a fundamental point: Interactions are not different in kind from main effects. If one investigates the P, V relation, unaware that temperature is relevant, one will surely find a strong main effect of P on V. Ambient temperatures do not vary enough to create conspicuous inconsistency. By the same token, an nth-order interaction very likely is the shadow of an interaction of order $n + 1$ or higher. The c in the gas law represents a fourth interacting variable, associated with molecular weight, and the stickiness mentioned earlier is a fifth.

What is called a main effect of X is most often an average—over the range of all other variables affecting the data—of inconstant X effects (i.e., of interaction

---

[3] Ordinality is troublesome, however, because the relations are monotone. In such cases, goodness-of-fit indexes are often unable to show that a linear model fits better than an interactive model or vice versa. (This is a generalization from simulations by Parker, Casey, Ziriax, & Silberberg, 1988.)

Table 1.

VOLUME IN EACH OF FOUR CELLS

	Raw volume			Residualized	
T	P = 1	P = 1.5	M	P = 1	P = 1.5
293	293	195	244	1.7	−1.7
273	273	182	228	−1.7	1.7
M	283	189	236	0	0

effects). If an early physicist had started with one of the common designs and with V as dependent variable, he might have crossed two convenient temperatures—of the room (20° C) and of ice water (0° C)—with pressures of 1 and 1.5 atmospheres.[4] To simplify, assume that an extremely large number of observations are averaged, and ignore the multiplier c. The results, after converting temperature to the Kelvin scale, are shown in Table 1.

The sum-of-squares partitions as follows:

Temperature	278	3%
Pressure	8899	97%
Residual	11	0.1%

It looks as if the interaction effect is vanishingly small; in a finite experiment, error variance would engulf the interaction. Anderson (1982) offered further demonstrations of nonlinear relations that common analyses report as linear.

RECOGNIZING POWER IN DESIGN, ANALYSIS, AND INTERPRETATION

Returning now to statistical inference, I need barely mention well-known impediments to establishing significance:

- ☑ Dichotomizing a continuous distribution sacrifices power.
- ☑ Power drops rapidly as the number of degrees of freedom for the numerator increases, as when predictors or treatments are kept in the form of multiple, unordered categories.
- ☑ Conventional p values become uninterpretable when many hypotheses are tested on the same sample.

---

[4] The saddle surface applies to the interaction of T and $1/P$. Making the formal changes necessary to recognize this would not alter the conclusions.

If one tests only for main effects, on the other hand, the power is reduced by any unexamined interaction, because interaction variance is assigned to error. Similarly, when one tests a first-order interaction and stops there, any higher order interaction inflates the error variance.

The Plausible Range for a Nonsignificant Effect

Instead of letting a low *p* value kill interest in a relationship, I advise forming confidence intervals for the regression equations or otherwise dramatizing the uncertainty of knowledge at this time. To illustrate, I borrow an argument from Krantz and Shinn (in preparation) that considers variables like those of Figure 1, except that social support replaces coping. For both predictors, 1 is *never* and 2 is *rarely*, on a 5-point scale. The regression coefficient relating distress to stressors, when no interaction term is fitted, is .255. At Support = 2, the data are better fitted with a slope of .32; however, at Support = 4, the data are best fitted with a slope of .18. The interaction contrast is .14. Choosing a confidence level of .25 (two-tailed), Krantz and Shinn calculated plausible upper and lower limits from the standard error. The upper limit identifies the population slope difference that would, in one eighth of all samples, generate a slope difference less than that observed. The outer limits for the slopes were .38 and .12, for a difference of .26. At these limits, the level of distress is 1.4 with either level of support, when Stressors = 2. When Stressors = 4 (*often*), distress values of 2.6 and 3.1 correspond to high and low support. The 0.5 difference is as large as the Stressor main effect between *rarely* and *often*. The upper limit, then, describes a practically important interaction. The lower limit yields a small positive difference; the zero-difference hypothesis that could not be rejected at the .05 level does not fall within the plausible (.25) range. There is no magic in the .25 level; it is the style of thinking that is to be encouraged.

Techniques for forming interval estimates of regressions and regression differences can be found in Cronbach and Snow (1977, pp. 86–93), Willson (1985), and Rutter and Pickles (chap. 7). Because the usual methods are difficult to stretch over some types of analysis, a flexible alternative deserves mention. The bootstrap (Efron & Tibshirani, 1986) is a "resampling" scheme. Suppose that variance components are being estimated for an adoption file to study G × E interaction. The bootstrap would form an alternative data set of the same size by sampling families *with replacement* from the original, then would estimate the components as before. The distribution of estimates from a large number of these resamples indicates the uncertainty in the original estimate.

The reader may have recognized that resampling could be applied to Krantz and Shinn's (in preparation) data. One would fit the b_0 . . . b_{12} model to several hundred bootstrap resamples from the original data, substitute Stressor values of 2 and 4 in the equations, and obtain a distribution of slope differences. The Krantz and Shinn analysis trusts a number of statistical assumptions (notably, uniform residual variances), whereas the bootstrap avoids assumptions. Although bootstrapping is comparatively expensive, it is especially valuable when the usual assumptions seem likely to be violated. Unfortunately, the bootstrap does not always prove out well. Prospective users should know of the Monte Carlo methods used to check on its accuracy and of some refined proposals for improving results (Efron, 1983).

Choosing Values for Predictor Variables

Power depends greatly on the choice of X and Y values (at least when one assumes a saddle surface and homogeneous residual variances). If X is a person variable, there is a larger effect size for it if data are collected at the extremes of the X distribution than if the same number of cases are drawn at random. Likewise, more extreme contrasts between treatment conditions produce greater effect sizes (and Fs). Those facts are well known. It is not so well known that, other things being equal, increasing the X and Y variances does much more to enhance the apparent strength of an interaction than that of a main effect.

By way of demonstration, return to the primitive experiment on the volume of a gas, but double the range of P and T, keeping the center of the data unchanged. The reader can verify that with temperatures of 30° C and $-10°$ C crossed with pressures of 0.75 and 1.75, the following sums of squares result:

Temperature	1562	2%
Pressure	79806	97.5%
Residual	400	0.5%

The part of the interaction that enters the residual sum of squares is still small, but it has increased by 36 times, whereas the other effects increased about 6 and 9 times, respectively. With any amount of error variance, the three F ratios will increase in those proportions. (Note, too, that if the effect *were* linear, doubling the range would increase main effects by a factor of only 4. Larger values arise here because the main effects are credited with even more of the interaction variance than before.)

A related point: In the saddle surface, the further the sample centroid is from zero on one or both scales, the more variance a linear model accounts for. The interaction effect (the regression coefficient for the product term) is the same at all distances, but with a smaller residual less variance is assigned to it and it looks unimportant.

Distinguishing Relationships at Multiple Levels

The bad news about the power of interaction analysis is usually accompanied by a recommendation to increase sample size. Unfortunately, studies with hundreds of cases can lack power if the effects are mediated by common influences within classrooms or other separated settings. Effects mediated by features of the group were important in the Brownell-Moser, Hedges, and Webb studies reviewed earlier. Regressions of a reading posttest on a pretest can be based on school means, class means within each school, or pupils within each class. The last two kinds of coefficient vary over groups. Nonuniform within-group regression coefficients imply that there is an interaction to be explained. The various interactions identified with these unequal slopes are thoroughly confused when an analysis ignores aggregate units. Effects at the school or class level are often comparatively large, yet few studies include enough classes or schools to set narrow bounds on across-aggregate parameters.

In recent years, the statistical community has advanced ingenious ways to extract information from hierarchical data. These methods should enable us to set aside the pupil-as-unit analyses that can either hide interactions or produce spurious ones (e.g., Cronbach & Webb, 1975). A recent book edited by Bock (1989) lays out several alternative methods of multilevel analysis. The new methods apply most clearly when individuals are nested within settings. Such data structures occur in hospitals, in family service agencies, and in results of mass-media campaigns in scattered communities. Note also that siblings are nested within families, but the small within-group Ns rule out some methods of multilevel analysis.

Among the analyses in Bock's (1989) book, one has special relevance to developmental psychology. Logically, we would expect infant vocabulary to develop more rapidly when mother talk is plentiful, but little evidence has been presented. Bryk and Raudenbush (in Bock, 1989, pp. 178–186) make a preliminary report on an 11-case study: Vocabulary at 26 months correlated highly with that at 16 months, but an index of mother's speech (LMS) at 16 months added only .08 to the squared correlation. Because vocabulary had been measured eight times between 12 and 26 months, it was possible to treat child as a ''level'' within which the eight measures were nested. One or more growth parameters for each child, which summarized adequately the eight scores, could be estimated. Such parameters related strongly and significantly to LMS. Specifics of the analysis have been modified substantially in a later paper (Huttenlocher, Haight, Bryk, Seltzer, & Lyons, 1989) with 11 additional cases. In both analyses, the influence of LMS varied with age. One could probably reconfigure the data to exhibit an ordinal interaction of child's status and LMS. The study is related to McCall's chapter 8 (this book) because of its handling of a longitudinal vector. The eight person variables are collapsed into a few summary variables; in principle, the mother (environment) could be treated the same way. Then, the two sets of parameters could describe a relatively simple joint function.

Allowing for Error in Variables

Apart from its economical use of information, the analysis just sketched gets strong results because (like that of Hedges) it estimates relations for parameters of the children's data rather than relations for fallible observations. Among earlier studies of interaction, almost none have allowed for error except those treating genotype as a latent variable.

Correcting for measurement error will change the strength (and perhaps the ordinality) of the Group $\times$ Predictor interaction. Sometimes the correction will change regressions from parallel to nonparallel, or vice versa (especially where groups have different standard deviations on X (Cronbach & Snow, 1977, pp. 33–35, 49). Evans (1985) presents dramatic examples of the masking of interactions by measurement error, correlated or uncorrelated.

In scientific work, it is advisable to go beyond reliability studies and to measure a construct with two or more indicators. Then, latent structure analysis (with LISREL, perhaps) will discard indicator-specific variance and report on the interaction effects of whatever construct both indicators embody. The researcher must be alert, however; sometimes it is indicator-specific "method variance" (e.g., mother's perception of a child's compliance) that has explanatory power. (What distorts reports on interaction is error and irrelevant variance in predictors; in measures of outcome, they increase error variance but do not systematically affect raw-score regressions or group means.)

Quasi-experiments and correlational analyses of observational studies are often analyzed by comparing regressions. The biases that enter estimates of treatment effects from studies with uncontrolled assignment, particularly from analyses of covariance, have been much discussed (Anderson et al., 1980). Little has been written, however, about biases in comparisons of slopes. Whenever treatment-group membership or other focal situational variable is correlated with the predictor, trouble is likely. The mathematics relevant to the following paragraph is sketched in chapter 6 of Cronbach (1982).

One can get pseudointeraction effects when (perhaps because of nonrandom assignment) contrasted groups are not equally representative of the relevant population. Moreover, with nonequivalent groups, real effects may be erased or reversed. If within-treatment regressions are parallel when two groups of cases are distributed similarly on the predictor X, the regressions will almost surely not be parallel when the study is run on groups having unequal standard deviations on X and vice versa.[5] That is, a pseudointeraction will arise from confounding in the design or a correlation in nature, rather than from a more fundamental cause.

For example, in the Terman file on women that I am currently analyzing, one might reasonably ask how strongly an indicator of lifetime happiness is related to level of education. I could then go on to a question of interaction: Is the strength of association (regression coefficient) different for homemakers and career women? I can make that comparison at a descriptive level, but the meaning is elusive because the distributions on the educational variable differ. The interpretative question is an unanswerable counterfactual: If equivalent groups had gone into the two life paths, would the strength of association be the same?

A STRUCTURED EXPLORATORY METHOD

I close by describing one more promising innovation. CART methodology (Breiman, Friedman, Olshen, & Stone, 1984) is a much improved version of the old Sonquist–Morgan Automatic Interaction Detector. The investigator concerned with a certain dependent variable D records a large number of independent variables that may, separately or jointly, be associated with it. The computer program builds a tree structure in stepwise fashion. Any variable, dichotomized, can sort cases so that low D is more prevalent in the left branch than the right.

All variables are tried, and the one that discriminates best is chosen for the top of the tree. Each branch is now split, giving a structure like the one in Figure 2, where the percentage is the prevalence of low D in the cell.

In the made-up example in Figure 2, even the second step describes interactive relations (i.e., joint effects of variables). On the left, the combination of high X with high Y implies a greater incidence of low D. On the right, low D is associated with low X and positive Z. At subsequent stages in the development of the tree, new variables enter or old variables reenter.

Tree-building obviously capitalizes on chance, and the great virtue of CART is a built-in cross-validation. By repeatedly forming trees on the basis of 90% of the cases and calculating hit rates on the holdout cases, the program prunes off lower branches that probably were generated by sampling error. The end product displays a tree that has moderate complexity and a nonspurious hit rate. The patterning of variables in the tree becomes the source of substantive hypotheses or of practical decision rules. Applications have ranged from classifying radar signatures of various warships to rules for emergency room disposition of cardiac patients. The procedure works for moderate samples just because it discounts probabilities that fall in the chance range; however, samples of at least 200 are

---

[5] An exception is to be made for studies in which groups were selected explicitly on X (Cronbach, 1982, p. 195).

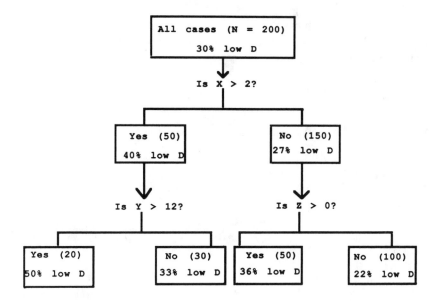

Figure 2. Tree to identify groups high and low on *D*.

desirable. Most important is that the analysis gives almost as much primacy to high-order interactions as to low-order interactions and main effects.

CONCLUSIONS

I have indicated a number of aspects of design and analysis that tend to lose sight of interactions that are present in nature. Remedies include the following:

1. Identifying the range of plausible models instead of giving primacy to a no-interaction hypothesis.
2. Analyzing in terms of latent variables.
3. Experimenting on cases from the extremes of the predictor distribution or on cases in the neighborhood of the likely saddle point.
4. Collecting qualitative information on settings and processes.
5. Pursuing the explanation of a phenomenon in an extended program of studies.

More subtle investigation not only can locate more interactions but can better describe and explain them. On the other hand, interactions may be "found" when there is no interaction in nature. This difficulty was mentioned in connection with sampling error and cross-validation, scale transformation, levels of aggregation, and contrasts of nonequivalent groups.

Fortunately, much has been learned in recent years about pitfalls and promising possibilities. Those who keep up to date will be rewarded with greater yields from their investigative effort.

References

Abelson, R. P. (1986). A variance explanation paradox. *Psychological Bulletin, 97*, 129–133.

Anderson, N. H. (1982). *Methods of information integration theory.* San Diego, CA: Academic Press.

Anderson, S., Auquier, A., Hauck, W. W., Oakes, D., Vandaele, W., & Weisberg, H. I. (1980). *Statistical methods for comparative studies: Techniques for bias reduction.* New York: Wiley.

Baron, R., & Kenny, D. (1986). The moderator–mediator variable distinction in social psychological research. *Journal of Personality and Social Psychology, 51*, 1173–1182.

Bock, R. D. (Ed.). (1989). *Multilevel analysis of educational data.* San Diego, CA: Academic Press.

Breiman, L., Friedman, J. H., Olshen, R. A., & Stone, C. J. (1984). *Classification and regression trees.* Belmont, CA: Wadsworth.

[6]Brownell, W. A., & Moser, H. E. (1949). *Meaningful versus mechanical learning: A study in grade III subtraction.* Durham, NC: Duke University Research Studies in Education, No. 8.

Bryk, A. S., & Raudenbush, S. W. (1988). Heterogeneity of variance in experimental studies: A challenge to conventional interpretations. *Psychological Bulletin, 104*, 396–404.

Busemeyer, J. R.(1980). Importance of measurement theory, error theory, and experimental design for testing the significance of interactions. *Psychological Bulletin, 88*, 237–244.

Busemeyer, J. R., & Jones, L. E. (1983). Analysis of multiplicative combination rules when the causal variables are measured with error. *Psychological Bulletin, 93*, 549–562.

Cohen, J. (1988). *Statistical power analysis.* Hillsdale, NJ: Erlbaum

Cook, T. D., & Campbell, D. T. (1979). *Quasi-experimental and experimental designs for field experiments.* Chicago: Rand-McNally.

Cox, D. R. (1984). Interaction. *International Statistical Review, 52*, 1–31.

Cronbach, L. J. (1982). *Designing evaluations of educational and social programs.* San Francisco: Jossey-Bass.

Cronbach, L. J. (1987). Statistical tests for moderator variables: Flaws in analyses recently proposed. *Psychological Bulletin, 102*, 414–417.

Cronbach, L. J., & Snow, R. E. (1977). *Aptitudes and instructional methods: A handbook for research on interactions.* New York: Irvington.

Cronbach, L. J., & Webb, N. M. (1975). Between-class and within-class effects in a reported Aptitude × Treatment interaction: Reanalysis of a study by G. L. Anderson. *Journal of Educational Psychology, 67*, 717–724.

Efron, B. (1983). Estimating the error rate of a prediction rule: Improvements in cross-validation. *Journal of the American Statistical Association, 78*, 316–331.

---

[6] Nonmethodological reference.

Efron, B., & Tibshirani, R. (1986). Bootstrap method for standard errors, confidence intervals, and other measures of statistical accuracy. *Statistical Science, 1*, 54–77.

Evans, M. G. (1985). A Monte Carlo study of the effects of correlated method variance in moderated multiple regression analysis. *Organizational Behavior and Decision Processes, 36*, 305–323.

Finney, J. W., Mitchell, R. E., Cronkite, R. C., & Moos, R. H. (1984). Methodological issues in estimating main and interactive effects: Examples from coping/social support and stress field. *Journal of Health and Social Behavior, 25*, 85–98.

Fornell, C., & Rust, R. T. (1989). Incorporating prior theory in covariance structure analysis: A Bayesian approach. *Psychometrika, 54*, 249–259.

Freeman, G. H. (1973). Statistical methods for the analysis of genotype–environment interactions. *Heredity, 31*, 339–354.

Hedges, L. (1987). The meta-analysis of test validity studies: Some new approaches. In H. Wainer & H. Braun (Eds.), *Test validity for the 1990's and beyond* (pp. 191–212). Hillsdale, NJ: Erlbaum.

Huttenlocher, J., Haight, W., Bryk, A., Seltzer, M., & Lyons, L. (1989). *Early vocabulary growth: Relation of language input and gender.* Unpublished manuscript, University of Chicago, Department of Education.

Krantz, D. H., & Shinn, M. (in preparation). *Important interaction effects are hard to detect.* Columbia University, Department of Psychology.

Levins, R., & Lewontin, R. (1985). The analysis of variance and the analysis of causes. In R. Levins & R. Lewontin (Eds.), *The dialectical biologist* (pp. 109–122). Cambridge, MA: Harvard University Press.

Meehl, P. E. (1991). Why summaries of research on psychological theories are uninterpretable. In R. E. Snow & D. E. Wiley (Eds.), *Improving inquiry in social science* (pp. 13–59). Hillsdale, NJ: Erlbaum.

Parker, S., Casey, J., Ziriax, J. M., & Silberberg, A. (1988). Random monotone data fit simple algebraic models: Correlation is not confirmation. *Psychological Bulletin, 104*, 417–423.

Roux, C. Z. (1984). Treatment × Unit interactions in the completely randomized and randomized block designs. In K. Hinkelmann (Ed.). *Experimental design, statistical models, and genetic statistics* (pp. 141–153). New York: Dekker.

Schemper, M. (1988). Non-parametric analysis of treatment-covariate interaction in the presence of censorship. *Statistics in Medicine, 7*, 1257–1266.

Schmidt, F. L., Pearlman, K., Hunter, J. E., & Hirsh, H. R. (1985). Forty questions about validity generalization and meta-analysis. *Personnel Psychology, 38*, 697–798.

Srivastava, J. (1984). Sensitivity and revealing power: Two fundamental statistical criteria other than optimality arising in discrete experimentation. In K. Hinkelman (Ed.), *Experimental design, statistical models, and genetic statistics* (pp. 95–117). New York: Dekker.

Stone, E. F. (1988). Moderator variables in research: A review and analysis of conceptual and methodological issues. In K. Rowland & G. R. Ferris (Eds.), *Research in personnel and human resources management* (Vol. 6, pp. 191–229). Greenwich, CT: JAI Press.

Stone, E. F., & Hollenbeck, J. R. (1989). Clarifying some controversial issues surrounding statistical procedures for detecting moderator variables: Empirical evidence and related matters. *Journal of Applied Psychology, 74*, 3–10.

Tukey, J. W. (1949). One degree of freedom for non-additivity. *Biometrics, 5*, 232–242.

Wahlsten, D. (1990). Insensitivity of the analysis of variance to heredity–environment interaction [with commentary]. *Behavioral and Brain Sciences. 13*, 109–162.

[6]Webb, N. M. (1978). *Learning in individual and small group settings.* Unpublished doctoral dissertation, Stanford University, Stanford, CA.

[6]Webb, N. M. (1989). Peer interaction and learning in small groups. *International Journal of Educational Research, 13,* 21–37.

Willson, V. L. (1985). The analysis of interactions in research. In C. R. Reynolds & V. L. Willson (Eds.), *Methodological and statistical advances in the study of individual differences* (pp. 275–295). New York: Plenum Press.

CHAPTER 7

PERSON–ENVIRONMENT INTERACTIONS: CONCEPTS, MECHANISMS, AND IMPLICATIONS FOR DATA ANALYSIS

MICHAEL RUTTER AND ANDREW PICKLES

CONCEPTS

Person–environment interactions have been conceptualized in a variety of different ways (Bornstein & Bruner, 1989; Rutter, 1983). At one (broad) extreme, they have been viewed in terms of the variety of ways in which individuals act upon and respond to their psychosocial and physical environment. At the other (narrow) extreme, the concept is restricted to some kind of synergistic interaction in the chemistry of the moment, by which individuals with a particular set of biologically determined characteristics either respond to environments in a qualitatively different way (disordinal interactions) or in a quantitatively greater or lesser way (ordinal interactions; Plomin, DeFries, & Fulker, 1988). Either extreme can be justified, but we prefer to conceptualize person–environment interactions as a set of processes defined simply as apparently similar sets of experiences having different consequences according to the characteristics of the individual.

Four aspects of this concept require particular emphasis. First, person–environment interactions refer to a situation as observed, rather than to a mechanism as inferred. The key consequence of this conceptualization is that the discovery of a person–environment interaction is always the starting point of a search for possible mediating mechanisms rather than an endpoint in which it is concluded that some form of biological synergism is taking place. The assumption is that observed interactions may arise through a variety of different mechanisms, of which biological synergism is only one, and that the research goal is to determine what these are.

Second, the "person" element in the equation constitutes whatever the individual brings to the situation that represents the experience, regardless of the origins of those individual characteristics. Thus, the characteristics may be genetically determined, the results of physical experiences, or the consequences of psychosocial encounters; they may also reflect maturational stage. This specification is necessary because it is known that the structure of the organism may be altered by stress experiences (Hunt, 1979), hormonal exposure (Ehrhardt & Meyer-Bahlburg, 1981; Greenough, Carter, Steerman, & DeVoogd, 1977), and sensory input (Blakemore, 1991), to give only three examples, and because reactivity to environmental factors is influenced by features such as sex, intrauterine growth, chronological age, nutrition, and patterns of early rearing (Chandra, 1983; Martyn, 1991; Suomi, 1991).

Third, the environment as observed (whether physical or psychosocial) refers to the objective, not the effective, environment. The point of this distinction is that, if there is a person–environment interaction, it usually means that the experience is in some real sense not comparable across the population. There is a substantial danger, in our view, of ruling out person–environment interactions as inoperative as soon as one knows the mechanism that is operating. That does not seem very helpful. The point is that "interaction" does not define a unitary process. Once the mechanism is known, it usually ceases to be interesting or relevant to refer to it as an interaction. The statistical identification of an interaction is no more than an indicator that there is a question of process that needs to be tackled. As we have indicated, the finding of a person–environment interaction is never an endpoint, but always a beginning. In other words, its presence alerts one to a possible mode of leverage in a course of investigations of the mechanisms involved; it is that characteristic that makes such an interaction of both theoretical and practical importance.

Fourth, we do not think that it is helpful to restrict consideration of person–environment interaction to those that are evident in findings applicable to the bulk of subjects falling within the "normal" range of some continuous measure. Just as the study of psychopathology can throw light on normal functioning, interactions that are clearly evident in extreme groups may be relevant to the behavior of those who are less extreme. However, many person–environment interactions apply only to small subsections of the population. This feature has certain important implications for the methods of statistical analysis that need to be used (see the next section). Loosely speaking, in such contexts, the conceptual and statistical tool kit of the epidemiologist can prove more incisive than that of the psycho-metrician.

THE PERVASIVENESS OF PERSON–ENVIRONMENT INTERACTIONS

Any consideration of person–environment interactions needs to begin with an appreciation that from the point of view of models of causation, interactions are likely to be very common (Rothman, 1976) and that, biologically speaking, they are indeed found to be so. This assertion may at first seem surprising in light of the conclusions from careful studies undertaken by such thoughtful investigators as Plomin and his colleagues that interactions seem decidedly uncommon (Plomin et al., 1988). We return later to the nature of this apparent paradox, but suffice it to say that we are conceptualizing interactions in a broader sense than did Plomin et al.; that interactions have been identified by a variety of means other than statistical interaction terms; and that the strength of these interactions has been assessed in terms other than the proportion of total population variance explained.

To substantiate our claim that person–environment interactions are biolog-ically pervasive, a few examples follow. It is well known, for instance, that a number of metabolic disorders require particular environmental conditions to be manifest. Thus, phenylketonuria gives rise to a mental handicap only when phe-nylalanine is present in the diet (Fuggle & Graham, in press). This tends not to be discussed as a person–environment interaction simply because all ordinary diets include substantial amounts of phenylalanine. Nevertheless, ordinary diets do have devastating effects in biologically vulnerable individuals, whereas they have no ill effects in other people. A comparable situation exists with respect to coeliac disease, in relation to the consequence of glutens in the diet (Losowsky, 1987). The flushing response to alcohol, seen in some individuals of Asiatic origin, constitutes another well-known example (Goedde & Agarwal, 1987), one that is thought to be important in terms of the lower rate of alcoholism in Asiatic races (Merikangas, 1990). These are not just genetic main effects that require an en-vironment within which they can be manifest. There are, of course, genetic effects either that do not need any particular sort of environment (as with the autosomal dominant condition of Huntington's disease) or for which effects are very com-parable across a wide range of environments (as, e.g., with genetic effects on intelligence). The examples given here, however, are of genetic effects that act by altering the person's response to particular environmental features and hence require those features for the phenotypic expression to be manifest.

The resistance to malaria that is a consequence of the sickle-cell phenomenon is an interesting variant of a person–environment interaction in that it represents a case of one disease providing protection against another (Rotter & Diamond, 1987). However, this is only one example of the general finding of marked individual differences in susceptibility to infection deriving from genetic influences, nutritional factors, drugs, intercurrent chronic disease, and previous exposure to the relevant pathogens (Greenwood, 1987). The last is important in terms of individual differences within any population, but it is also relevant to differences among populations. For example, because the population had not acquired adequate immunity from previous exposure, the mass emigration from Tristan da Cunha following the volcanic eruption was accompanied by heavy morbidity from infectious disease when the islanders reached the United Kingdom (Black, Lewis, Thacker, & Thould, 1963; Samuels, 1963).

Person–environment interactions are also evident in the effects of diet on cholesterol levels, in terms of both markedly raised levels in response to ordinary diets in individuals suffering from familial hypercholesterolaemia (FH) and individual differences in response to low or high cholesterol diets among people without FH (Katan & Beynen, 1987; Mistry, Miller, Laker, Hazzard, & Lewis, 1981). It is known that there are important genetic influences on lipid metabolism (see Bock & Collins, 1987); the extent to which these operate through modifying responses to variations in diet is not known, but it is likely that this constitutes part of the process. However, it is not only genetic factors that influence the body's response to diet. Studies in baboons have shown that breast-fed and formula-fed animals differ in their response to high cholesterol diets in adult life (Mott, Jackson, McMahan, & McGill, 1990). Yet another example is provided by the well-established greater vulnerability of boys, compared with girls, to a wide range of physical hazards spanning malnutrition, infection, and irradiation (Earls, 1987).

Immune reactions provide another domain within which person–environment interactions are widely evident. For example, both small-for-gestational-age and malnourished infants show a reduced immune response following BCG vaccination (Chandra, 1983). Also, the effects of diet in infancy on later atopic disease seem to be present only in children with a family history of allergies (Lucas, Brooke, Morley, Cole, & Bamford, 1990). Furthermore, exposure to the hepatitis B virus during infancy commonly results in a chronic antigen carrier state but only rarely produces overt hepatitis, whereas the reverse is the case following infection in adult life (Martyn, 1991).

Age differences in susceptibility to environmental influences are also well known in neural development, as shown both by experimental animal studies and by the effects of strabismus in humans. Patterned visual input drives the structural organization, as well as the function, of the visual pathways in the brain (Blakemore, 1991). Similarly, animal studies show that very early endocrine influences organize brain development in ways that influence later sex role behavior (Ehrhardt & Meyer-Bahlburg, 1981; Greenough et al., 1977). Neither visual nor endocrine influences have the same effect at later ages. The mechanisms involved in these effects, as evident in the field of somatic medicine, are diverse, but the point that we want to make is that such interactions are very common.

In the psychological arena, too, it is likely that person—environment interactions are widespread, although their systematic study has been very limited. Let us give several different examples. The relevance of maturational features is shown by the well-established observation that an adverse response to separation experiences tends to be more marked during the preschool years, but after the age of about 6 months (Rutter, 1981). Gender differences are apparent in the greater vulnerability of boys to the effects of family discord and disruption (Zaslow and Hayes, 1986) and in the observation that shyness in boys tends to be accompanied by negative interpersonal relationships, whereas shyness in girls is more often associated with positive ones (Radke-Yarrow, Richters, & Wilson, 1988; Stevenson-Hinde & Hinde, 1986). The effects of prior experience are demonstrated by the different physiological response shown by experienced parachute jumpers compared with novices (Ursin, Baade, & Levine, 1978) and by the protective effects of early physical stress, as shown in Levine's rodent studies (Levine, Chevalier, & Korchinn, 1956). Various early physical stressors lead not only to structural and functional changes in the neuroendocrine system, but also to enhanced resistance to later stressors (Hunt, 1979). A variety of studies have shown that recidivist delinquents and psychopaths have a reduced physiological responsivity to stress (Venables, 1987). There has recently been much interest in the phenomenon of behavioral inhibition, characterized by an increased physiological and behavioral response to stress and challenge (Kagan, Reznick, Snidman, Gibbons, & Johnson, 1988). Monkey studies indicate that individual differences in reactivity are not apparent in familiar environments but become strikingly manifest under conditions of stress and challenge (Suomi, 1991).

A different sort of example is provided by the evidence that the effects of rearing by a deaf parent tend to have beneficial consequences for deaf children, whereas they do not for hearing children (Meadow, 1975). Another different kind of example of an interaction (albeit one in which the stimulus is internal, although the mediating mechanism of the stimulus may not be) is provided by the evidence that whereas boys tend to respond positively to puberty, girls tend to respond negatively (Graham & Rutter, 1985). Also, it seems that the rise in depressive psychopathology during adolescence is more marked in females than in males and that in girls, it possibly may be related to puberty as well as to chronological age, whereas in boys it is not (Rutter, Angold, Harrington, Nicholls, & Taylor, 1989). Longitudinal studies (Elder, 1986) were striking in showing the protective effect in disadvantaged (but not other) individuals of a period of service in the armed forces; military service seemed to provide a means of extending education and of postponing marriage (making it less likely that the spouse would be from a similarly disadvantaged background). Also, college education seems to have a greater effect on later occupational level and on personality characteristics in disadvantaged subjects than in other people (Caspi, 1991).

It is clear too that there are important individual differences in the likelihood that adults will develop emotional disorders following acute or chronic life stressors. Increased vulnerability has been found to be associated with higher levels of neuroticism (Ormel, Stewart, & Sanderman, 1989), with the experience of psychosocial adversity (Ghodsian, 1990; Quinton & Rutter, 1976), or with a combination of the two (Rodgers, 1990).

Such individual differences in response to psychosocial hazards are sometimes dismissed by behavioral scientists as irrelevant to the issue of person–environment interactions because the person variable is not obviously genetic or structurally organismic. However, that is an inappropriate response. The medical examples that we have given emphasize that in many cases the crucial person characteristics have been experientially determined and that, when the biological processes are well understood, the organismic changes associated with the experiences become apparent. For example, this is true for immune responses and for the neuroendocrine changes associated with exposure to stress experiences (Hunt, 1979).

It may seem that the psychological examples of person–environment interactions that we have given are less striking than the examples from medicine and neurobiology. However, that is because most of the study of interactions in the behavioral sciences has relied on finding statistically significant interaction terms in multivariate analyses that lack an adequate conceptualization both of environmental variables and of the ways by which interactions might operate. The biological examples were chosen to indicate that this may not be the best way forward; rather, there needs to be a focus on processes and mechanisms in which both epidemiological and experimental methods have crucial roles to play and in which there is much to be gained from drawing lessons from findings in other domains (see Bock & Whelan, 1991, for examples regarding the effects of early experience on adult functioning).

POSSIBLE MECHANISMS INVOLVED IN PERSON– ENVIRONMENT INTERACTION DIFFERENCES IN THE EFFECTIVE ENVIRONMENT

Differences in the Effective Environment

It is usually supposed that person–environment interactions can have meaning only if the environmental stimulus is the same for all people. We deliberately chose examples to illustrate that this is a difficult criterion to apply. Thus, the variations in phenylalanine levels in a diet have no meaning to most people, but they are crucial to those with phenylketonuria because they lack the biochemical mechanisms to deal with phenylalanine. Is the stimulus the same, or is it not? What about the example of the protective effect on children of rearing by a deaf parent? In both deaf and hearing children, there is the communality that good communicative experiences foster language development; the contrast is that, because of the handicap of hearing impairment, there is a difference in what constitutes good communication. Does that mean that the environmental stimulus is the same or different?

Let us move a little farther afield. Would we accept as a person–environment interaction the example of boys and girls responding differently to puberty? One could well say that the experience here is not comparable, because the hormonal changes are different in the two sexes and are in any case internal and not environmental. However, this is not a sufficient reason for exclusion, because the differences arise in part as a result of variations in the cultural acceptability of the physical changes that come about as a result of the hormonal effects.

In our view, there is not much to be gained in attempting to draw a hard and fast line on the circumstances in which stimuli would be regarded as exactly comparable across individuals. In a sense, they can never be quite the same, and, if that is the criterion, there can never be person–environment interactions. Rather, it is more fruitful to start with the assumption that the observation of person–environment interactions alerts one to the need to study how the environmental effects operate and to recognize that the very existence of an apparent interaction provides a useful means of investigating the mechanisms involved. Considerations of variations in what constitutes the *effective* environment alerts one to the possibility that the interaction effect may derive from individual differences in the salience of what is objectively the same stimulus.

The examples of phenylketonuria and of deaf children are instances when the salience is physiologically determined. However, variations in salience may more often be experientially determined. Immunity to infectious disease constitutes an obvious examples in the realm of physical experiences. Our own work provides several examples in the psychosocial field (Quinton & Rutter, 1988). In a longitudinal study extending from childhood into early adult life, it was found that positive school experiences had a marked protective effect in institution-reared children, whereas they had little or no effect in children from the general population. Although the mechanisms involved are not known, it seems likely that the positive school experiences exerted their protective effect because they provided sources of self-esteem and self-efficacy. The institution-reared children had few such sources, and hence the benefits of those obtainable at school were striking. By contrast, children in the general population tended to have many such sources of self-esteem and self-efficacy, and one more at school made little difference. In the same study, it was found that the psychological characteristic of "planning" (a tendency to make definite decisions about key life choices such as work, career, and marriage) exerted a protective effect in the institution-reared sample but not in the comparison group. Once more, the mechanisms are not known, but it seems plausible that the different circumstances of the two groups were crucial. The institution-reared youngsters were faced with many psychosocial hazards in their environment, and they tended to lack effective parents to guide them; accordingly, their own choices were crucial. By contrast, the controls faced far fewer psychosocial hazards and had families who would help them take the right steps even if they lacked the necessary initiative themselves.

DIFFERENCES IN PERSON–ENVIRONMENT INTERACTION PROCESSES

Temporal Aspects

Temporal Differences in Person–Environment Interaction Processes

Most psychosocial adversities or stressors are better thought of in terms of processes that act over time rather than as a happening that resides in the psychological chemistry of the moment. This may be illustrated by findings on family discord that suggest that boys are more vulnerable than girls (Zaslow & Hayes, 1986). The available empirical evidence is not sufficient for any firm conclusions on how this difference arises, but it is obvious that there are several different alternatives. Thus, within families with a given level of discord, boys may be more likely to be drawn into the conflict and to be the target of parental negative feelings and actions. This possibility is suggested by our own finding that temperamentally difficult children were more likely than temperamentally easy ones to be the target of parental criticism, irritability, and hostility (Rutter, 1978).

Hetherington, Cox, & Cox (1982) found that in discordant families, parents were more likely to quarrel in front of their sons than their daughters. That is, of course, a person–environment correlation rather than an interaction. However, the point that we wish to emphasize is that this distinction is very dependent on the level of knowledge and on the type of variables being examined. If the environment is considered in terms of overall family discord, there is no person–environment correlation because boys are no more likely that girls to be reared in such households. It is only when the variable is redefined in terms of active involvement in negative interpersonal interchanges that the correlation appears.

Thus, it is important to look beyond the immediate personal response to the environmental stimulus to the effects on other people in the social environment that are engendered by the subject's response. We have already referred to the evidence that shy behavior in boys tends to be associated with negative personal interactions with other people, whereas in girls it tends to be associated with positive interactions (Stevenson-Hinde & Hinde, 1986). Furthermore, it was found that mothers back away from negative behavior shown by their sons (Maccoby and Jacklin, 1983), which tends to increase the boys' oppositional tendency. This difference was, however, not found in the daughters. The relevance of these findings for person—environment interactions is that individual differences in responses to environmental circumstances may sometimes reside as much in the processes that take place over time as in initial reactivity (also see chap. 8).

Different Reaction Patterns Across Time

There is another alternative. Suppose that there is no sex difference in exposure to discord, but that boys and girls tend to react in different ways. Thus, boys are more likely to respond with negative oppositional behavior, whereas girls are more likely to respond with emotional distress. The reactions of boys may, as a consequence, be more likely to persist as definite psychopathology, just because their style of response is less likely to elicit a sympathetic and supportive response from parents. Is this a correlation or an interaction? In truth, it is not quite either. The resulting sex difference, in this hypothesized sequence of events, arises because there is an initial disordinal interaction (i.e., boys and girls respond in different ways) followed by a second-stage disordinal correlation (or transactional effect) in which the childrens' responses elicit different reactions in the parents. It does not seem to us helpful, therefore, to have a cut-and-dried distinction between interactions and correlations. The important things is to focus on the mechanisms over time that are involved, to appreciate that these may be multistage reactions operating over time, and to recognize that there may be more than one explanation when the process is considered as a whole (also see chap. 2).

We have emphasized the need to consider the possibility that individual differences in reactions to the environment may lie not so much in the degree or direction of response, but in the pattern of behavior elicited. It will often not be appropriate to pool these on the assumption that they represent alternative manifestations of the same basic phenomenon. The reason why such a pooling is likely to be misleading in many cases is because the pattern of response may have crucial implications for what happens thereafter. For example, in the already-mentioned longitudinal study of institution-reared children, it was found that girls showed a very marked tendency to react to their unhappy family circumstances by early marriage and pregnancy, whereas this was unusual in boys (Rutter, Quinton, & Hill, 1990). This sex difference was important because early marriage tended to make it more likely that the marriage would be to a deviant spouse and therefore formed part of a process associated with continuing social problems (Pickles & Rutter, 1991). Conduct disturbance in childhood also had a different effect on spouse selection in the two sexes (Pickles & Rutter, 1991). Girls with conduct disturbance tended to marry deviant spouses and end up without marital support, whereas this was not found for boys with conduct disorder. Once again, the implication is that the processes need to be examined over the course of multiple links in a chain, rather than just in terms of an interaction at any one moment in time.

Intrinsic Individual Differences in Susceptibility

The third type of possibility is that there is some kind of intrinsic individual variation in susceptibility or vulnerability to particular kinds of environmental features. It is difficult to know how common this source of person–environment interaction is likely to be. Undoubtedly, part of the difficulty stems from the problems that are inherent in the delineation of the crucial person and environment features. Until they can be so identified, it will inevitably be difficult to differentiate main effects from interactions. An example from internal medicine illustrates the point. One of the interesting secular trends that has been noted is the shift from a preponderance of myocardial heart disease in middle-class individuals to a preponderence in the socially disadvantaged (Barker & Osmond, 1986). It was hypothesized that this might be a consequence of people from poor backgrounds having less adequate nutrition in childhood and thereby being more vulnerable to the ill effects of affluent diets in midlife (the access to such diets being greater today than it was in generations past). This hypothesis is in keeping with animal data that show that patterns of nutrition in infancy program later differences in lipid metabolism (Mott et al., 1990).

Longitudinal data in humans also have provided some support for this hypothesis (Barker, Winter, Osmond, Margetts, & Simmonds, 1989). Men with the lowest weights at birth, and also those with the lowest weights at 1 year of age, had the highest death rates in middle life from ischaemic heart disease. The standardized mortality ratios fell from 111 in men who weighed 18 pounds or less at 1 year to 42 in those who weighed 27 pounds or more. The possibility of an interaction is suggested by the fact that the risk in relation to weight in infancy is the opposite to that in adult life (i.e., the risk increases with low weight in infancy but with excessive weight in adult life.) However, the mechanisms in both early life and adulthood remain unclear. There is a slight association between low birth weight and increased blood pressure in childhood (Whincup, Cook, & Shaper, 1989), but the effect is small, and it seems doubtful whether this could be sufficient to account for the greater effect on mortality from ischaemic heart disease many years later. The point of this example is that the study of possible person–environment interactions provides a means for examining mechanisms. The presence of an interaction says nothing in itself about the processes involved, and hence constitutes the starting point (albeit one with important clues) for further enquiries, but it should not be a conclusion on mechanism. Clearly, the same applies in the psychological arena.

IMPLICATIONS FOR DATA ANALYSIS

Theory-Driven Planned Comparisons

It follows from what we have said about concepts that the least satisfactory way to study person–environment interactions is just to rely on putting an interaction term into the overall summarizing multivariate analyses. Instead, we argue the need for theory-driven planned comparisons focusing on the subgroups in which interactions are thought likely to operate. Most of the examples of person–environment interactions that we have given apply only to particular subsegments of the population in relation to certain specific circumstances, with respect to particular outcome variables. This is certainly not a plea for interaction fishing expeditions in the hope that the meaningful interactions will turn up if a sufficient number of mixes of variables are examined. The dangers of spurious false positive effects would be much too great, as is well known. Rather, analyses to consider the possibility of interactions should be part of an overall plan of investigation designed to study processes and mechanisms.

In most circumstances, it will be preferable to determine the ways in which effects "work" in particular subsamples rather than to go straight to an overall multivariate analysis. This has been evident, for example, in the study of sex differences in a variety of aspects of psychological development. Similarly, the preferability of this method is apparent in looking at age differences in relation to stressful separation experiences in childhood. Theory has suggested that very young infants are less likely to be affected because they have yet to develop selective attachments, whereas older children are likely to be less at risk because they are cognitively able to maintain relationships over periods of absence. It is preferable to examine this possibility directly rather than to start by modeling the effects of age as a dimensional variable. However, for this planned comparison approach to be feasible, it is essential to have clear conceptualizations of what are likely to be the crucial personal characteristics and the crucial environmental features, and to have some hypothesis of what sort of mechanism might be reflected in a person–environment interaction. Sometimes effects are missed because the concepts that defined the analysis were mistaken. For example, much of the genetic analyses of possible environmental effects on schizophrenia used schizophrenia in the parent as the relevant environmental, as well as genetic, risk variable. It now seems clear that this is not a significant environmental risk factor (Gottesman & Shields, 1982). The twin data (which show monozygotic [MZ] concordance rates of only about 50% and which give rise to heritability estimates that are short of unity) make clear that environmental influences are indeed important, but these influences are not indexed by schizophrenia in the parent. On the other hand, there is evidence that overinvolved, highly critical family relationships associated with poor communication are substantial risk factors in terms of the relapse of schizophrenia (Falloon, 1988; Leff & Vaughn, 1984). Whether they are also risk factors for the initial development of schizophrenia is not known with any certainty, but it is plausible that they might operate at that stage of the process. Alternatively, it has been shown that obstetric complications are associated with schizophrenia, and it has been argued that they may constitute the environmental risk factor (Murray, Lewis, Owen, & Foerster, 1989). Appropriate studies need to be undertaken to examine both possibilities, and these should provide the opportunity to determine whether this environmental risk factor operates in the absence of a genetic risk, or only in its presence.

However, Brown, Harris and Lemyre (1991) found that environmental vulnerability factors operate in interaction with acute life stressors only with respect to clinically significant depressive disorders, and not for lesser or different varieties of dysthymia. Although it may seem elementary to note the need to conceptualize appropriately the relevant person characteristics, environmental features, and psychopathological outcomes, it is crucial.

Other chapters in this volume (see chapters 3, 4, and 5) consider what might be the critical individual and environmental characteristics that give rise to person–environment interactions, and one might ask similarly what kind of theory is needed to study interactions. In our view, that is not a useful way of approaching the issue. Person–environment interactions do not constitute a meaningful homogenous class and certainly do not reflect a single mechanism. This means that no single theory can be applicable to all forms of interaction. Nevertheless, it is crucial to start with a set of hypotheses on the nature of the processes that might be involved. Whenever possible, these hypothesized processes should be linked to appropriate theoretical models. Similarly, the organismic and environmental characteristics chosen for study should be driven by the specific theory or specific postulated mechanism that is thought to be applicable. Thus, a different sort of theory (and of statistical analysis) will be needed for interactions based on normally distributed quantitative variations in a specific form of intrinsic susceptibility (that might perhaps be the case in the cholesterol metabolism examples given earlier); on a qualitative variation in intrinsic variability (as with phenylketonuria or coeliac disease); on a sequential process (as with some examples of immune response or carcinogenesis); on maturation—related variations in susceptibility deriving from the increased vulnerability at times of brain growth that plays a part in structural and functional organization (as with the effects of unilateral visual restriction in infancy on later binocular stereoscopic vision); and on a difference in the meaning or salience of the relevant environmental variable (as with deaf children's response to rearing by deaf or hearing parents). We have deliberately chosen medical examples to bring out the basic biological principles, but it is obvious that these apply similarly in the fields of psychology and psychiatry. It is also apparent that there is little point in seeking to identify classes of person or environmental variables that are likely to exhibit interaction; necessarily, they will vary according to the process or mechanism involved.

Dimensions or Categories, Syndromes or Behaviors

In the standard forms of regression analysis, the relationships examined are those among dimensional variables. Often, that is the most appropriate conceptual approach to follow, but sometimes it is not. In the first instance, the extremes of dimensions may have a meaning that is quite different from variations within the middle of the distribution. For example, this is obviously the case with the dimension of intelligence, where the below-50 IQ range functions differently from that above it (Nichols, 1984; Plomin, Rende, & Rutter, in press; Rutter & Gould, 1985). Thus, single major genes predominate in the case of severe retardation, whereas they are of little importance in accounting for variations within the normal range of intelligence. Also, fecundity and life expectancy are markedly reduced for severely retarded individuals, but are not for those in the mildly retarded range. However, it is important to note that the issue is not simply one of extremes of dimensions but also one of a difference between person characteristics (or constellations of variables, or syndromes) and single behaviors. For example, the level of activity is of little importance in predicting the degree of response to stimulant medication, but the presence of early-onset pervasive overactivity is associated with a significantly and substantially greater drug response (Taylor et al., 1987). Similarly, reduced physiological activity in response to experimental stress does not show a very systematic relationship with the level of aggression or delinquency as measured in dimensional terms, but it is evident as a feature of constellations of aggressivity, overactivity, and inattention (Magnusson, 1988).

It should be noted that this is not necessarily a difference that is best expressed in terms of a category rather than a dimension because the behavioral constellation may represent an underlying dimension. The difference concerns the relevance of combinations of behaviors rather than single traits. Of course, the plea is not for multiple analyses putting together variables in all manner of different ways, but rather for concepts that are derived either from theory or from findings of previous empirical research. However, it is important to recognize that there are a variety of methodological hazards to be negotiated when amalgamating, transforming, or truncating variables. For example, there is an extensive literature indicating an interaction between low birth weight and social disadvantage (Sameroff & Chandler, 1975). The implication has been that the effects of organic brain damage are potentiated by the co-occurrence of poor patterns of upbringing. There may be such an interaction, but the earlier findings may have been an artifact of measurement error, given that low birth weight constituted only a very weak indirect measure of organic brain dysfunction. This possibility arises because, although moderately low birth weight (which carries a very low risk of brain damage) is strongly associated with social disadvantage, very low birth weight (where the risk of brain damage is much higher) is not. With the advent of modern methods of noninvasive brain imaging, it is now possible to have direct measures of neonatal brain pathology (Costello et al., 1988); now that these are available, it is important to reexamine the question of brain damage–social disadvantage interactions.

There are parallel sets of problems associated with the assumption that the risk factors that operate in the general population are the same ones that are important in individuals at risk, because of some person-based risk factor. For example, in our own studies, we found that children with severe head injury were at markedly increased risk for psychiatric disorder (Rutter, Chadwick, & Shaffer, 1983). The fact that this was evident on the basis of longitudinal data, after taking account of a range of possible confounding variables, indicates that the causal inference was almost certainly correct. However, unlike the situation with cognitive impairment, the dose–response relationship was weak and inconsistent. The overall pattern of findings strongly suggested that severe head injury did not lead directly to psychiatric disorder, but rather in some way increased the vulnerability to other risk factors. Nevertheless, we were unable to find any kind of interaction between organic brain damage (however measured) and psychosocial risk variables such as family discord or parental mental disorder. The conclusion is that we were investigating the wrong set of psychosocial risk variables.

Other evidence suggests that, rather than these familywide environmental risks, it would have been more profitable to focus on nonshared influences (Plomin & Daniels, 1987). In the case of children suffering severe head injury, the most influential influences may involve overprotective responses to handicap in the child (Shaffer, Chadwick, & Rutter, 1975). Overprotection may not be of great risk importance in the population as a whole, but in the special case of children recovering from a severe head injury, it may play a greater role. Of course, this hypothesis needs to be put to the test, but the point is that when other evidence suggests that person-environment interactions likely play a part in the risk process, the failure to find a significant statistical interaction should not close the matter (see chap. 6). On the other hand, when they amalgamate or truncate variables, or pool heterogenous data, researchers need to be aware of the possibilities of removing or creating interactions that may be misleading or artifactual, as well as real. This issue is considered in more detail in the appendix to this chapter.

DESIGNS FOR GENE–ENVIRONMENT INTERACTIONS

Adoption designs have generally been favored for the study of gene–environment interactions because the genetic contribution from the biological parents can be clearly separated from the environmental contribution from the adoptive parent

(Plomin, 1986; Plomin et al., 1988). This is a powerful advantage, but several limitations need to be noted. First, just because of the lack of correlation between biological parent genes and environment, relatively few genetically vulnerable subjects will be exposed to sufficiently high-risk environments. As a consequence, only a small proportion of the population variance could be explained on the basis of gene−environment interactions even when the interaction effect is strong in the subgroup for whom genetic and environmental risk factors co-occur.

Second, adoptive parents are selected to exclude those with psychopathology and those likely to provide a poor rearing environment. Insofar as that policy is effective (and it will be only partially so), it will mean that there will be disproportionately few children from a severely disadvantaged environment. If gene−environment interactions operate mainly through the combination of high-risk factors, adoption designs will have weak power to detect their operation. Third, selection policies for adoptive parents are likely to result in reduced environmental variance in adopted samples. This may well lead to a reduced estimate of environmental effects on population variance (see Plomin, DeFries, & Loehlin, 1977). But this is by no means inconsistent with a marked environmental effect on level, as shown by the findings on children from low-IQ mothers adopted into superior homes (Caron & Duyme, 1989; Schiff & Lewontin, 1987). It is important to appreciate that a different approach will be required to test gene−environment interactions in that connection because the causes associated with effects on level may not be the same as those that apply to individual differences (Rutter & Giller, 1983; Rutter & Madge, 1976). For example, it is obvious that the processes that explain changes over time in levels of unemployment (as in the massive rise in unemployment in the United Kingdom in the 1970s and mid-1980s) are quite different from those that explain why one individual is out of work, whereas another is not at any one time. Similarly, nutritional factors are probably unimportant (and genetic factors predominant) with respect to individual differences in height among Caucasian boys in London, but nutritional changes are likely to constitute the main reason for the 10-cm rise in average height of London boys during the first half of this century (Tizard, 1975).

The issue, then, is whether there are person variables that affect responsivity to these environmental influences on level. A comparison of environmental effects between groups chosen to vary in the postulated person variable then represents one way of tackling the interaction question. In the case of biological parental social level (a proxy measure of genetic background) and adoptive parental social level (as the environmental influence), using a cross-fostering design, there does not seem to be any interaction (Caron & Duyme, 1989), but there could be an interaction with other more sensitive measures of genetic background (see chap. 3) or environmental influences (see chap. 4).

Fortunately, it is possible to tackle the detection of gene−environment interactions in various other ways, making use of the contrasting predictions that derive from different models (Kendler & Eaves, 1986). For example, if genes control sensitivity to the environment (see also Loehlin, Willerman, & Horn, 1982), it may be expected that in the situation in family studies when the proband is reared in a protective environment and relatives in a predisposing one, the risk of psychopathology is lower in MZ cotwins than in siblings. This seemingly paradoxical finding arises because individuals who become ill in a protective environment are likely to have an insensitive genotype, because the MZ cotwins therefore are more likely than siblings to have an insensitive genotype and because individuals with an insensitive genotype are at a particularly low risk for psychopathology, relative to other genotypes, in a predisposing environment. Of course, to make use of these predictions it is necessary to identify and measure accurately the genetic features and environmental risk factors. Measurement of the genetic features is likely to rely on biological trait markers, but little is known about these so far. Without knowledge of the genetic feature, the interaction with an environmental risk factor will present itself as the risk factor having an apparent variability in its effect. This variability can be represented as a random effect in a multilevel model (Bock, 1989). It is possible to extend this approach to unknown environmental risk factors as well, but not surprisingly, the power of the analysis declines substantially. Thomas, Langholz, Mack, and Floderus (1989) discuss this in the context of twin data on age of onset.

Twin studies may also be used in novel ways, as shown by Heath, Jardine, & Martin (1989), who showed that the genetic predisposition to depressive symptomatology was substantially less in married twins than in unmarried individuals, especially after the age of 30 years. Also, Kendler, Neale, Heath, Kessler, and Eaves (1991) used questionnaire data from the Virginia Twin Study to contrast effects according to whether the pairs were concordant for depressive symptoms and concordant for either independent or dependent life events. Structural equation modeling suggested that genetic and familial environmental factors had a greater effect on depression in high-stress than in low-stress environments. The data could not separate gene–environment interactions from common environment-specific environment interactions (i.e., an interaction between the broader environment impinging on both twins and the stress factor specific to one twin), but the findings pointed to some kind of synergistic effect.

We have focused on gene–environment interactions because of their great biological importance (see Bell, 1990, for a discussion of their role in maintaining diversity and of how such interactions are likely to lead to gene–environment correlations or covariance). Their study in nonexperimental situations indicates the need for multiple research strategies and for designs that will test for interactions in ways other than showing a significant statistical interaction term in some analysis of variance (ANOVA) or regression analysis. This need applies similarly to other types of person–environment interactions, where the payoff is likely to be even greater because of the peculiar difficulties of studying the interplay between genes and environments outside of the experimental laboratory.

Interactions and Their Statistical Description

All too often, a broader debate on the presence or absence of a particular interaction narrows to one of the p value of one form or other of statistical test. We argue that this is almost never appropriate, and illustrate that there should be a continuing interplay among theory, postulated mechanisms, the purpose of the investigation, and the apparently abstract statistical technicalities. We consider in some detail interaction effects among categorical measures and, in so doing, explain some of the differences among the various forms of generalized regression model appropriate for such data. The spirit of our argument applies equally to analyses involving continuous measures. We focused on categorical measures because it is easier to conceptualize simple mechanisms for such data and also because of the widespread use of cross-tabulation methods. It is with such a cross-tabulation that our discussion begins.

Table 1 shows data for the effects of two factors, a severe life event and having three children less than 14 years old, on the development of depression in women. Brown and Harris (1978) argued that the impact of the provoking agent (life events) was much greater in the presence of the vulnerability factor (three children less than 14) than in its absence (i.e., 42.9% − 0.0% is greater than 16.8% − 1.7%), and they found a highly significant chi-square of 7.8 using the Grizzle–Starmer–Koch, (G–S–K; Grizzle, Starmer, & Koch, 1969) approach. On the other hand, Tennant and Bebbington (1978) analyzing the same table using log-linear methods, found a wholly insignificant chi-square of 2.0, reflecting the fact that with both factors present, the proportion depressed (strictly speaking, the odds ratio for depression) is very close to what would be expected from multiplicative factors acting independently—with, very roughly, life events increasing the rate by a factor of 12 (20.1%/1.6%), and three children less than 14 increasing the rate by a factor of 3.0 (22.0%/7.4%). What explains such divergent findings and how can they be reconciled?

The first element of the explanation lies in understanding that the G–S–K and log-linear approaches combine the effects of the two factors on the outcome proportion in different ways, the former using an additive scale and the latter using a logistic scale. This means that the probability of depression is linked to the explanatory variables using different functions, and these combine the main effects of the impact of provoking agent and vulnerability factors in different ways in calculating the expected rate of outcome. In fact, these are just two of a whole range of possible link functions. Figure 1 shows how the value of a goodness-of-fit chi-square for the main effects model (and thus the test of interaction) varies

Table 1.

RISK OF DEPRESSION IN RELATION TO VULNERABILITY AND PROVOKING FACTORS

	Vulnerability factor[a]								
	Absent		Present		Total	
Severe life event	% Depressed	N	% Depressed	N	% Depressed	N
Absent	1.7	4/235	0.0	0/20	1.6	4/245
Present	16.8	24/143	42.9	9/21	20.2	33/164
Total	18.5	28/378	22.0	9/41	21.8	37/409

[a]Three children younger than 14 years of age.

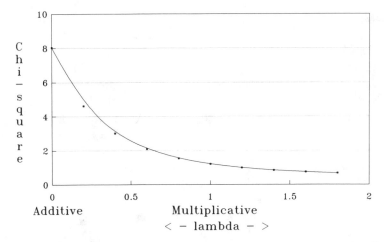

Figure 1. Vulnerability and provoking agent: test of interaction for generalized relative risk models.

if one considers a more general link function, the generalized relative risk function of Breslow and Storer (1985). This link function possesses an additional parameter lambda that gives, for certain values of lambda, the additive and logistic functions as special cases. It is clear that whether a statistically significant interaction is identified depends on the value of lambda, and thus on the link function. With any of the link functions commonly in use, the conclusions reached will be very similar, provided that all cell proportions are within the 20%–80% range. However, with a base rate of, say 12%, and independent main effects that each raise the rate to 36%, the combined effect of both yields expectations of 60%, 68%, 70%, and 79% using the additive, probit, logistic, and complementary log–log functions, respectively (see McCullagh & Nelder, 1983, and the appendix for more details). An observed rate of, say 70%, will, given an adequate sample size, show no interaction, positive interaction, or negative interaction depending on the link function used. These figures are not untypical of those found in many epidemiological and clinical studies. How do we choose among them?

It is useful to consider some idealized causal models that lead naturally to one scale or function rather than to another (Walter & Holford, 1978). Suppose there are two causal risk factors A and B and a common background risk factor C. Each generates disease-causing events randomly and independently in time with rates ra, rb, and rc. A little calculus gives the probability of disease in one unit of time in the presence of just one risk factor, say C, as $1 - \exp(-rc)$, the functional form that corresponds to the complementary log–log scale. Because it is necessary for only one event of any type to occur for disease to ensue, and if the individual rates of Type A and B events are low (such that the chance of both occurring in the same interval of time is small), then the increment in the probability of disease when exposed to both A and B is just the sum of the increments when exposed to either one separately. Thus, a natural scale on which to search for interactions in effects where the factors can be conceptualized as, say, physical or psychological "insults" to the organism may be the additive one (or, less approximately, the complementary log–log). The impact of severe life-events on depression would seem to correspond well with this model, offering some support for Brown and Harris's (1978) approach. The interaction term might then suggest that a severe life event when caring for several children places women at unusually elevated risk of being "hit."

Alternatively, the risks may represent reductions in the rate of occurrence of normal protective or nurturing factors, with disease occurring whenever any one of these factors is missing. The probability of disease is then equal to the probability of nonoccurrence of the event, an expression of the form $\exp(-rc)$, and increments in the probability of disease when exposed to Factors A and B are multiplicative with respect to the base rate and are combined on the logistic scale. This derivation of the logistic scale that implicitly underlies the log-linear analysis does not suggest the log-linear approach as being especially appropriate for the depression data.

A third possibility is based on the notion of disease onset occurring when some unobserved continuous variable, like stress, exceeds a certain value. If there are many factors that contribute to the stress level (allowing a central limit theory justification for a normally distributed unobserved or latent variable) and the presence of Factors A and B simply add a certain amount to this, then the natural scale and link function to use is the standard normal integral or probit function.

On balance, the first and last of these conceptualizations might be the most plausible for our data. However, some further considerations suggest more compelling arguments for the use of the logistic or multiplicative model. As we have argued, the mechanisms underlying many psychological and developmental processes may involve a set of stages or a sequence of events and changes before the final outcome is observed. If one risk factor increases the rate of transition from an initial to an intermediate stage and another then acts upon those in the intermediate stage, increasing their rate of transition to the final outcome stage, then the effects of the two risk factors together combine naturally in a multiplicative fashion in terms of their effect on the overall rate from initial to final stages. Such a multistage theory has been long proposed for carcinogenesis (Armitage & Doll, 1961), with cells having to go through a series of stages before cancerous growth itself begins. The finding of a multiplicative effect of asbestos dust and cigarette smoking on lung cancer is then understood as each having an independent effect on different cell transitions (Peto, 1977). In the context of the data on Table 1, the multiplicative model suggests that having three or more children less than 14 years of age increases the rate of transition into an intermediate state of increased vulnerability. Thus, if we consider the possibility that the process is a multistage

Table 2.

HIERARCHICAL AND NONHIERARCHICAL LINEAR-LOGISTIC MODELS
FITTED TO THE DATA FROM TABLE 1

Model	Prediction equation	Scaled deviance
Null model	$y = a$	51.63
Main effects models	$y = a + b_1X_1$	44.18
	$y = a + b_2X_2$	7.27
	$y = a + b_1X_1 + b_2X_2$	2.00
Nonhierarchical interaction	$y = a + b_1X_2 + b_2X_2X_1$	0.66
Standard interaction	$y = a + b_1X_1 + b_2X_2 + b_3X_1X_2$	0.00

Note. Dummy variables: $X_1 = 1$ or 0 (vulnerability factor); $X_2 = 1$ or 0 (provoking agent).

one, then a multiplicative (linear logistic or log-linear) model without interaction offers a view of the data that is only subtly different from the "one-hit" additive model with interaction. Focusing on the significance of the interaction term alone results in a needless polarization of interpretation.

Until now, whichever scale was chosen, the significance of the interaction has been assessed after the inclusion of the main effects for each factor. However, the vulnerability-provoking agent theory suggests that in the absence of the provoking agent, the rates of the vulnerable are the same as those for the nonvulnerable. Thus, no main effect for the vulnerability factor is posited, and a test of the main effects model (with three parameters: a constant and two main effects coefficients) against the saturated model that includes the regular interaction term is not the relevant test. The main effect for vulnerability will incorrectly absorb part of the variance because of the real interaction, and the residual variance attributable to the standard interaction term is frequently not large enough to achieve significance. The conclusion that the main-effects model "fits," that both main effects are significant, and that there is no interaction would in this instance be incorrect. Rather, the concept suggests that the comparison that we should make is of a model in which the vulnerable–nonvulnerable pairs are equated (two parameters) with a model that allows the pair in the presence of the provoking agent to differ (three parameters). Such models are easily fitted (Breen, 1984), and Table 2 shows that although the main effects model fits well, the equally parsimonious nonhierarchical model that already contains a highly significant interaction term fits even better. The consideration of the effects of one factor within the separate groups defined by the other factor provides a preliminary approach to such models.

Attempts to choose empirically between the various forms of models with different link functions, each with and without hierarchical or nonhierarchical interactions, will rarely yield an unequivocal choice because expected or predicted rates from at least some of the models will be very similar or will differ only in cells with low rates of occurrence. A convincing statistical rejection of one model over all others is thus rare, and the choice often rests on other factors. In addition to available theory and the conceptualization of the mechanism, the purpose of the study also influences whether a model with an interaction is to be preferred over another without. Where the context of the analysis is public health and the purpose is to draw to the attention of policymakers subgroups of the population who are already exposed to one factor and who will experience substantially elevated absolute risks if exposed to a second factor, the additive model is likely to be the more appropriate (Blot & Day, 1979; Rothman, 1976). From this point of view, the identification of the mechanism that generates the ''synergism'' is not the immediate concern. This explains much of the continuing use in epidemiology of the additive model (often under the name of the ''excess mortality model'').

Forward or Backward Approaches to the Examination of Interaction Effects

There is a general acceptance among statisticians and researchers alike that parsimonious explanatory models are to be preferred to complex ones with all manner of qualifications and contingencies. There are two main reasons for this preference. First, there is an awareness that when multiple variables are being put together in a wide range of combinations, it is highly likely that chance effects will lead to a spurious increase in explanatory power when special qualifications are added. Second, the ability to generalize from one population to another is markedly hampered when the explanatory model is unduly complex. It is for these reasons that there has been a general preference for explanatory models with the fewest possible interaction terms.

There seem to be two main schools of practice in this connection: the regression school, which performs forward selection, and the ANOVA school, which performs backward selection. The regression school adds main effects to the model and then generally restricts tests of interactions among variables to those of particular theoretical importance or those with already-demonstrated significant main effects. The ANOVA school, in contrast, argues that main effects cannot be interpreted if they are also involved in interactions, and so starts with all interactions present, removing only those that are nonsignificant. The force of this argument is well illustrated by the depression example given earlier, but it applies in many other domains (see, e.g., Lucas et al., 1990). As noted earlier, if the reality is that one of the independent variables has a zero effect in the absence of the second variable, the finding of a main effect creates a wholly misleading impression of an effect that does not rely on an interaction. Similarly, if there is a disordinal interaction (i.e., if the effects are different in direction according to the presence or absence of the second variable), there will be no main effect (because the two will cancel each other out) and, hence, if main effects are tested for first, there will seem to be no need to go on to look for interactions.

If all interactions are tested first (particularly if there are several variables to be considered), there is a substantial risk of identifying interactions as significant when, in reality, they have arisen by chance just because of the number of tests being undertaken. If, to avoid this problem, simultaneous test procedures are used to account for multiple tests, the power of the tests of the effects that are of primary interest can be substantially reduced. That is because one is, of necessity, controlling for the operation of multiple tests, many of which are of little plausibility or interest. Clearly, the most satisfactory answer needs to be guided by theory or by previous empirical research to have a focused approach to the study of particular interactions. In the absence of good theory or previous findings, the preferred practice may well be to use backward model selection where there are many subjects and few variables, but to use the forward approach otherwise.

Sequences and Differential Outcomes

In the examples that we gave near the beginning of this chapter, there were several instances in which person-environment interactions operated either through sequences over time or through effects on differential outcomes. We wish here simply to provide a reminder that the methods of data analysis must take these possibilities into account. We mentioned earlier the finding that whereas girls tended to seek "escape" from stressful family circumstances through early marriage and pregnancy, boys were much less likely to adopt this response. This constitutes an example both of a difference in type of response in boys and girls and of a difference that is likely to set in motion a different chain of events. The implication is that, quite often, it will be most important to examine person-environment interactions in terms of sequences over time rather than at any one moment. As indicated throughout this chapter, the search needs to be not for a statistically significant interaction effect as such, but rather for mechanisms that reflect differences in the ways in which people of particular characteristics respond to apparently comparable environmental circumstances. However, there is a problem here to be kept in mind. In our longitudinal study (Rutter & Quinton, 1984) of families with a mentally ill parent, the findings at the start of the study showed a substantial Sex × Family Discord interaction. That is to say, boys appeared to be much more vulnerable than girls to family discord. However, by the end of the 4-year study, although the difference was still in the same direction, the effect was much less marked and fell well short of statistical significance.

One might well argue that what this means is that boys and girls are both vulnerable to family discord, but that boys tend to respond earlier than do girls. Another possible explanation of this declining sex difference is suggested from survival analysis literature, where a common finding with proportional hazard models is that they are not proportional: The size of an estimated relative risk decreases with time. Yet another possible explanation has been shown to be the presence of frailty or heterogeneity (Lancaster & Nickell, 1980). With samples that possess variability in exposure or sensitivity to risks not described by explanatory variables already in the model, the expectation should be that constant sex differences will appear as a declining relative risk as measured by a proportional hazards analysis, giving rise to a Time × Sex interaction. Whatever the explanation, one implication is that an analysis at just one point in time may misinterpret the nature of the interaction (as with early analysis of the family discord data) or miss it entirely (as with analyses at later time points).

Size of Effects

The last point to be made concerns the strength of effects of person-environment interactions. Behavioral scientists are used to thinking of strength of effects in terms of proportion of population variance explained. As Cohen (1988) pointed out, there are situations in which this can be highly misleading. He cited Rosenthal and Rubin's (1982) example of a particular treatment that reduced the death rate from 65% to 35%. The phi coefficient for the resulting 2 × 2 table was 0.3, explaining 9% of the variance. That seems a very small proportion, and yet obviously in real terms the effect on mortality was very substantial indeed. A reduction in death rate from 55% to 45% will give rise to 1% variance accounted for, but again the effect is obviously an important one. This illustrates the old and well-recognized point that how one presents figures may make a big difference in the impression given of the strength of an effect, even though the alternative statistics derived from the same figures mean the same thing (Rutter, 1977).

There are, in addition, two rather different points about strength of effects that need to be mentioned. Cohen (1988) quoted from Abelson (1985), who found that individual differences in batting skill in baseball accounted for a mere .00317% of the variance of the outcome in the likelihood of getting a hit on any one individual at bat. That seems miniscule, and it is obvious that individual skills make much more difference than that to the outcome of baseball games (or indeed in any other sport). The explanation seems to be that cumulative effects within individual players and for the team as a whole lead to greatly enhanced effects on overall team performance. Of course, this cumulative effect is dependent on the availability of circumstances in which such effects could take place. However, for the reasons given above, these may be more common than is usually thought.

Another consideration is that the proportion of variance explained is crucially dependent on the number of subjects in key cells and on the role of modifying variables (Rutter, 1987). For example, in the American National Perinatal Collaborative Study, Down's syndrome accounted for a tiny fraction of 1% of the population variance in intelligence (Broman, Nichols, & Kennedy, 1975). Obviously, that does not mean that this chromosomal abnormality has an unimportant effect on IQ. To the contrary, it virtually always leads to substantial mental handicap. What the figure does mean is that Down's syndrome is rare in the population as a whole, and hence can account for only a trivial proportion of population variance. The effect of moderator variables is shown by the association between exposure to the tubercle bacillus and acquisition of the disease of tuberculosis. It is not possible to get tuberculosis without the tubercule bacillus, and that is hence the all-important cause. On the other hand, in the case of any one instance of exposure to the bacillus, only a small proportion of individuals acquire the disease. This is because a whole variety of other variables, such as individual vulnerability, modify the susceptibility to the bacillus. These examples all apply to main effects rather than to person-environment interactions. However, it is obvious that they will apply at least as strongly to interactions. For example, phenylketonuria provides a direct parallel to the Down's syndrome example; the interaction will necessarily appear exceedingly weak in terms of proportion of variance explained, because the condition is rare, but in reality the interaction is exceedingly strong when the condition is present. The clear implication for all of these considerations is that the strength of effects needs to be considered in several different ways.

Whatever the effect size being presented, the provision of a confidence interval helps to ensure balanced interpretation. Thus, where tests of interaction may lack power, as they often do in comparison with tests of main effects, the nonsignificance of the finding will be confirmed by the occurrence of the zero effect size within the interval. However, also included in the interval will be large interaction effects, the possible existence of which cannot reasonably be ruled out. Such intervals may be highly asymmetric and, in more complex models where effects are described by several parameters, may represent curiously shaped regions of plausible values. The profile likelihood approach, an example of which is described in the appendix, provides a simple but general approach to the calculation of such intervals and regions (also see chap. 6).

CONCLUSIONS

We have given numerous examples from a wide range of fields that organism–environment interactions are common and that their occurrence is informative about the detailed mechanisms underlying the process under study. They represent an important potential line of attack in almost any scientific investigation. We thus argue that the researcher should consider carefully the possible occurrence of such interactions in almost any study, not only at the stage of data analysis, but at the design and conceptual stages as well.

We have suggested five main points as useful in such considerations. First, there are diverse ways in which similar sets of experiences can give rise to different consequences according to the characteristics of the individual. There are *quantitative* differences in responsivity, as reflected in the phenomenon of behavioral inhibition, in sex differences in vulnerability to physical hazards, in the response of children with pervasive hyperactivity to stimulant drugs, and in the potentiating effect of one psychological adversity on another. Then there are *qualitative* differences in responsivity. These include experientially determined physiological differences between experts and novices in their anticipatory response to parachute jumping; gender-related differences in pattern, as shown by the behavioral differences between boys and girls in their reaction to discord and adversity; and abnormal metabolic processing, as with phenylketonuria. A third type of difference reflects variation in the *salience* or meaning of the environmental stimulus. This is evident, for example, in the value for deaf children of being reared in a deaf environment, in species differences in responses to separation experiences, in the different effects of being in the armed forces and having a college education in disadvantaged and advantaged youths, and in the difference across cultures in the temporal connections between puberty and dating.

Another type of individual difference in response is a function of variations in the *opportunity* for the environmental factors to make a difference. This seemed to be the case in the differences we found between institution-reared children and controls in the protective effect provided from positive school experiences (Quinton & Rutter, 1988). Finally, there are the effects that derive from experiences that operate at different points in a *multistage* process. This seemed to apply to the apparent potentiation in the combined carcinogenic effect of asbestos and tobacco. In the psychological arena, it was evident in the different social correlates of shyness in boys and girls and in the greater likelihood of young women (compared with men) to react to family adversity by marrying deviant men and becoming pregnant—events that laid the basis for later stresses that, were more likely to impinge on women.

Second, there are numerous ways of statistically representing the same data; typically, some ways will suggest the need for a formal statistical interaction term, whereas others will not. An interaction term is just one element in an overall statistical model or description of the data, and it cannot be understood without reference to the rest of that model. Any correspondence between a particular form of synergism and an interaction term rests closely on the degree of correspondence between the theoretical conceptualization of the overall process and the overall model. The actual analyses we find ourselves doing may lack such correspondence. On the one hand, some forms of synergism can be represented by commonly used statistical models with no interaction terms. On the other hand, what at first sight appear to be synergisms generating significant interaction terms within some analysis may not in fact reflect catalytic effects in the chemistry of the moment at all, but rather the combination of disparate "main" effects operating multiplicatively at different points in a multistage process.

Third, the choice and interpretation of the statistical results and the manner in which they are presented require consideration of a broad range of factors. A parsimonious description is not necessarily the one with the fewest interaction terms, because that description may involve individual main effects or a combination of main effects that are neither necessary nor scientifically plausible. A model that includes an interaction term may represent a mechanism for which there is much support from other sources, or may sensibly isolate subpopulations of interest to those involved with public health or intervention implications. We have shown how the magnitude of any interaction effect can seem to be very different according to the choice of measure of effect size. Again, this choice should be appropriate to the mechanism and purpose. In all cases, a greater use of confidence intervals would convey a fairer picture of the precision of our knowledge.

Fourth, we have emphasized how the search for organism–environment interactions should be driven by theoretical considerations specific to the research topic and the study population available. These considerations will have implications for the sample design, measurements, and statistical analysis. In particular, as our examples illustrate, in many cases the effects apply to only very small subsets of the general population. The magnitude of the interaction effect for these subsets can be dramatic, even though the proportion of the overall population variance explained may be small.

Finally, we emphasize how, having satisfied ourselves that within some appropriately structured analysis there is evidence of an interaction, the next step is almost always to introduce new concepts and measures to "explain" the observed interaction. Although the interaction effect as defined using the original concepts and measures will remain, subsequent analyses using the new concepts and measures may, but need not, involve any interaction.

References

Abelson, R. P. (1985). A variance explanation paradox: When a little is a lot. *Psychological Bulletin, 97*, 129–133.

Aitkin, M., Anderson, D., Francis, B., & Hinde, J. (1989). *Statistical modelling in GLIM*. Oxford, England: Oxford University Press.

Armitage, P., & Doll, R. (1961). Stochastic models for carcinogenesis. In *Proceedings of the Fourth Berkeley Symposium on Mathematical Statistics and Probability: Biology and problems of health* (pp. 19–27). Berkeley: University of California Press.

Baker, R. J., & Nelder, J. A. (1978). *GLIM: Generalized linear interactive models* (Release 3). Oxford, England: Numerical Algorithms Group.

Barker, D. J. P., & Osmond, C. (1986). Infant mortality, childhood nutrition and ischaemic heart disease in England and Wales. *Lancet, 1*, 1077–1081.

Barker, D. J. P., Winter, P. D., Osmond, C., Margetts, B., & Simmonds, S. J. (1989). Weight in infancy and death from ischaemic heart disease. *Lancet, 2*, 577–580.

Bell, G. (1990). The ecology and genetics of fitness in *Chlamydomonas*: I. Genotype-by-environment interactions among pure strains. *Proceedings of the Royal Society of London, 240B*, 295–321.

Black, J. A., Lewis, H. E., Thacker, C. K. M., & Thould, A. K. (1963). Tristan Da Cunha: General medical investigations. *British Medical Journal, 2*, 1018–1024.

Blakemore, C. (1991). Childhood infection and adult disease. In G. Bock & J. Whelan (Eds.), *The childhood environment and adult disease* (pp. 129–147). New York: Wiley.

Blot, W. J., & Day, N. E. (1979). Synergism and interaction: Are they equivalent? *American Journal of Epidemiology, 110*, 99–100.

Bock, G., & Collins, G. M. (Eds). (1987). *Molecular approaches to human polygenic disease*. New York: Wiley.

Bock, G., & Whelan, J. (Eds). (1991). *The childhood environment and adult disease*. New York: Wiley.

Bock, R. D. (1989). *Multilevel analysis of education data*. New York: Academic Press.

Bornstein, M. H., & Bruner, J. S. (Eds.). (1989). *Interaction in human development*. Hillsdale, NJ: Erlbaum.

Box, G. E. P., & Cox, D. R. (1964). An analysis of transformations [with discussion]. *Journal of the Royal Statistical Society, 143A*, 383–430.

Breen, R. (1984). Fitting nonhierarchical and association log-linear models using GLIM. *Sociological Methods and Research, 13*, 77–107.

Breslow, N., & Storer, B. E. (1985). General relative risk functions for case-control studies. *American Journal of Epidemiology, 122*, 149–162.

Broman, S. H., Nichols, P. L., & Kennedy, W. A. (1975). *Preschool IQ: Prenatal and early developmental correlates*. Hillsdale, NJ: Erlbaum.

Brown, G. W., & Harris, T. O. (1978). *Social origins of depression*. London: Tavistock.

Brown, G., Harris, T. O., & Lemyre, L. (1991). Now you see it, now you don't: Some considerations on multiple regression. In D. Magnusson, L. Bergman, G. Rudinger, & B. Törestad (Eds.), *Problems and methods in longitudinal research: Stability and change*. Cambridge, England: Cambridge University Press.

Caron, C., & Duyme, M. (1989). Assessments of effects of socioeconomic status in IQ in a full cross-fostering study. *Nature, 340*, 552–554.

Caspi, A. (1991). Continuity and change in behavioral development. In G. Bock & J. Whelan (Eds.), *The childhood environment and adult disease* (pp. 209–219). New York: Wiley.

Chandra, R. K. (1983). Nutrition, immunity, and infection: Present knowledge and future directions. *Lancet, 1*, 688–691.

Cohen, J. (1988). *Statistical power analysis for the behavioral sciences* (2nd ed.). New York: Academic Press.

Costello, A. M. de L., Hamilton, P. A., Baudin, J., Townsend, J., Bradford, B. C., Stewart, A. L., & Reynolds, E. O. R. (1988). Prediction of neurodevelopmental impairment at four years from brain unltrasound appearance of very preterm infants. *Developmental Medicine and Child Neurology, 30*, 711–722.

Cox, D. R. (1970). *Analysis of binary data*. London: Chapman & Hall.

Earls, F. (1987). Sex differences in psychiatric disorders: Origins and developmental influences. *Psychiatric Developments, 1*, 1–23.

EGRET. (1989). Seattle, WA: Statistics and Epidemiology Research Corporation.

Ehrhardt, A. A., & Meyer-Bahlburg, H. F. L. (1981). Effects of prenatal sex hormones on gender-related behavior. *Science, 211*, 1312–1318.

Elder, G. H. (1986). Military times and turning points in men's lives. *Developmental Psychology, 22*, 233–245.

Everitt, B. S., & Smith, A. M. R. (1979). Interactions in contingency tables: A brief discussion of alternative definitions. *Psychological Medicine, 9*, 581–584.

Falloon, I. R. H. (1988). Expressed emotion: Current status. *Psychological Medicine, 18*, 269–284.

Fuggle, P., & Graham, P. (in press). Metabolic and endocrine disorders and psychological functioning. In M. Rutter & P. Casaer (Eds.), *Biological risk factors in developmental psychopathology*. Cambridge, England: Cambridge University Press.

Ghodsian, M. (1990). *Childhood, adolescent and adult factors associated with depression at 23*. Manuscript submitted for publication.

Gottesman, I. I., & Shields, J. (1982). *Schizophrenia: The epigenetic puzzle*. Cambridge, England: Cambridge University Press.

Goedde, H. W., & Agarwal, D. P. (Eds.). (1987). *Genetics and alcoholism*. New York: Alan R. Liss.

Graham, P., & Rutter, M. (1985). Adolescent disorders. In M. Rutter & L. Hersov (Eds.), *Child and adolescent psychiatry: Modern approaches* (2nd ed., pp. 351–367). Oxford, England: Blackwell Scientific.

Greenough, W. T., Carter, C. S., Steerman, C., & DeVoogd, T. J. (1977). Sex differences in dendritic patterns in hamster preoptic area. *Brain Research, 126*, 63–72.

Greenwood, B. M. (1987). The host's response to infection. In D. J. Weatherall, J. G. G. Ledingham, & D. A. Warrell (Eds.), *Oxford textbook of medicine* (2nd ed., pp. 5.1–5.13). Oxford, England: Oxford University Press.

Grizzle, J. E., Starmer, C. F., & Koch, G. G. (1969). Analysis of categorical data by linear models. *Biometrics, 25*, 489–504.

Heath, A. C., Jardine, R., & Martin, N. G. (1989). Interactive effects of genotype and social environment on alcohol consumption in female twins. *Journal of Studies on Alcohol, 50*, 38–48.

Hetherington, E. M., Cox, M., & Cox, R. (1982). Effects of divorce on parents and children. In M. Lamb (Ed), *Non-traditional families* (pp. 233–288). Hillsdale, NJ: Erlbaum.

Hunt, J. V. (1979). Psychological development: Early experience. *Annual Review of Psychology, 30*, 103–143.

Kagan, J., Reznick, J. S., Snidman, N., Gibbons, J., & Johnson, M. O. (1988). Childhood derivatives of inhibition and lack of inhibition to the unfamiliar. *Child Development, 59*, 1580–1589.

Katan, M. B., & Beynen, A. C. (1987). Characteristics of human hypo- and hyper-responders to dietary cholesterol. *American Journal of Epidemiology, 125*, 387–399.

Kendler, K. S., & Eaves, L. J. (1986). Models for the joint effect of genotype and environment on liability to psychiatric illness. *American Journal of Psychiatry, 143*, 279–289.

Kendler, K. S., Neale, M. C., Heath, A. C., Kessler, R. C., & Eaves, L. J. (1991). Life events and depressive symptoms: A twin study perspective. In P. McGuffin, & R. Murray (Eds.), *The new genetics of mental illness* (pp. 146–164). Oxford, England: Heinemann Medical Books.

Lancaster, T. (1985). Generalised residuals and heterogeneous duration models with applications to the Weibull model. *Journal of Econometrics, 28*, 155–169.

Lancaster, T., & Nickell, S. (1980). The analysis of re-employment probabilities for the unemployed. *Journal of the Royal Statistical Society, 143A*, 141–165.

Leff, J., & Vaugh, C. (1984). *Expressed emotion in families: Its significance for mental illness*. New York: Guilford Press.

Levine, S., Chevalier, J. A., & Korchin, S. J. (1956). The effects of early shock and handling on later avoidance learning. *Journal of Personality, 24*, 475–493.

Loehlin, J. C., Willerman, L., & Horn, J. M. (1982). Personality resemblances between unwed mothers and their adopted-away offspring. *Journal of Personality and Social Psychology, 42,* 1089–1099.

Losowsky, M. F. (1987). Malabsorption. In D. J. Weatherall, J. G. G. Ledingham, & D. A. Warrell (Eds.), *Oxford textbook of medicine* (2nd ed., pp. 12.98–12.114). Oxford, England: Oxford University Press.

Lucas, A., Brooke, O. G., Morley, R., Cole, T. J., & Bamford, M. F. (1990). Early diet of preterm infants and development of allergic or atopic disease: Randomised prospective study. *British Medical Journal, 300,* 837–840.

Maccoby, E. E., & Jacklin, C. (1983). The "person" characteristics of children and the family as environment. In D. Magnusson & V. L. Allen (Eds.), *Human development: An interactional perspective* (pp. 75–91). New York: Academic Press.

Magnusson, D. (1988). *Individual development from an interactional perspective: A longitudinal study.* Hillsdale, NJ: Erlbaum.

Martyn, C. N. (1991). Childhood infection and adult disease. In G. Bock & J. Whelan (Eds.), *The childhood environment and adult disease* (pp. 93–102). New York: Wiley.

McCullagh, P., & Nelder, J. A. (1983). *Generalized linear models.* London: Chapman & Hall.

Meadow, K. P. (1975). The development of deaf children. In E. M. Hetherington (Ed.), *Review of child development research* (Vol. 5, pp. 441–508). Chicago: University of Chicago Press.

Merikangas, K. R. (1990). The genetic epidemiology of alcoholism. *Psychological Medicine, 20,* 11–22.

Mistry, P., Miller, N. E., Laker, M., Hazzard, W. R., & Lewis, B. (1981). Individual variation in the effects of dietary cholesterol on plasma lipoproteins and cellular cholesterol homeostasis in man. *Journal of Clinical Investigation, 67,* 493–502.

Mott, G. E., Jackson, E. M., McMahan, C. A., & McGill, H. C. (1990). Cholesterol metabolism in adult baboons is influenced by infant diet. *Journal of Nutrition, 120,* 243–251.

Murray, R., Lewis, S., Owen, M., & Foerster, A. (1989). The neurodevelopmental origins of dementia praecox. In P. McGuffin, & P. Bebbington (Eds.), *Schizophrenia: The major issues* (pp. 90–107). London: Heinemann Medical Books.

Nichols, P. L. (1984). Familial mental retardation. *Behavior Genetics, 14,* 161–170.

Ormel, J., Stewart, R., & Sanderman, R. (1989). Personality as modifier of the life change-distress relationship: A longitudinal modelling approach. *Social Psychiatry and Psychiatric Epidemiology, 24,* 187–195.

Peto, R. (1977). Epidemiology, multistage models and short-term mutagenicity tests. In H. H. Hiatt, J. P. Watson, & J. A. Winsten (Eds.), *Origins of human cancer* (pp. 1403–1430). Cold Spring Harbor, NY: Cold Spring Harbor Laboratory.

Pickles, A., & Rutter, M. (1991). Statistical and conceptual models of "turning points" in developmental processes. In D. Magnusson, L. Bergman, G. Rudinger, & B. Törestad (Eds.), *Problems and methods in longitudinal research: Stability and change* (pp. 32–57). Cambridge, England: Cambridge University Press.

Plomin, R. (1986). *Development genetics, and psychology.* Hillsdale, NJ: Erlbaum.

Plomin, R., & Daniels, D. (1987). Why are children in the same family so different from each other? *Behavioral and Brain Sciences, 10,* 44–54.

Plomin, R., DeFries, J. C., & Fulker, D. W. (1988). *Nature and nurture during infancy and early childhood.* Cambridge, England: Cambridge University Press.

Plomin, R., DeFries, J. C., & Loehlin, J. C. (1977). Genotype–environment interaction and correlation in the analysis of human behavior. *Psychological Bulletin, 84,* 309–322.

Plomin, R., Rende, R. D., & Rutter, M. (in press). Quantitative genetics and developmental psychopathology. In D. Cicchetti & S. Toth (Eds.), *Rochester Symposium on Developmental Psychopathology: Vol. 2. Internalizing and externalizing expressions of dysfunction.* Hillsdale, NJ: Erlbaum.

Prentice, R. L., & Mason, M. W. (1986). On the application of linear relative risk regression models. *Biometrics, 42,* 109–120.

Quinton, D., & Rutter, M. (1976). Early hospital admissions and later disturbances of behavior: An attempted replication of Douglas' findings. *Developmental Medicine and Child Neurology, 18,* 447–459.

Quinton, D., & Rutter, M. (1988). *Parenting breakdown: The making and breaking of inter-generational links.* Aldershot, England: Avebury.

Radke-Yarrow, M., M., Richters, J., & Wilson, W. E. (1988). Child development in the network of relationships. In R. A. Hinde & J. Stevenson-Hinde (Eds.), *Relationships within families: Mutual influences* (pp. 48–67). Oxford, England: Clarendon Press.

Rodgers, B. (1990). Influences of early-life and recent factors on affective disorder in women: An exploration of vulnerability models. In L. Robins & M. Rutter (eds.), *Straight and devious pathways from childhood to adulthood* (pp. 314–327). Cambridge, England: Cambridge University Press.

Rosenthal, R., & Rubin, D. B. (1982). A simple, general purpose display of magnitude of experimental effect. *Journal of Educational Psychology, 74,* 166–169.

Rothman, K. (1976). Causes. *American Journal of Epidemiology, 104,* 587–592.

Rotter, J. I., & Diamond, J. M. (1987). What maintains the frequencies of human genetic diseases? *Nature, 329,* 289–290.

Rutter, M. (1977). Prospective studies to investigate behavioral change. In J. S. Strauss, H. M. Babigian, & M. Roff (Eds.), *The origins and course of psychopathology* (pp. 223–247). New York: Plenum Press.

Rutter, M. (1978). Family, area and school influences in the genesis of conduct disorders. In L. Hersov, M. Berger, & D. Shaffer (Eds.), *Aggression and antisocial behaviour in childhood and adolescence* (pp. 95–113). Oxford, England: Pergamon Press.

Rutter, M. (1981). *Maternal deprivation reassessed* (2nd ed.). Harmondsworth, Middlesex, England: Penguin Books.

Rutter, M. (1983). Statistical and personal interactions: Facets and perspectives. In D. Magnusson & V. Allen (Eds.), *Human development: An interactional perspective* (pp. 295–319). New York: Academic Press.

Rutter, M. (1987). Continuities and discontinuities from infancy. In J. Osofsky (Ed.), *Handbook of infant development* (2nd ed., pp. 1256–1296). New York: Wiley.

Rutter, M., Angold, A., Harrington, R., Nicholls, J., & Taylor, E. (1989, April), *Age trends in patterns of psychopathology in child psychiatric clinic attenders.* Paper presented at the Society for Research in Child Development symposium on effects of pubertal timing and social factors in adolescent development, Kansas City, KS:

Rutter, M., Chadwick, O., & Shaffer, D. (1983). Head injury. In M. Rutter (Ed.), *Developmental neuropsychiatry* (pp. 83–111). New York: Guilford Press.

Rutter, M., & Giller, H. (Eds.). (1983). *Juvenile Delinquency: Trends and perspectives.* Harmondsworth, Middlesex, England: Penguin Books.

Rutter, M., & Gould, M. (1985). Classification. In M. Rutter & L. Hersov (Eds,), *Child and adolescent psychiatry: Modern approaches* (2nd ed., pp. 304–321). Oxford, England: Blackwell Scientific.

Rutter, M., & Madge, N. (1976). *Cycles of disadvantage.* London: Heinemann.

Rutter, M., & Quinton, D. (1984). Parental psychiatric disorder: Effects on children. *Psychological Medicine, 14,* 853–880.

Rutter, M., Quinton, D., & Hill, J. (1990). Adult outcome of institution-reared children:
    Males and females compared. In L. Robins & M. Rutter (Eds.), *Straight and devious
    pathways from childhood to adulthood* (pp. 135–157). Cambridge, England: Cam-
    bridge University Press.
Sameroff, A. J., & Chandler, M. J. (1975). Reproductive risk and the continuum of
    caretaking casualty. In F. D. Horowitz (Ed.), *Review of child development research*
    (Vol. 4, pp. 187–244). Chicago: University of Chicago Press.
Samuels, N. (1963). Experiences of a medical officer on Tristan Da Cinha, June–October,
    1961. *British Medical Journal, 2*, 1013–1017.
Schiff, M., & Lewontin, R. (1987). *Education and class: The irrelevance of IQ genetic
    studies.* Oxford, England: Clarendon Press.
Shaffer, D., Chadwick, O., & Rutter, M. (1975). Psychiatric outcome of localized head
    injury in children. In R. Porter & D. Fitzsimons (Eds.), *Outcome of severe damage
    to the central nervous system* (pp. 191–213). Amsterdam: Elsevier–Excerpta Medica–
    North Holland.
Stevenson-Hinde, J., & Hinde, R. A. (1986). Changes in associations between character-
    istics and interactions. In R. Plomin & J. Dunn (Eds.), *The study of temperament:
    Changes, continuities and challenges* (pp. 115–129). Hillsdale, NJ: Erlbaum.
Suomi, S. J. (1991). Early stress and adult emotional activity in rhesus monkeys. In G.
    Bock & J. Whelan (Eds.), *The childhood environment and adult disease* (pp. 171–
    183). New York: Wiley.
Taylor, E., Schachar, R., Thorley, G., Wieselberg, H. M., Everitt, B., & Rutter, M.
    (1987). Which boys respond to stimulant medication? A controlled trial of methyl-
    phenidate in boys with disruptive behaviour. *Psychological Medicine, 17*, 121–143.
Tennant, C., & Bebbington, P. (1978). The social causation of depression: A critique of
    the work of Brown and his colleagues. *Psychological Medicine, 8*, 565–575.
Thomas, D. C., Langholz, B., Mack, W., & Floderus, B. (1989). *Bivariate survival
    models for analysis of genetic and environmental effects in twins.* Unpublished
    manuscript, Department of Preventative Medicine, University of Southern Cali-
    fornia, Los Angeles.
Tibshirani, R., & Hastie, T. (1987). Local likelihood estimation. *Journal of the Americal
    Statistical Association, 82*, 559–567.
Tizard, J. (1975). Race and IQ: The limits of probability. *New Behaviour, 1*, 6–9.
Ursin, H., Baade, E., & Levine, S. (1978). *Psychobiology of stress: A study of coping
    men.* Academic Pres: New York.
Venables, P. H. (1987). Autonomic nervous system factors in criminal behavior. In S. A.
    Mednick, T. E. Moffitt, & S. A. Stack (Eds.), *The causes of crime: New biological
    approaches* (pp. 110–136). Cambridge, England: Cambridge University Press.
Walter, S. D., & Holford, T. R. (1978). Additive, multiplicative and other models for
    disease risk. *American Journal of Epidemiology, 108*, 341–349.
Whincup, P. H., Cook, D. G., & Shaper, A. G. (1989). Early influences on blood pressure:
    A study of children aged 5–7 years. *British Medical Journal, 299*, 587–591.
Zaslow, M. J., & Hayes, C. D. (1986). Sex differences in children's response to psycho-
    social stress: Toward a cross-context analysis. In M. E. Lamb, A. L. Bronn, & B.
    Rogoff (Eds.), *Advances in developmental psychology*, (Vol. 4, pp. 285–337). Hills-
    dale, NJ: Erlbaum.

APPENDIX   *(by Andrew Pickles)*

Some Statistical Considerations for Interaction Effects With a Categorical Outcome

Different Link Functions

In ordinary linear regression, an interaction effect between two explanatory variables X_1 and X_2 on some outcome variable y is estimated by a parameter such as c in the following equation:

$$y = a + b_1 X_1 + b_2 X_2 + c X_1 X_2 + e$$

An essentially similar approach can be adopted for the estimation of interaction effects where the outcome is a categorical variable by the use of generalized linear models (McCullagh & Nelder, 1983). Generalized linear models allow outcomes or dependent variables that have discrete or bounded values to be related to an ordinary linear regression-type prediction equation (the above equation without the error term e) by the use of appropriate transformations or link functions and error terms. For binary data, the values from the prediction equation are transformed to the 0–1 range of a proportion, and this is then used as the expected value or mean of some binomial distribution. This chapter makes clear that the estimated value for the parameter c (and all of the other parameters) depends on the choice of transformation. The equations that define the various link functions mentioned are as follows, where (i) is the link function and (ii) its inverse and we abbreviate the prediction equation to just $a + bx$ for simplicity:

Linear-additive	(i)	$p = a + bx$
	(ii)	$p = a + bx$
Logistic	(i)	$\log [p/(1 - p)] = a + bx$
	(ii)	$p = \exp (a + bx)/[1 + \exp (a + bx)]$

which also corresponds to the multiplicative relative risk model if bx is replaced by $\log[R(x)]$, where $R(x)$ is the relative risk.

Probit	(i)	$F^{-1} (p) = a + bx$
	(ii)	$p = F (a + bx)$ $F(.)$ is the normal cumulative distribution function (CDF)
Complementary-log-log	(i)	$\log[- \log(1 - p)] = a + bx$
	(ii)	$p = 1 - \exp[-\exp(a + bx)]$

Figure 2A shows these various scales (standardized to the logistic scale at probabilities .25 and .5). This shows clearly how similar the functions are in the range 0.2 to 0.8, and implies that if all of the observed proportions fall within this range, then if a main effects only model is adequate in one model, it will also be adequate in the others. Thus, conflict about the presence or absence of

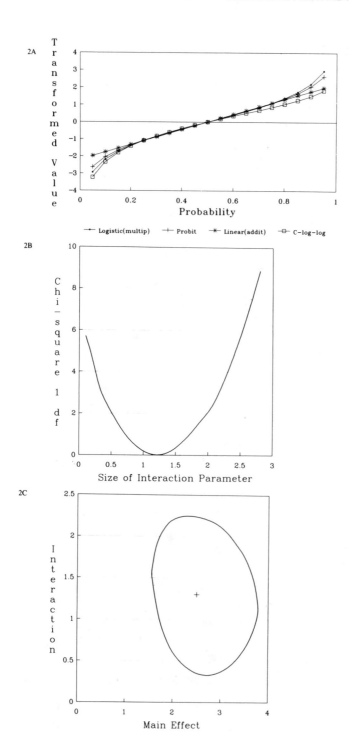

Figure 2.
Figure 2A = comparison of link functions (data from Brown & Harris, 1978). (Figure 2B = likelihood confidence interval from profile likelihood: nonhierarchical interaction [data from Brown & Harris, 1978]. Figure 2C = confidence region for estimated main effect and interaction: non-hierarchical model [$X_2 + X_2X_1$]; data from Brown & Harris, 1978. Used by permission.)

interaction effects should arise only if one or more of the observed proportions fall outside of this range. The great majority of the debate has been concerned with the occurrence of events that in the absence of risk factors have very low base rates. Under such circumstances, odds ratios closely approximate relative risk, and the logistic or log-linear model is then "multiplicative" in the relative risks and directly contrasted with models with "additive" relative risks.

If we regard a main effects explanation as more parsimonious than a model that requires interactions, searching for a link function that fits without an interaction may be sensible. As well as the standard parametric link functions, four of which have been mentioned with regard to categorical data, there are other more general approaches that either use a wider class of transformation, such as the Box–Cox approach (Box & Cox, 1964) or use a nonparametric or locally smoothed link function (e.g., Tibshirani & Hastie, 1987). We illustrated such an approach using the generalized relative risk model of Breslow and Storer (1985). In fact, this is an example of the power link function (see McCullagh & Nelder, 1983):

$$\log[p/(1 - p)] = a + b.\log[R(x)],$$
$$\text{where } \log[R(x)] = [(1 + bx)^k - 1]/k \text{ for } k \neq 0$$
$$= \log(1 + bx) \text{ for } k = 0$$

and k is the parameter lambda of Figure 1.

Statistical Considerations in the Choice of Link Function

This chapter suggests some theoretical and contextual considerations in the choice of link function. However, there are also some simple statistical criteria that distinguish the link functions, of which we now mention three.

Invariance Under Sampling Design It would seem desirable that whatever the sample design, be it prospective, case-control/retrospective, simple random sampling, or stratified, we should be able to estimate the same effect. Does choosing one transformation or link function rather than another effect this?

Consider the case of a simple 2×2 table with sample cell proportions labeled below as a to d, where $a + b + c + d = 1$. Our principal interest lies in the population proportions or probabilities, say A to D, in particular the difference in the conditional probabilities of caseness for the exposed $B/(A + B)$ and unexposed $D/(C + D)$. On an additive scale (linear link), this corresponds to the simple difference. For the multiplicative (logistic link), this difference is $\log(D/C) - \log(B/A)$ or $\log(AD/BC)$. The table would look as follows:

	Sample outcome (caseness)		Population outcome (caseness)	
	−	+	−	+
Risk				
−	a	b	A	B
+	b	d	C	D

Cox (1970) argued the following. A simple random sample (SRS) of the population allows the estimation of each of the cell probabilities A to D by their corresponding sample proportions a to d. Any link function or measure of the difference of the conditional probabilities can be used with such a design. However, SRS is rarely used, particularly where risk factor, outcome, or both are rare.

A prospective study of a fixed (say equal) number of risk-exposed and risk-unexposed individuals will often be more efficient, but then the marginal proportions a + b and c + d (because we fixed them to be equal) will bear no relation to the population values A + B and C + D. The sample proportions b/(a + b) and c/(c + d) still estimate the corresponding population quantities of primary interest and thus the test of interaction will be testing the same effect in this design as it would under SRS for a wide range of link functions.

In a similar fashion to the prospective design, a retrospective study of a fixed number of cases and controls also does not allow the estimation of each of the population cell proportions, nor are the margins a + c and b + d informative, but now it is the proportions C/(A + C) and D/(B + D) that can be estimated. From such a design, the simple difference in the conditional probabilities of interest (B/[A + B] and D/[C + D]) cannot be directly estimated. However, we can still estimate log(A/C), log(B/D), and log(A/C) − log(B/D) = log(AD/BC). This is the same difference on the logistic scale that the other sampling designs give us. Thus, a multiplicative test of interaction is testing the same effect under all three designs, whereas an additive test of interaction applied to retrospective data does not, in general, test for the same effect as that under SRS or a prospective design. In this respect, use of the additive model restricts the scope for comparison and replication.

Another way of viewing this is that we can leave the beta coefficient fixed, independently vary the constant in the logistic model, and produce a family of situations in which the overall proportion of successes is arbitrary. This cannot be done for the linear probability model. A different experimenter using a different range of stimuli/prevalence would be likely to find a different stimulus–response relationship. These arguments extend to the analysis of tables with higher order interaction effects.

Amalgamation, Truncation, Ordering, and Latent Variables Categorical measurements need not be binary, but may involve several categories. A 3 × 2 × 2 table of data that shows no three-way multiplicative interaction may show such interaction if cells are amalgamated to form a 2 × 2 × 2 table. A table showing no additive interaction will continue to show no such interaction when amalgamated. However, if the table is truncated rather than amalgamated, one category of the first dimension simply being dropped, then a table showing no multiplicative interaction will remain without multiplicative interaction, but one without additive interaction may exhibit additive interaction after truncation.

Both of these standard multiplicative and additive treatments ignore the potential ordering in the categories of a dimension and thus neither may in fact be appropriate.

Models of dichotomous outcomes based on a latent variable crossing a threshold are easily extended to ordered categories by the inclusion of several thresholds of increasing "severity." Such threshold response models can be constructed using many link functions but are usually based on the univariate logistic or probit functions. These models in fact represent an extreme form of orderedness in which the "errors" that influence crossing one threshold are the same as those crossing the next (i.e., there is just one underlying latent dimension). Categories can be more loosely "ordered" by having thresholds on different latent variables that are correlated. This is, for example, how anxiety and depression could well be represented. Few of the many possible univariate link functions generalize satisfactorily to this more complicated multivariate situation. The multivariate probit, based on the multivariate normal distribution, offers great generality but quickly becomes computationally cumbersome as the number of categories increases beyond about four.

   Collapsing Over Another Risk Factor The parameter estimates from a multiplicative model are not, however, invariant to collapsing over the dimension of another independent risk factor (although certain functions of the parameters, notably elasticities, are still consistently estimated). A similar effect occurs with proportional hazards survival models with an omitted variable, commonly referred to as "frailty" in the survival literature. For a wide class of models, a consistent finding is that the coefficients for the observed risk factors are attenuated but that the degree of attenuation changes with the duration of survival. This can give rise to the impression that a risk factor although in fact possessing constant relative risk at the individual level, shows an effect that varies with duration (Lancaster & Nickell, 1980); note that again the elasticities may remain unaffected (Lancaster, 1985).

Confidence Intervals for Effects

For several of the models discussed, a sensible confidence interval will be asymmetric around some point estimate of the interaction effect or may need to be presented in conjunction with some other parameter estimate, for example a main effect. In either case, the usual procedure of taking the point estimate plus or minus two standard errors as a confidence interval may be inadequate. Plotting the profile likelihood allows these complexities to be examined (see Aitkin, Anderson, Francis, & Hinde, 1989, p. 199, for an example). Programs such as GLIM (Baker and Nelder, 1978) and EGRET (1989) allow the setting of an offset, essentially the fixing of a parameter to a specified value. A model can therefore be fitted with a fixed size for the interaction effect and the goodness-of-fit obtained. Plotting this goodness-of-fit for a range of values of the interaction gives, for the nonhierarchical interaction model and the Brown and Harris (1978) data, the results shown in Figure 2B. All the values of the interaction effect that do not fit significantly worse than the best-fitting value fall within the likelihood interval. Where another effect is simultaneously of interest, the model must be fitted to a grid of values of the offset, and the profile likelihood interval shows a region of plausible values, such as that shown in Figure 2C.

CHAPTER 8

SO MANY INTERACTIONS, SO LITTLE EVIDENCE. WHY?

ROBERT B. McCALL

A case can be made for the proposition that interactions between organisms and environments are the rule in nature, not the exception. Indeed, individual differences exist for essentially every behavioral and physical variable that researchers know, and rarely, if ever, does an environmental event or manipulation produce identical effects on all individuals experiencing it. Organismic and environmental factors would interact, it seems, in producing almost any phenomenon if they were measured with sufficient precision on a sample containing sufficient variability. Indeed, this book is filled with specific examples.

At the same time, when samples of essentially normal individuals are studied, relatively few interactions are empirically well documented by a consistently replicated research literature. For example, Plomin and Hershberger (see chap. 3 in this book) report that researchers in the field of behavior genetics often look for interactions but rarely find them. Similarly, relatively few replicable Aptitude × Instructional Method interactions are documented consistently (Cronbach & Snow, 1977).

This anomaly, described most vividly by Plomin (see chap. 3; Plomin & Daniels, 1984), became known to the conferees as "Plomin's paradox," and it was defined succinctly by Wachs to mean "so many interactions, so little evidence."

The premise of the paradox—namely, that interactions are very common, if not pervasive—was accepted by the conferees, who then offered numerous explanations for the lack of empirical evidence for interactions. This chapter reviews many of these potential explanations, introducing more elaborate a... sions in subsequent chapters. In addition, I have mixed in some personal speculation about other possible reasons for this lack of evidence and offered some modest direction as to how to find these elusive interactions.

In my opinion, the reasons we do not find many replicable interactions fall into two broad categories. One category is that nature conspires against it, and the second is that researchers conspire with nature.

ON THE NATURE OF INTERACTIONS

The first step toward understanding interactions as they occur in nature is to specify what we are looking for.

Definitions and Distinctions

Interactions

The concept of organism–environment interaction can mean many different things (Bornstein & Bruner, 1989; Wachs & Plomin, this volume), but an *interaction* is commonly defined in the same way that the term is defined in the analysis of variance. That is, two variables, such as organism and environment, are said to interact if different environments produce different effects on different categories of organisms. That is, outcomes (i.e., phenotypes or consequences) are differentially or uniquely contingent on both organismic and environmental factors.

Note that the term *organism* is intended to be quite broad. It includes essentially any individual or categorical differences among subjects existing before the environmental event or manipulation of interest occurs. It represents the set of characteristics endogenous to subjects at the time of the assessment or manipulation, and it may include differences among or within species caused by genetic, biological, biochemical, sexual, racial, and life history factors, among others. Analogously, *environment* is also conceived broadly and could include biochemical (e.g., drugs, foods), physical, and social events that occur exogenously to subjects being studied at the time of the observation.

Additive Versus Interactive Effects

To sharpen the definition, it is necessary to distinguish between "additive" effects of organism and environment, which might be symbolized by O + E, and "interactive" effects, which might by symbolized by O × E.

Both organism and environment may have an effect on the outcome. However, if differences in outcomes can be totally predicted within sampling error by adding the main effects of organism to the main effects of environment, then there are additive main effects, or O + E, not an interaction. On the other hand, if outcomes are not totally predicted within sampling error by adding the main effects of organism and environment, then an interaction, or O × E, is said to have occurred.

Interaction, Covariation, and Transaction

It will be useful to recall the distinctions made in the introduction to this book among "interaction," "covariation," and "transaction." Covariation is essentially the nonindependence in naturalistic contexts of organismic and environmental factors. For example, good genes and good environments covary so that genetically intelligent parents not only contribute genes for higher levels of intelligence to their children but also tend to provide superior intellectual environments for their children. Conceptually, covariation represents the overlapping additive contributions of organismic and environmental factors. Thus, the more covariation, the more additive effects, and by implication, the fewer interactive effects, that will be discovered.

"Transaction" refers to the mutual influence during development of organism and environment. Such transaction may produce covariation. It includes, for example, the reciprocal influence between mothers and infants. I propose, for the present discussion, that it also includes "niche-picking," in which organisms select their own environments, which, in turn, influence those organisms.

The focus of this chapter is on interactions and why researchers do not seem to find replicable empirical documentation of many interactions. I contend in the remainder of this chapter that although interactions are a conceptual necessity, nature favors convariation, which is sometimes achieved through transaction and which tends to produce a predominance of additive rather than interactive organism–environment effects.

A Concept of Natural Interactions and Covariations

In the conceptual extreme, all phenotypes are the products of organism–environment interactions. Specify any behavioral phenomenon, for example, and it will occur for some but not other organisms (e.g., species) in some but not other environmental circumstances; one needs only to be sufficiently extreme in selecting the organisms and environments. Even within a species, one will always be able to think of some combination of organismic and environmental circumstances that will be associated with more or less of the phenotype in question. Thus, every phenomenon requires a specific combination—that is, an interaction—of organism and environment.

This means that essentially all phenomena are interactions at some level or another, and some of these interactions will be observed in research data. However, some researchers have the impression that fewer interactions have been observed than one might expect, and my task in this chapter is to speculate why more interactions are not empirically demonstrated. Thus, the focus is on why we might not find interactions.

A main reason, I suspect, is that nature "conspires" against revealing interactions because covariation of organism and environment is very adaptive, especially when major characteristics of the species are concerned. Indeed, the consequence of evolution and the survival of the fittest is a nonrandom distribution of organisms across environments (i.e., organisms and environments covary), and some combinations lead to one kind of outcome and other combinations lead to other kinds of outcomes. Recall, however, that in the analysis of variance, the model for defining interactions, the "independent" variables (i.e., organism, environment) indeed must be "independent." In contrast, I allege that they are often not independent but that they covary. When that is the case, organism main effects will be related to environmental main effects. However, interactions are produced by the "odd" combinations, which accentuate or contradict main effects. Not only does covariation mean that such odd combinations will be less frequent in the sample and thus less influential in producing interactions, but the concept of adaptation implies that even such odd combinations should tend to produce adaptable outcomes—outcomes not so different from the predominant combinations.

This is obvious both at the species level and in the extreme (i.e., odd organism–environment combinations that produce extreme outcomes may not survive). However, does this apply to variations within a species and across environments in which combinations produce outcomes less crucial to survival? I believe it does, at least to a certain extent. That is, I suspect that the more a characteristic is crucially adaptive, the greater the covariation and the less likely one will find interactions. Conversely, the less crucial to survival and adaptation a characteristic is, the less tendency there is toward covariation and, presumably, the more likely are interactions. Furthermore, within a species, not only may evolution have left few examples of some types of organisms in the population, but individual organisms will adapt to their individual environments or seek out compatible environments, which produces covariation or minimizes extreme or odd outcomes, both of which tend to minimize observable interactions.

I believe that nature follows a few simple principles that result in covariation, which, in turn, minimizes observable interactions in research samples.

1. *The necessary organismic and environmental circumstances for a phenomenon are commonly provided and "dominant."* Although most phenomena are the result of interactions, the required organismic and environmental circumstances are usually available and "dominant." The interaction, then, although a conceptual necessity, is a practical irrelevancy.

Take language development, for example. On the organismic side, a human being with certain sensory and brain systems physically intact is required. On the environmental side, this organism must be exposed to and actively engage a language environment. This organism–environment combination (i.e., interaction) is required for language to develop. However, although both of these factors are necessary, both naturally coexist, producing covariation rather than interaction. It is only the unusual genetic or physical anomaly or the extreme environment that illustrates the interaction; otherwise, covariation is the observation.

This example pertains to the extreme and gross outcome of the presence or absence of language in children. That is, nearly all human children are "wired" for language, nearly all children are exposed to an interactive language environment, and consequently, nearly all children talk. However, children are born with variable potential for language fluency, they are reared in environments that vary in the support and nurturance of language fluency, and they vary in their verbal fluency. These are certainly main effects for organism and environment. Are there interactions? I suspect there are, but I also suspect that covariation makes it difficult to observe many of these interactions. The covariation is a result of the genetic–environment correlation (children with good genes tend to be reared in good environments) and of niche-picking in which capable children select environments that support their organismic dispositions.

Interactions are most commonly illustrated with examples involving unusual genetic anomalies or unusual environmental circumstances, perhaps because extreme and unusual circumstances are needed to observe the "odd" combination. Phenylketonuria (PKU) is such an example. The required genetic circumstance is rare—approximately 1 in 10,000 live births. This condition produces the inability of the child to metabolize phenylalanine into tyrosine, producing excessive amounts of phenylpyruvic acid, which leads by some mechanism to mental retardation. Because phenylalanine is present in many foods, PKU originally appeared empirically to be a genetic main effect because all individuals with the genetic circumstance developed the retardation. Later, when the biochemical mechanism and the necessary environmental circumstance (phenylalanine) were specified, a special diet devoid of phenylalanine was created. Genetically disposed children kept on a phenylalanine-free diet did not develop the retarded characteristics. PKU retardation is an example of a Genetics × Environment interaction, but it involves only about 1 in 10,000 individuals. The other 9,999 exhibit nature's adaptive conspiracy of covariation, at least for avoiding retardation by this mechanism.

Schizophrenia may be another example, although knowledge of the nature of this interaction is considerably less precise. It seems likely that both genetic and environmental factors are involved, and it is likely that they interact. Although schizophrenia is more frequent in genetic descendants of schizophrenics, it is less likely than would be predicted on the basis of straight genetic transmission. Presumably, some environmental circumstance, in combination with the genetic disposition, is required. Similarly, being reared by at least one schizophrenic parent is not a sufficient environmental factor, and even the combination of these genetic and environmental factors may not be totally sufficient to produce the disorder. It may be that genetic dispositions vary in strength, with some individuals destined to become schizophrenic regardless of their environmental circumstances, whereas others require a combination (i.e., an interaction) of genetic disposition and environmental circumstance. Conversely, no environment may be able to produce schizophrenia in those lacking the genetic disposition, although certain environments will make a contribution toward that outcome for certain genotypes. In any case, once again, for most individuals, the covariation of genetic and environmental combinations for normality is very common; typically, only an exceptional combination of circumstances (i.e., diathesis and stress; see chap 7) produces the disorder.

2. *The reaction ranges for organismic and environmental factors are very large for many characteristics.* Most of the above examples have been all-or-none, present-or-absent phenomena, but most characteristics we study are graded, not dichotomous. Intelligence, for example, is unlikely to be produced by one or two genes, environments vary substantially in the extent to which they support intellectual skills, and the outcome itself (i.e., intelligence) is multifaceted and varies along many graded continua.

For many such behaviors, the reactions ranges of the required genetic and environmental circumstances are very large. That is, certain genetic circumstances are necessary and do make a contribution, but the environment can have an enormously broad influence in most genetic circumstances. Again, from a conceptual standpoint, intelligence is the result of an interaction at some level of analysis, but from a practical standpoint, most of the differences among individuals are associated with genetic and environmental main effects, which operate within the large reaction ranges ranges permitted by the other factor and which tend to covary with one another (see next section).

3. *Developmental organism–environmental transaction tends to produce covariation and changing interaction patterns.* As stated earlier, I believe there is a natural developmental drift toward covariation within individuals, the result of the developmental processes of transaction and niche-picking, and the accumulated result may minimize interactions in some cases or produce them in others. Either way, interactions may tend to be developmental, appearing mainly over developmental time or primarily during one or another developmental

period. The proposition that organisms and environments tend toward covariation with development is simply a rephrasing of the biological principle of individual organism–environment adaptation or Piaget's principles of assimilation and accommodation.

Again, take IQ as an example. The fact that IQ has substantial heritability for a behavioral trait means that one begins with some degree of covariation, at least among family members who will provide some portion of the intellectual environment for their child. In the course of development, the transactions between those parents and the child that are pertinent to the development of intelligence increase covariation. For example, bright parents provide intellectually stimulating environments for their children, and very bright children often elicit extra stimulation from their parents (e.g., Fowler, 1981). Later, children "niche pick," seeking out environments or experiences that match their intellectual levels, which increases covariation. Furthermore, the environment (i.e., other people) is likely to shape the children's responses and behaviors to fit their intellectual levels. The result is substantial genetic and environmental covariation, vastly overshadowing and perhaps obscuring any interaction.

Ordinarily, one might expect that the developmental process of a transaction will produce greater covariation, which will lead to less interaction, which is presumably the case in the IQ example just given. However, it may produce more, not less, interaction in some circumstances. Consider the classic study by Cooper and Zubek (1958), which is a prototypical illustration of an interaction. Two strains of rats, one bred to be "maze-bright" and the other to be "maze-dull," were exposed to either rich or poor environments. The rich environment helped the maze-dull animals when they tested on certain learning tasks, but maze-bright animals achieved well regardless of environment. Analogously, children born with perinatal complications often show no long-term ill effects with respect to mental development compared with infants who did not have perinatal problems if those distressed infants are reared in upper-middle-class homes. Infants having perinatal complications who are reared in less educated homes tend not to "catch up" (e.g., Hunt & Cooper, 1989; Sameroff & Chandler, 1975). Here is a phenomenon (developmental performance or standing) that starts out as a main effect (perinatal complications produce depressed performance during infancy) but developmentally is an interaction with family environment.

The point here is that some natural development processes, including transaction and niche-picking, likely lead toward greater covariation of organismic and environmental circumstances, which have the tendency to reduce the strength or presence of interactions, but under certain circumstances, these processes may produce interaction. In any event, the presence and intensity of an interaction may require developmental study to observe it.

Conclusion

The hypothesis has been proffered that although most phenomena are the result
of an interaction of some sort, nature, through evolution or developmental processes, tends toward covariation because covariation is more likely associated
with survival, adaptation, balance, harmony, well-being, and other positive characteristics. The more crucial the characteristic is to the species or to the organisms,
the greater will be the percentage of organisms exposed to the adaptive organismic–
environmental combinations, the wider will be the reaction ranges of both organismic and environmental factors that will permit an adaptive outcome, and the
more motivated will be organisms and members of their social environments to
achieve covariation. Because covariation minimizes interactions, the result is that
interactions in normal groups of subjects are difficult to find empirically. Although
interactions may be a conceptual necessity for most phenomena, they also may
be a practical irrelevancy. Nature does not leave important characteristics up to
chance combinations, nor does it endow the crucial genetic and environmental
factors with narrow reaction ranges. Mechanisms exist to produce covariation at
the species level, as well as with respect to individual differences within a species.

ON APPROPRIATE RESEARCH METHODS AND
DATA ANALYSIS

If nature conspires against revealing interactions, as described earlier, researchers
conspire with nature by using research methods that either appropriately match
nature and therefore tend not to reveal interactions or are not very sensitive to
those interactions that nature potentially allows researchers to view. Next is a
listing of aspects of research design and analysis that limit researchers' ability to
empirically document interactions, plus some modest suggestions on what to do
to increase the likelihood of empirically describing interactions when they exist.

Sampling Issues

Sampling limitations may account for the failure to find some interactions in
several ways.

1. *Some interactions may involve extreme groups that are not represented or that are underrepresented in most research samples.* Given
   the disposition in nature toward covariation through hereditary and developmental mechanisms, it follows that interactions are most likely to
   be observed when extreme organismic and environmental factors are
   present in the sample. Indeed, some of the clearest examples of interactions involve genetic abnormalities or extreme environments that are

likely to be absent or rare in most samples (see, e.g., chapters 6 and 7).

Rutter and Pickles (chap. 7) cite a variety of medical examples demonstrating that an abnormality is observed in an organism when a particular genetic organismic circumstance occurs in combination with a particular environmental circumstance. Typically, one or both of these circumstances are extreme and rare. The PKU example just given illustrates a case of a very rare genetic circumstance (approximately 1 in 10,000) combined with a very common environmental condition (i.e., the presence of phenylalanine in most foods). The schizophrenia example illustrates a case in which both genetic and environmental circumstances are relatively rare, and the genetic and environmental combination necessary to produce the phenotype of schizophrenia is even more unusual (of course, the $O \times E$ combination will always be more unusual than the $O \times E$ alone, except when the organismic or environmental factor is pandemic, as in the PKU example).

Obviously, to reveal such interactions, one needs samples that contain enough cases of the positive and negative (or alternative) organismic and environmental circumstances to reveal an interaction, and this requires some understanding or theory of the nature of the interaction. Therefore, investigators are not likely to discover interactions involving rare or extreme circumstances in most descriptive fishing expeditions.

In the absence of such understanding, either researchers will fail to sample the unusual cases that demonstrate the interaction or such rare phenomena may appear to be nearly totally genetic (or environmental). PKU appeared to be a homozygous recessive genetic main effect that resulted in retardation in the phenotype until the biochemical mechanism was discovered and the presence of phenylalanine in most diets was specified. Then a diet could be produced lacking phenylalanine, and the interaction was observed. Similarly, tuberculosis (TB) once appeared empirically to be a noninteractive genetic condition dependent on an inherited biochemical susceptibility to the TB bacillus, which was so environmentally pervasive that almost every individual came into contact with it. After the role of the TB bacillus was identified and public health measures (e.g., sewers and soap) were introduced widely, the requirement of having both the biochemical disposition and the environmental exposure to the bacillus became more obvious in epidemiological studies. Indeed, now such studies tend to show TB to be more of an environmental phenomenon because the bacillus is only present in rare, dismal health environments.

Not only do these examples show the need for understanding a phenomenon before sampling can be designed to reveal the interaction, but the empirical presence of an interaction may depend on circumstances that vary with the secular period of time in which the study is conducted and on factors that determine the distribution of unusual circumstances in samples that can be reasonably obtained at that time. Not finding an interaction does not mean that an interaction is not an underlying mechanism but only that a necessary organismic or environmental component is extremely pervasive or extremely rare in the sample, at that point in history, or in the organisms' development. Perhaps a pure organismic or environmental main effect should not be accepted as such, but it should stimulate thought and perhaps a search for an interaction.

Another pattern of results may signal the presence of an interaction. In the field of predicting childhood mental disorder from assessments early in infancy, typically the following is found: (a) Retrospectively, disordered individuals have in their backgrounds higher-than-expected rates of both the genetic–organismic and the environmental circumstances that dispose them toward disorders; (b) prospectively, neither genetic–organismic nor environmental circumstances predict very accurately the manifestation of the disorder; and (c) interaction effects are not found or are not strong.

This pattern of results suggests that many individuals have the genetic or the required environmental characteristics during infancy that produce disorder in childhood, but substantially fewer have the interactive combination that results in the later manifestation of disorder. Many infants experience perinatal trauma or insult, but most of these infants also experience sufficiently positive environments to progressively "grow out of" this early condition, in the same manner that rich environments produced benefits for Cooper and Zubek's (1958) maze-dull rats. Such a pattern of results suggests that one should look for the necessary combination of early genetic–organismic and environmental factors that leads to disorder or to positive outcomes.

2. *Some phenomena are interactive, but one or both of the necessary circumstances are almost always present.* Some of the most crucial characteristics are the result of interactions, but it takes an unfortunate biological or environmental accident or tragedy to demonstrate an interaction because both required factors are almost always present in natural contexts. Language development requires both a human organism with certain intact sensory and physical systems and active engagement with a language environment, two factors that are present for essentially all individuals. It is only when the rare biological or environmental anomaly occurs (deaf–mute individuals, Helen Keller, children locked in closets or darkened rooms during their early years of life, and children provided with television but with no social engagement with language) that the need for both factors—that is, the interaction—is revealed.

3. *The hypothesized developmental trajectory toward covariation described earlier may be more commonly achieved in the middle ranges of genetic and environmental variables than in the extremes.* One

might speculate that extreme organismic dispositions are less likely to accommodate to natural environmental circumstances than are mid-range dispositions. Buss and Plomin (1984, p. 88) made a similar proposal, namely, that those in the middle range of a temperamental dimension are more likely than those in the extremes to be influenced by the environment because they are more likely to accommodate to the social rewards that are available. Notice that if the distribution of individuals along the dimension peaks in the middle of the range, many more people will tend toward covariation than tend to be exceptions to it, making the examples of interaction relatively rare in broad-based samples.

Furthermore, these infrequent deviations from covariation raise statistical issues. Rutter and Pickles (chap. 7) point out that typical statistical methods that reflect significance or effect size (i.e., most standard correlational and analysis-of-variance techniques) may not be appropriate as methods for demonstrating interactions in such cases because the number of exemplars of odd outcomes is small relative to the total sample size. The amount of variance accounted for by such an interactive factor would be proportionately modest, perhaps so small that statistical significance would not be achieved. Furthermore, interactions that are observed might not be consistently replicated because they depend on the presence of unusual cases being included in the sample.

The best solution is to have a sufficiently explicit theory or hypothesis so that one can isolate individuals who fit the hypothesized combination and to compare them as a group with those who do not. Similarly, in cases in which dichotomous factors are involved, one must identify groups on the basis of the presence or absence of a specific set of symptoms or disposing characteristics versus those not having the complete set—again, a task made easier by a clear understanding of the phenomenon. To generate such hypotheses, one might examine outliers for unusual combinations of background factors that might be directly investigated in subsequent research.

4. *It is possible that a particular environmental circumstance has an interactive influence only on people who fall within a particular range of the organismic variable (and vice versa).* For example, broad, general environmental factors may operate as a main effect with respect to developing lower to average IQs, different and perhaps highly specific environmental circumstances may be necessary to produce extremely high IQs. Specifically, early in the history of enrichment programs, it was discovered that a great variety of interventions for disadvantaged children that mimicked middle-class environments could be successful in raising IQs toward the average of 100. However, these same methods did not raise IQs much above 100; other environ-

mental circumstances apparently were required to produce above-average IQs. Perhaps a special combination of organismic and environmental circumstances are required to produce brilliance that are different from those circumstances that produce average intelligence. This possibility is recognized in work on retardation in which a specific environmental circumstance may promote development for normal children but in which that same environmental circumstance may not promote or may even hinder development for certain handicapped children (Wachs, 1988).

Measurement Issues

Whenever an expected phenomenon in any behavioral field is not found, one of the possible explanations is that the wrong variables were measured or that they were measured in an insensitive or inappropriate manner. Certainly, this criticism can be made of studies in the field of organism–environment interactions.

1. *The genetic or environmental factor may not be measured at all.* Typical studies in population behavioral genetics do not measure the environment at all (see chap. 1). Instead, estimates of the percentage of individual difference variance are derived by calculating associations between pairs varying in their average genetic relationship. The result is an estimate of "broad-sense heritability"; estimates of "environmental" contributions are really estimates of "nongenetic" variation, which includes environmental effects plus error. Although estimates of interactions are possible in some designs, the environmental component of such an interaction is typically not specifically measured, which precludes finding interactions with any specific environmental characteristic. Perhaps this explains in part why interaction effects are not typically found in behavioral genetic research.

However, "environmental research" is no better. Most studies of environmental factors and interventions do not measure genetic or organismic circumstances. Not only does this strategy obviate finding interactions, but sometimes the measures of environment also measure genetics or organismic factors (as one might expect to result from the disposition toward covariation). For example, socioeconomic class, as measured by years of education or job status, is often interpreted as an environmental variable, even though it certainly covaries with genetics for many outcome measures. Obviously, designs in which either organismic or environmental variables are not measured at all are unable to uncover interactions.

2. *Even when measured, organism and environment are often assessed with general and indirect methods.* Measurements of genetics, for ex-

ample, may apply to the average pair of related individuals in the study, not to any individual pair. Siblings and dizygotic twins, for example, share half of their genes on the average, but an individual pair may be more or less than 50% similar genetically. Also, when environment circumstances are assessed, such measurements may be very general (i.e., socioeconomic status, years of education) or highly specific (percentage of responses by the parent to the infant's social overtures). Imprecision may reduce sensitivity to interactive effects (see chap. 4), but highly specific measurements may not encompass the interactive variable. Again, it helps to have an accurate theory or a precise understanding of the phenomenon that will dictate appropriate and sensitive measurements.

Typically, the "environment" in twin or sibling studies refers only to those aspects of the family environment that the two siblings share and perceive similarly. However, a single environmental event may be perceived differently by and produce very different outcomes in two siblings, which contributes to nongenetic variance in such designs, but not to an interaction. Such variation is an environmental effect, not an interaction, if only one sibling is assessed (as in traditional environment designs) or if both are assessed (as a pair in traditional behavioral genetic designs), but the phenomenon may also be an interaction if viewed with more specific research designs.

Consider an obvious example of a nonshared (or at least nonequivalent) event for siblings: the birth of a younger sibling into the family. If the organismic variable is child characteristics (e.g., existing child, child just born), the event of the birth of that baby will have a different effect on the existing sibling than on the just born for virtually any behavioral variable one can name (e.g., McCall, 1984). Less trivially, it is likely that most major environmental events will influence older children differently than younger ones within a family, which is an interaction with age of child (and its organismic and life-history correlates). Such interactions are rarely studied directly because investigators do not often include both siblings in their assessments or they relegate the nonsimilar response of the siblings to the nongenetic "main effect" in behavior genetic analysis. Such interactions account for substantial portions of individual-difference variance in mental performance and other characteristics (e.g., McCall, 1983; Rowe & Plomin, 1981).

3. *An environmental variable may be defined too globally to reveal interactions.* Suppose the variable of interest is stress, but the researcher is not particularly concerned with how the stress is produced. It may be produced in one way for some individuals (e.g., divorce) and in another way for other individuals (e.g., family violence)—whatever "works" (i.e., whatever circumstances produce stress for a particular

person). The environmental factor of stress may not interact with organismic differences, but the specific conditions used to produce the stress may well interact (e.g., Pianta, Egeland, & Sroufe, 1990). Yet, that interaction would not be revealed in a study in which the primary variable is simply stress, not the particular circumstances that produce it. How one defines the environmental or organismic variable may determine whether an interaction is observed.

4. *Researchers define the environment by events that they observe or manipulate, but the functional environment may depend on how individuals perceive those circumstances.* The U.S. Marine Corps' "confidence course" used in basic training consists of a series of vaulting, climbing, and other activities that the trainee must negotiate in a sequence and within a given period of time. Some trainees view the exercise as a challenge, and for them reaching the performance criterion may well enhance their self-confidence. Other trainees, however, may be intimidated by the exercise and not meet criterion, or if they meet criterion, they may never want to see the course again. For them, it does not build self-confidence. In this case, the same environmental intervention may be viewed and experienced very differently by different individuals, and those differences in perceptions are organismic interactions. However, as long as the "confidence course" is treated as a single environmental episode and differential perceptions and their relationship to life history are ignored, these important interactions will be relegated to the within-subjects error term.

Insensitive Research Designs

Naturally, how a study is designed may influence whether interactions are found, and many of the designs commonly used are insensitive to potential interactions. I have discussed similar issues in the previous section for observational research, but what about experimental studies?

Just as accidents, mutations, and tragedies are "nature's experiments" and more likely to reveal interactions, so too might one hypothesize that true experiments are more likely to reveal interactions than naturalistic observations. If nature conspires toward covariation that masks interaction, the heart of experimental research is random assignment of organisms to environmental conditions, which essentially obviates covariation. Then why are more interactions not found in experimental research? Because researchers do not look for them.

1. *Some main effects are really interactions.* Question: When might a main effect really be an interaction? Answer: When the researcher only studies one level of a factor.

Suppose one wants to study the effects of divorce on children. A sample of boys aged 4–5 years whose parents have divorced approximately 1 year earlier is selected for study and matched with a similar sample of children whose parents have not divorced. Comparisons are made on a variety of dependent measures. The results are interpreted as a main effect of divorce, an environmental factor. In this study, only one level of many organismic and life-history factors, such as the age of the children, their sex, their temperament, and other factors, was examined. Had children of several ages and sexes, for example, been assessed, interactions might well have been found. Thus, one reason investigators do not observe many interactions is that they do not sample or manipulate certain variables.

Other examples abound. When studying a phenomenon in rodents that is influenced by activity level, researchers typically use only male rats because the activity of the female is directly related to the estrous cycle, which will add unwanted variability to the results. Consequently, interactions between sex and the treatment of interest are never examined. Similarly, studies of physical aggressiveness in humans often rely on male subjects because males display more physical aggression than females. If both physical and verbal aggressiveness or both overt and passive aggression were measured and both male and female subjects were studied, interactions might be observed.

Researchers also tend to shy away from manipulating or including several independent variables in research designs, even when they are known to be relevant. Students are sometimes told to design two- or maybe three-factor studies, but never four- or five-factor studies, because "how would you interpret the higher order interactions you are likely to get?" Most researchers (and journal editors) would prefer a simple, straightforward result, and they tend to design simple experiments that may not include all of the potentially interactive variables. Obviously, if one wants to find organism–environment interactions, one must study organismic and environmental variables that are likely to be involved in such interactions.

Finally, even when interactions are present, some researchers ignore them or even rescale the data to eliminate them (see chap. 1; Fulker, 1979; Jinks & Fulker, 1970; Mather & Jinks, 1982).

2. *Developmental studies may be more sensitive to interactions than studies of single ages*. It follows from the conceptual analysis of developmental changes in covariation that interactions may be more apparent at some stages of development than at others.

Cronbach (see chap. 6) cites the study by Huttenlocher and others (in Bock, 1989) on children's vocabulary between 12 and 26 months of age. Developmental profile across age was more likely to be involved in certain interactions than was status at the eldest age. Indeed, Sackett (see chap. 2) defines interaction to be a differential effect on the growth process of individual organisms.

In a study of similarity in IQ within sibling pairs, McCall (1970) found that siblings were substantially more similar to one another with respect to the general level of IQ performance averaged across age (similar to an assessment made at only one age) than with respect to the developmental pattern of IQ change across age. This study suggested that genetics, for example, may play a more important role with respect to general level than with respect to changes over age, and interactions may be more common for developmental pattern than for general level.

It is also possible, as Sackett (see chap. 2) points out, that a particular environmental circumstance may have an effect at one age but not at another, or it may have one effect at one age and a different effect at another age. Children are more interested in members of the opposite sex after puberty than before, so it is likely that environmental events having heterosexual implications will have very different effects, and interactions may be more common, at one age than at another.

The concept of developmental changes in covariation raises some additional interesting and thorny methodological issues. As indicated earlier, it is not clear whether progressive increases in covariation will result in fewer or more interactions over the course of development. Generally, it would seem that early in infancy is the time to observe interactions if one believes that developmental processes will tend to dilute them. However, counterexamples have been presented in which interactions actually emerged during the course of development. Another issue is when to start looking for interactions and how frequently to measure subjects during the course of that process.

It would be convenient to be able to specify the age periods most likely to contain interactions and the factors most likely to signal the presence of interactions, but I am not hopeful that such signposts will be found. Interactions, I suspect, will depend on the particular phenomenon in question, how the variables are measured, the design strategy, and all of the other factors mentioned here. So, without pilot data and theory, finding interactions looks like a hit-or-miss proposition. It seems that one needs to do research before one knows enough to design sensitive and appropriate research. Actually, however, I believe that this is no more of a problem when studying interactions than when studying any other developmental phenomenon; knowledge and theory, or at least shrewd insight, always help.

Statistical Issues

How data are analyzed (or not analyzed) can determine whether interactions are found.

1. *Variance associated with an interaction in the analysis of variance may be shared with main effects.* Suppose one has an analysis-of-variance design with equal numbers of cases in each cell. Suppose further that the data are totally random (i.e., no effects are present) and that the grand mean is 10. Now imagine that a substantial amount (e.g., 50) is added to each score in one cell of the design. Conceptually, this represents the addition of a "pure" interaction: Only subjects having a specific level of Factor A and a specific level of Factor B are different from the other subjects. Yet, when the analysis of variance is calculated, the addition of this "pure" interaction will not only produce an interaction effect, but it will also tend to produce main effects for Factors A and B. Furthermore, in designs having unequal cell size and using least squares statistical procedures, main and interactive effects are not independent and the sequence of effect extraction can influence the size of the statistical interaction.

These two examples illustrate that the statistical assessment of interaction is not totally independent of the assessment of main effects in many statistical analyses; a "pure" interaction effect actually may be "shared" with main effects and therefore diluted in the analysis. Although I doubt that this observation accounts for much of the failure to find interactions, it is nevertheless a potential contributor to the problem.

2. *Researchers sometimes do not analyze data for interactions when they could.* Suppose a researcher developed an educational program or intervention and evaluated it by giving a pretest and a posttest to both a treatment and a control group. Typically, one assesses the effects of such an environmental intervention by comparing the mean posttest score for the treatment versus the control group, assuming pretest scores were comparable for the two groups. Although rarely done, it is also possible to calculate the correlations between pre- and posttest scores separately within each group. If these correlations are high and similar for the treatment and control groups, then one might assume that the treatment program had similar effects on all subjects. However, if the correlation is substantially lower in the treatment than in the control group, then one has evidence that the treatment program influenced different subjects by different amounts. This Treatment × Subjects interaction is a reflection of an Organism × Environment interaction.

This is not the only context in which interactions are not typically assessed. Indeed, in most repeated-measures designs, the error term for a repeated factor is a Subjects × Factor interaction mean square that is not assessable as an effect within the analysis of variance. However, repeated-measures analyses of variance assume homogeneity of covariance across levels of the repeated factors (McCall & Appelbaum, 1973), and violations of that assumption, which can be assessed by calculating the correlations, is at least indirect evidence of the existence of a Subjects × Factor interaction in the same way as described above. Obviously, additional independent measures of the subjects, especially specific organismic measures, would help specify and interpret such interactions.

3. *Interaction in regression analysis may be represented by a term that reflects only one particular form of interaction.* For example, in multiple regression, a main effect for variable X and a main effect for variable Y may be entered into the model plus an XY term to represent an interaction. This is typical in behavioral genetic research, for example. However, a multiplicative effect is only one type of interaction. The actual interaction may be X^2Y, the interaction may only involve extreme groups, or low values of X in the presence of Y may produce one result but high values of X in the presence of Z may produce another result. The term XY may be relatively insensitive to these other forms of interactions. The main solution to this problem, unhappily, requires that one "knows one's interactions" so they can be accurately modeled in the analysis.

CONCLUSIONS

This discussion of possible reasons why interactions are difficult to find empirically converges on two major conclusions:

1. *Although interactions may be conceptual necessities for most phenomena, from a practical standpoint nature conspires against interactions being major, robust, empirical phenomena.* One reason for this is that although specific organismic and environmental circumstances must be present for a phenomenon to occur, those circumstances either are often pervasively present in naturalistic contexts or, in the case of anomalies, are very rare. Furthermore, there is a tendency in nature toward organismic–environmental harmony or covariation, which may reduce the potential magnitude of interaction effects (although it may also produce them in other circumstances). This may occur through heredity itself, which tends to provide children with dispositions that are similar to those of their parents and to the environments their parents create for them. It can also occur through developmental adjustment and accommodation of parent and child to one another (i.e., transaction), and it can be the result of niche-picking by individuals who select environments that are similar to their organismic dispositions.

Therefore, interactions may exist, but I speculate that there is a tendency for them to be minimized and masked by organismic–environmental covariation.

2. *Although some scholars have deliberately tried to design research to reveal interactions, it is not a common objective.* Consequently, they tend not to use sampling procedures, measurements, designs, and statistical techniques that would be most sensitive to and appropriate for revealing interactions. Furthermore, it is ironic that experimental research may be more likely to be able to find interactions because random assignment of subjects reduces covariation but that experimentalists are less likely to want to find interactions, tend to design studies to minimize the presence of Organism × Treatment interactions, and tend not to use statistical procedures that would reveal interactions.

References

Bock, R. D. (Ed.). (1989). *Multilevel analysis of educational data.* San Diego, CA: Academic Press.

Bornstein, M. H., & Bruner, J. S. (Eds.). (1989). *Interaction in human development.* Hillsdale, NJ: Erlbaum.

Buss, A. H., & Plomin, R. (1984). *Temperament: Early developing personality traits.* Hillsdale, NJ: Erlbaum.

Cooper, R. M., & Zubek, J. P. (1958). Effects of enriched and restricted early environments on the learning ability of bright and dull rats. *Canadian Journal of Psychology, 12,* 159–164.

Cronbach, L. J., & Snow, R. E. (1977). *Aptitudes and instructional methods: A handbook for research on interactions.* New York: Irvington.

Fowler, W. (1981). Case studies of cognitive precocity: The role of exogenous stimulation in early mental development. *Journal of Applied Developmental Psychology, 2,* 319–367.

Fulker, D. W. (1979). Nature and nurture: Heredity. In H. Eysenck (Ed.), *The structure and measurement of intelligence* (pp. 102–132). New York: Springer.

Hunt, J. V., & Cooper, B. A. B. (1989). Differentiating the risk for high-risk preterm infants. In M. H. Bornstein & N. A. Krasnegor (Eds.), *Stability and continuity in mental development: Behavioral and biological perspectives* (pp. 105–122). Hillsdale, NJ: Erlbaum.

Jinks, J., & Fulker, D. (1970). Comparison of the biometrical, genetical, MAVA and classical approaches to the analysis of human behavior. *Psychological Bulletin, 73,* 311–349.

Mather, K., & Jinks, J. (1982). *Biometrical genetics* (3rd ed.). London: Chapman & Hall.

McCall, R. B. (1970). IQ pattern over age: Comparison among siblings and parent–child pairs. *Science, 170,* 644–648.

McCall, R. B. (1983). Environmental effects on intelligence: The forgotten realm of discontinuous nonshared within-family factors. *Child Development, 54,* 408–415.

McCall, R. B. (1984). Developmental changes in mental performance: The effect of the birth of a sibling. *Child Development, 55,* 1317–1321.

McCall, R. B. & Appelbaum, M. I. (1973). Bias in the analysis of repeated-measures designs: Some alternative approaches. *Child Development, 44,* 401–415.

Pianta, R., Egeland, B., & Sroufe, L. A. (1990). Maternal stress in children's development: Prediction of school outcome and identification of protective factors. In J. Rolf, A. Masten, D. Cicchetti, K. Neuchterlein, & S. Weintraub (Eds.), *Risk and protective factors in the development of psychopathology* (pp. 215–235). Cambridge, England: Cambridge University Press.

Plomin, R. & Daniels, D. (1984). The interaction between temperament and environment: Methodological considerations. *Merrill-Palmer Quarterly, 30,* 149–162.

Rowe, D. C., & Plomin, R. (1981). The importance of nonshared (E_1) environmental influences in behavioral development. *Developmental Psychology, 17,* 517–531.

Sameroff, A. J., & Chandler, M. J. (1975). Reproductive risk and the continuum of caretaking casualty. In F. D. Horowitz (Ed.), *Review of child development research* (Vol. 4, pp. 187–249). Chicago: University of Chicago Press.

Wachs, T. D. (1988). Environmental assessment of developmentally disabled infants and preschoolers. In T. D. Wachs & R. Sheehan (Eds.), *Assessment of young developmentally disabled children* (pp. 321–346). New York: Plenum Press.

CHAPTER 9

SYNTHESIS: PROMISING RESEARCH DESIGNS, MEASURES, AND STRATEGIES

THEODORE D. WACHS

In this final chapter, I attempt to integrate the diverse views and topic areas presented in this volume. The primary goal is to develop recommendations for developmental researchers who are interested in the study of organism–environment interaction. To improve the synthesis, each of the contributing authors to this volume was sent a draft copy of this chapter for their comments. In those cases where there was not consensus, disagreements have been noted and alternative viewpoints have been expressed. However, ultimately, the conclusions expressed in this final chapter represent my interpretation of agreements and disagreements, as well as my attempts to reconcile disagreements in a way that would further the study of organism–environment interaction. In deriving conclusions, specific chapters will be referred to by the name of the chapter authors (without a reference date); readers wishing to see the arguments underlying conclusions should refer back to the specific chapters for greater detail.

This final chapter is divided into six major sections: definitional aspects, environmental considerations, organismic considerations, statistical considerations, criteria for developing theory-driven research on organism–environment interaction, and resolution of the Plomin paradox.

THE DEFINITION OF ORGANISM–ENVIRONMENT INTERACTION

Although both organismic and environmental factors influence individual development, the multidetermined nature of development is not what is meant by interaction. Rather, organism–environment interaction can be defined much more precisely, although the specific definition varies depending on whether we are viewing interaction at an operational, a conceptual, or a statistical level. Thus statistically, as noted by McCall, if developmental outcomes can be predicted by simply adding the separate influences of organism and environment, we do not have an interaction. Rather, Cronbach and McCall define interaction as the predictive information that remains after the main effects of organism and environment are removed. This does not mean, however, that finding a statistical interaction is sufficient to explain what is meant by interaction. As noted by Rutter and Pickles, statistical interactions alert the researcher to the possibility that main effect models may be insufficient to explain what is occurring. To explain why a main effects model is not satisfactory, interactions also need to be defined at a conceptual level. For example, conceptually, organism–environment interaction can be defined as a series of processes leading to objectively similar environments producing different effects on different individuals (Rutter & Pickles). The idea that different processes may underlie differential reactivity can be seen in the operational definitions of interaction presented in this volume, as in Plomin's concept of interaction as being differential heritability for a trait in different environments, Sroufe's notion of group differences emerging only in certain environments, and McCall's emphasis on environmental factors being salient only for individuals falling within a particular range of organismic characteristics.

Disagreements among the chapter authors focus primarily on the question of how ubiquitous organism–environment interaction is. For example, Cronbach has raised the possibility that "main effects" may actually be nothing more than interactions that are masked by insufficient range for one or more of our variables. However, McCall has suggested that if traits have large reaction ranges, individual differences will primarily be a function of main effects, which leaves little room for interaction. Although the possibility that main effects may be nothing more then hidden organism–environment interaction has obvious appeal for researchers interested in interaction, this question is perhaps best considered as one that is more appropriate for empirical test and that is thus not central to the definition of organism–environment interaction.

Given the level of agreement on the definition of organism–environment interaction at a statistical and conceptual level, the problem noted by Wachs and Plomin of multiple definitions for the term *interaction* does not seem to stem from the imprecision of the term per se. Rather, the problem is one of labeling processes other than organism–environment interaction by the same term. For example, the use of the term *interaction* to characterize patterns of parent–child relations (see Chapter 1) does not appear to reflect organism–environment interaction as much as it does organism–environment transaction. Given both historical precedent and the existence of a relatively precise definition of *interaction*, I would argue that this term may best be reserved for developmental processes involving the differential reactivity of individuals to the environment. Restriction of the term *interaction* to a relatively narrow usage is more than just a semantic quibble. Subsuming different processes under a single term can only lead to poor communication among researchers interested in the question of determinants of individual development (Kagan, 1989). The restricted definition used here suggests the need to develop other terms for processes involving relations between caregivers and children or the cultural transmission of knowledge across generations.

Although restricting the definition of interaction may be viewed as a means for increasing the preciseness of the definition, some chapter authors argue that such preciseness is misleading. This issue is discussed in the following section.

Organism–Environment Interaction and Organism–Environment Covariance: Can These Be Separated?

In chapter 1, Wachs and Plomin distinguished organism–environment interaction from organism–environment covariance (the overlapping contribution of organism and environment) at both a conceptual level and in terms of research strategy. Other chapter authors have also noted the relevance of this distinction (McCall, Rutter, & Pickles). In contrast, Sroufe has cogently argued that the distinction between interaction and covariance may be misleading in the sense that it may artificially disentangle what is actually entangled in nature. Specifically, if interaction is the differential reactivity of different children to the same environment, Sroufe (see also Rutter & Pickles) argues that the environment cannot necessarily be the same, because different children will perceive and construct their own environments in different ways. Sroufe goes on to point out that children simultaneously select and interpret their environments and that these processes cumulate across time. Thus, for Sroufe, the distinction between covariance and interaction is blurred because covariance, interaction, and organism–environment transaction are all interrelated. McCall makes a similar point when he notes that, conceptually, although most aspects of development may result from the interaction between organism and environment, from an empirical standpoint, interaction may be swamped by the greater salience of organism–environment covariance.

Although interaction and covariance may well be intertwined, it is not inappropriate to continue to look for interactions, especially if the goal is to understand processes underlying development. One potential approach would be to look at interaction and covariance developmentally.[1] Specifically, a number of authors, although not antagonistic to Sroufe's view, have noted the possibility

---

[1] Ideally, of course, as pointed out by McCall, experimental studies would offer a perfect way of disentangling the potential confound between interaction and covariance, through random assignment of different individuals to different treatment conditions. However, as also pointed out by McCall, most experimental research is designed to avoid obtaining interactions rather than illustrating them.

that interaction could, theoretically, precede covariance (McCall; Rutter, & Pickles). For example, Rutter and Pickles have suggested that the differential reactivity of boys and girls to objectively similar family stress (interaction) may ultimately lead to different parental treatment of boys and girls (covariance). A similar point may be implicit in Sackett's point regarding developmental processes that produce an organism that ultimately adapts characteristic modes of relating to its environment.

Taking a developmental perspective suggests that organism–environment interaction may be more apparent earlier in the life span (i.e., the infancy period) than later in life, when prior differential reactivity by children to parent behaviors (interaction) may lead to differential treatment (increased covariance). This hypothesis could be tested by obtaining detailed measures of children's characteristics and their objective environment across time. For example, both Crockenberg (1987) and Wachs and Gandour (1983) have reported interactive effects of tempermental difficulty and specific aspects of the environment (maternal anger–control; environmental contingencies) on infant development. In both of these studies, infants with different organismic characteristics (easy versus difficult temperament) reacted differently to objectively similar environmental stimulation. If a developmental perspective is correct, as these infants grow older, one would expect to find greater differentiation of the objective environment for toddlers or preschoolers with easy or difficult temperaments (differential rate of maternal anger–control, or environmental contingencies for easy vs. difficult infants). If McCall is correct, one should also find smaller interaction effects as the covariation increases. Thus, if a developmental perspective is taken, the conceptual distinction between organism–environment interaction and covariance can be maintained while simultaneously accepting Sroufe's arguments on the cumulative interrelateness of conceptually distinct processes such as interaction and covariance. Furthermore, taking a developmental perspective on this question is congruent with one of the major themes of this book: that the processes underlying organism–environment interaction may be more salient in some developmental periods than in others.

It should also be noted that an emphasis on the early part of life as a prime hunting ground for interactions does not necessarily rule out significant interactions later in life. The complexities inherent in postulating a transition from interaction to covariance have been deftly laid out by McCall in his chapter. These include the possibility that some aspects of early development may initially be driven by main-effect conditions, such as perinatal complications, whereas later development is more appropriately viewed as governed by a cumulative interaction between early status and subsequent experiences. Thus, the interaction–covariance hypothesis described above is only one of many potential developmental models predicting at which age periods organism–environment interaction may become especially salient. As noted by Sackett, alternative models may be more valid for other populations, environments, or outcome variables. For example, if one assumes that infant development is strongly canalized, strong canalization should result in less organismic variability and more functionally equivalent environments, leading to few organism–environment interactions in the infancy period.

The existence of alternative models offers the possibility of testing which models are most appropriate for specific organismic, environmental, or outcome parameters. For example, McCall has hypothesized that individual characteristics that have had survival value in the evolutionary history of the species may be less sensitive to organism–environment interactions than individual characteristics that are less survival driven. By using individual characteristics that have greater or lesser survival value in the evolutionary history of the species, it should be possible to test the validity of such a model.

The critical point is that the comparative salience of interaction, covariance, and main effects is testable if the tests are developed from hypothesis-driven research about the nature of the developmental process. Equally critical to keep in mind is the possibility that although the underlying mechanism for a phenomenon may involve interaction, whether the predicted interaction actually appears in our test may well depend on the particular context in which the test is done (McCall; Rutter & Pickles). An excellent example of how context can influence the pattern of observed results is seen in the fable of the birds and the berries, as originally set forth by Cronbach (personal communication, 1989), modified by Rutter (personal communication, 1990) and freely adapted by me (who is fully responsible for any ambiguities or lack of clarity). The fable appears in the box. As can be seen from the fable, although interactions may be conceptually necessary, it is important for the researcher to be sensitive to the question of whether the context in which the research is done will favor the appearance of main effects, covariance, or interactions.

THE FABLE OF THE BIRDS AND THE BERRIES

Premise: Bluebirds can eat blueberries and blackberries but thrive on blueberries and do less well on blackberries; blackbirds thrive on blackberries and do less well on blueberries.

There are two islands in the middle of the vast ocean, on one of which there are blueberries and on the other of which there are blackberries. The islands are reasonably close together and there is differential migration between the islands. Because each bird prospers on a different sort of berry, this leads to the bluebirds being largely found on the blueberry island and the blackbirds on the blackberry island. *Conclusion*: A demonstration of organism–environment covariance.

A volcano destroys one of the islands and the birds on that island are forced to migrate to the other. The remaining island has only blueberries. As a consequence, the bluebirds prosper and blackbirds do not, growing less well and diminishing in number. *Conclusion*: A demonstration of organism–environment interaction.

A scientist is interested only in blackbirds. He releases blackbirds on two deserted islands, one of which has lost its blackberry crop due to disease whereas the other has not. He returns several months later to find the blackbird colony thriving on one island and decimated on the other. *Conclusion*: A demonstration of an island main effect.

Moral: Although the basic biological mechanism remains a constant, changes in context will govern whether we conclude that we are dealing with interaction, covariance, or main effects.

Although sensitivity to context and the conceptualization of alternative models are critical, it is equally critical to use suitable research designs, suitable methodologies, and suitable statistical techniques in studies investigating organism–environment interaction. Clearly, the study of interaction entails all of the conceptual, measurement, and statistical difficulties involved in studying organisms and in studying environments. What is of critical interest are the special issues that are specifically relevant to studying interactions between organisms and environments. It is to these special considerations that I now turn.

ENVIRONMENTAL CONSIDERATIONS

As noted by both McCall and Wachs, in many studies supposedly investigating organism–environment interaction, measures of the environment are either missing (e.g., environment operationalized as residual variance) or inappropriate (e.g., social class). Although there are a variety of ways to assess the environment, the appropriateness of available methods for investigating organism–environment interaction is not an absolute but depends on other design features such as the range of organismic traits being considered. For example, if one is comparing near the extremes of a trait continuum, less precise environmental measures may be satisfactory, whereas if the researcher is comparing individuals in the middle of the trait distribution, highly precise environmental measures may be required. One means of increasing preciseness is to aggregate measurements of the environment whenever possible, to maximize stability of environmental assessments (Wachs). Similarly, particularly for older children, both McCall and Wachs have noted the importance of utilizing the child's perception of the environment, given that the child's perception may be a more accurate reflection of the *effective environment* (i.e., those aspects of the environment that actually influence development) than are objective assessments. There is also a strong emphasis in this volume on the need for a longitudinal framework when studying organism–environment interaction (Sackett). For example, McCall hypothesizes that interactions may be more characteristic of patterns of developmental change than of general level of performance at a given age. This argument suggests that the use of patterns of environmental change across time may be a potentially more sensitive measure of environmental influences than environmental characteristics measured at only one point in time.

Those recommendations are primarily methodological in nature. A number of chapter authors also suggest utilizing more conceptually driven environmental measures as a better way of improving environmental measurement in studies of organism–environment interaction. For example, both McCall and Wachs have emphasized the importance of broadly defining the environment so as to include not only social transactions between caregiver and child but also physical and biological features of the environment, as well as ecological–environmental features that lie beyond the immediate home environment of the child (e.g., social support for parents, family stress, and cultural patterns or values). A similar point is made by Sroufe when he describes using naturally occurring environmental circumstances, such as disorganization in summer camp structure or individual characteristics of the child's peers, as another aspect of the child's environment. The critical point made by each of the above contributors is that current theoretical formulations argue for a more differentiated view of the environment, both within and across levels of the environment, than has been traditional in studies of organism–environment interaction.

Another conceptual aspect relating to the measurement of environment is contained in the argument made by McCall that the greater the covariance existing between organism and environment, the more difficult it will be to identify organism–environment interactions. If McCall is correct, one potential approach to this problem emerges in the chapter by Plomin. Specifically, noting that many environmental measures may correlate with individual genotypes (gene–environment covariance), Plomin suggests utilizing measures of the environment that have a lower probability of being "contaminated" by genetic factors.[2] Working from both an empirical and a conceptual framework, Plomin suggests that these measures could include factors such as parental control, uncontrollable life events, and nonshared environmental variance. Similarly, Wachs has noted the possibility that physical features of the environment and ecological context variables may also be less contaminated by genetic influences. Thus, by appropriate selection of environmental variables, it may still be possible to illustrate interactions at age periods where organism–environment covariance may be the dominant process. Again, this emphasizes the need to use a more theoretically driven differentiated view of the environment when selecting environmental measures to use in studies of organism–environment interaction.

ORGANISMIC CONSIDERATIONS

Many of the same points raised for environmental factors can also be made on the organismic side of the equation. Again, in many studies supposedly investigating organism–environment interactions, inappropriate organismic measures may

---

[2] However, as pointed out by Rutter and Pickles (personal communication, 1990), if differential reactivity applies primarily to environmental factors that are "contaminated" by genetic factors, then researchers may be even more likely to miss interactions if they use only noncontaminated environmental measures.

be utilized (McCall). This problem may be particularly acute in behavioral genetic studies, in which indirect proxies of child genetic characteristics, such as biological parent phenotype, are often used (Plomin). Even in situations where direct measurement of individual child characteristics are made, psychometric problems with available instruments may make it difficult to distinguish between organismic characteristics and measurement error. This is why authors have repeatedly recommended using extreme groups in studies of organism–environment interaction.

Similarly, as with environment, a number of authors recommend utilizing a broad definition of organismic factors, encompassing individual differences in genotype, biological factors, maturational stage, sex, and prior developmental influences (Sroufe; McCall; Sackett; and Rutter & Pickles). A number of examples of nontraditional organismic factors that should be considered in studies of organism–environment interaction have also been suggested. These include the intergenerational history of the organism (Sackett) and the level of adaptation achieved by an individual child at time of exposure to specific environmental influences (Sroufe). Sroufe has also argued for the use of attachment as a relevant organismic characteristic. Attachment may be a highly sensitive individual characteristic because it may characterize the cumulative life history of the individual child. Sroufe provides a number of examples of how individual differences in attachment relate to differential reactivity to specific environmental circumstances.

Ideally, we should have direct measurements of organismic characteristics, such as the genetic probes described by Plomin. In the interim, perhaps the most appropriate strategy is the use of extreme groups. Certainly, with the use of extreme groups, differences between groups are less likely to be due to measurement error and are more likely to reflect real differences in the trait under study. Furthermore, individuals at the extreme of a distribution may be less likely to accommodate to environmental circumstances, resulting in less organism–environment covariance and a greater probability that interactions will be found (McCall).

STATISTICAL CONSIDERATIONS

One obvious though generally ignored consideration, noted in a number of the chapters, is that a nonsignificant statistical interaction term does not necessarily rule out the existence of interactions. Given that the interpretation of main effects must be qualified when there is interaction, failure to detect an existing interaction may result in misleading conclusions. The most obvious reason for finding a nonsignificant statistical interaction term when interaction actually exists is a lack of power in the design to detect interactions (Cronbach). Power considerations become particularly critical if there are a large number of variables involved, if a continuously distributed sample is dichotomized, or if the sample size is relatively small. However, increasing power involves more than simply reducing the number of variables or increasing the sample size. For example, just looking for first-order interactions may be oversimplistic because first-order interactions may be masked by higher order interactions (Sackett). Thus, if individual variables are studied in isolation rather than as part of a system of interlocking variables, we may miss critical interactions. However, the researcher runs into an immediate dilemma in the sense that studying clusters of variables as part of a system almost inevitably results in a loss of power. Although power may be raised by utilizing large sample sizes (Plomin), large sample sizes may preclude the use of highly sensitive environmental measures (Wachs). Thus, again researchers are on the horns of a dilemma: Power may be increased through increasing sample size, but at the cost of reducing the preciseness of environmental measures. Approaches have been discussed in this volume that may allow us to avoid some of the problems inherent in the tradeoff between power and preciseness. For example, aggregated data may be useful in increasing the power in small sample studies. Alternatively, if specific marker variables are used, results can be aggregated across small sample studies through meta-analytic procedures as a way of integrating the precision of small sample studies with the power found in larger sample studies.

Equally serious, but more subtle, is the possibility that a nonsignificant interaction term may reflect the fact that standard statistical procedures can underestimate the amount of interactive variance present in a study. A number of examples of this problem are noted in this volume. McCall has pointed out that in some statistical procedures, the Subject × Factor interaction term is counted in the error term. Similarly, as noted by both Plomin and McCall, standard regression techniques utilize a multiplicative interaction term. However, if existing interactions involve only certain subgroups within a population, or only appear over a narrow range of environmental, temporal, or organismic measures, then the standard multiplicative interaction technique will not detect these interactions because of the small number of exemplars involving interaction relative to the total sample size of the study.

Given the problems associated with identifying organism–environment interactions using traditional statistical techniques, are there more sensitive statistical procedures or models? Traditionally, interactions are tested after variation associated with main effects has been entered into the model (with some exceptions, as in the unequal n least squares solution of the mutivariate analysis of variance; McCall, personal communication, 1990). However, Rutter and Pickles argue that there may be situations where it is appropriate to test for interactions ahead of main effects. Specifically, if the conceptual model underlying the research suggests that certain combinations of factors will have no influence as a main effect (e.g., vulnerability per se should not have a significant impact on development in the absence of life stressors), then testing for interactions after main effects is inefficient, does not allow the researcher to take advantage of the preciseness of the theory, and may well result in wrong conclusions.

An alternative solution, suggested by Rutter and Pickles, may be used in those situations in which one believes that interactions are occurring only for a specific subgroup or within a specific range of environments. Under these conditions, the most appropriate procedure would be the comparison of models that allow for interaction versus those that do not. For example, if one believes that interactions are occurring only for a subgroup of individuals who are biologically vulnerable to stress, one might compare results obtained with a main effects model (i.e., is there a differential outcome for vulnerable vs. nonvulnerable subjects per se?) versus a model in which vulnerable versus nonvulnerable differences would occur only in the presence of a specific environmental stressor. Support for the latter model would lend validity to a hypothesis of organism–environment interaction, as well as provide evidence on the processes underlying the interaction. Obviously, to make these kinds of specific comparisons it is necessary to have some a priori basis for comparing specific main effect versus interactive models.

In the absence of precise theory, for situations in which there are a large number of subjects and few variables, it may be appropriate to start out by testing for interactions rather than main effects, given the possibility that initial testing for main effects may preclude subsequent testing for interactions (for examples of when this might occur, see the chapter by Rutter & Pickles).[3] Similarly, in the absence of precise theory, both Cronbach and McCall suggest examining interactions both within and between groups. Traditionally, assessing interaction involves between-groups comparisons. However, there may also be differential reactivity to treatment within a specific treatment group. For example, McCall proposes looking at the correlations between pre- and posttest measures in both treatment and control groups. If the correlations are similar, this suggests that the treatment had equal effects for all individuals. However, if the pre- and posttest correlations are lower or higher in the treatment groups than in the control groups, this suggests that the treatment program may have had different influences on different individuals. Thus, looking at within-group variability may be an alternative means of illustrating the existence of organism–environment interaction.

A final alternative, proposed both by Cronbach and by Rutter and Pickles, is to avoid analyses that focus on percent variance accounted for (which is not synonymous with effect size; see Rutter & Pickles) or that depend on a single go–no-go answer (i.e., models that assume that if the interaction term does not reach the .05 level of significance, there is no point in exploring further for interactions). Rather, these authors suggest using *confidence intervals* to indicate which explanatory models can be discarded versus which explanatory models require further testing. Rather than assuming that a nonsignificant interaction term

---

[3] The risk, of course, is that not all significant interactions may be valid. For example, as noted by Cronbach, when contrasted groups are not equally representative of the population, a pseudosignificant significant interaction term may appear in the analysis.

means no interaction, it may be more plausible to look at interaction in terms of whether the range of potential values can include large as well as zero-order values. One advantage of using a confidence-interval approach is that it allows one to test the validity of interaction-process models even though an individual interaction term is nonsignificant (Rutter & Pickles). This is particularly true for interactions that are restricted to one portion of the distribution, in that confidence intervals may indicate which portions of the distribution are most sensitive to interactions. Several examples of the use of confidence intervals, as described earlier, are found in chapter 6.

The Use of Theory-Driven Research

One theme running through many of the chapters in this book is the need for research on organism–environment interaction that is *theory driven*. Theory-driven research can be defined as consisting of studies that are based on a priori hypotheses about the nature of interaction. There are a number of reasons why it is important to have theory-driven research. First, different statistical models presume different types of interactions (Rutter & Pickles). Selecting the appropriate statistical model may reveal existing interactions; selecting an inappropriate model may mask existing interactions. This presupposes some hypotheses about the way in which interaction works in the population under study (i.e., theory-driven research). Theory-driven research on organism–environment interaction is needed also because not all environmental, organismic, or outcome variables will enter into interactions at all time periods (McCall; Plomin; Rutter & Pickles; Sackett; Wachs). Rather, interaction may be relevant only for certain subgroups, for certain environments, or within certain time periods. Thus, if one is to accurately target which organismic, temporal, environmental, or outcome variables enter into interactions, at the very least it is critical to have some a priori notion of the characteristics of environmental, temporal, organismic, or outcome variables that are more likely to predispose to interactions.[4] Finally, as pointed out by Maxwell (1990), testing for specific interactions allows the researcher "substantially" more statistical power than do tests for global interactions.

A final argument for theory-driven research has been made by Rutter and Pickles, who stress that the research goal should not be to discover interactions per se but to understand the processes that produce interactions. Simply identifying an organism–environment interaction may or may not tell researchers about process because multiple processes may be involved in producing the interaction.

---

[4] Although these a priori notions may come from formal theory, both Cronbach (chap. 6) and McCall (personal communication, 1990) have argued that good descriptive research may be a highly fruitful source for hypothesis generation about the nature of interaction. Discussion of this point is found later in this chapter.

Rutter and Pickles argue that interactions that do not simultaneously inform researchers about process will be of very limited value. The most appropriate way to understand process is to approach the study of interactions from a theoretical perspective. Although the importance of studying organism–environment interaction within a theoretical framework seems obvious, there are two major problems with developing theory-driven research: One problem is methodological and the other is conceptual.

Methodological Barriers

Certain methods that may be highly sensitive for revealing existing interactions may have the potential to mask the processes underlying these interactions. A prime example is studies of extreme groups. Extreme groups tend to be underrepresented in many research studies. However, as documented by Sroufe, organism–environment interactions are more readily revealed when either extreme environment or extreme group studies are used. There are a number of reasons for this. For example, power may be increased when extreme group or extreme environment designs are used, either through an increase in variance (which may also increase main effects; see Cronbach) or through a more accurate classification of subjects or environments, which would reduce errors of measurement (Wachs).

Although the use of extreme groups is a strategy that can increase the probability of identifying organism–environment interactions, the cost of this benefit may be a lessened ability to understand the processes underlying interaction across the full range of individual characteristics or environments. This is because the nature of processes influencing development in extreme groups may not be the same as processes operating in less extreme groups (Rutter & Pickles; Wachs). For example, Rutter and Pickles argue that the processes influencing variability in IQs below 50 (major biomedical or gene effects) are quite distinct from the processes influencing intellectual development in the normal range. Thus, by studying only extreme groups we may be increasing our ability to detect interactions, but the processes underlying detected interactions may apply only to extreme groups. This would not be a disadvantage if interactions occur only at the extremes or if the goal of the research is to identify interactions or to understand processes involved in differential reactivity in extreme groups; it would, however, be a disadvantage if the goals of the research encompass an understanding of process in the middle ranges of a distribution. In this latter case, the theoretical costs of extreme-group research may outweigh the empirical benefits. Alternatives to extreme-group research, which may aid researchers in illustrating both interactions and processes, are presented later in this chapter.

Conceptual Barriers

Although the advantages of theory-driven interaction research seem obvious, the major problem is *what theory*? As noted by Wachs and Plomin, most major developmental theories are primarily main effect in nature, often regarding interaction as nuisance or error variance. Existing theories that are more interactive in nature, such as the diathesis-stress model of schizophrenia, are often embarrassingly vague about specifying what the critical environmental, organismic, or temporal variables are. If existing theories do not translate easily into theory-driven organism–environment interaction research, is a call for theory-driven research nothing more then a scientific platitude? I would maintain that the state of affairs is not as bleak as it seems. Although no satisfactory model or theory of organism–environment interaction exists at present, one of the major contributions of the chapters in this volume is to delineate three essential features of such a theory of interaction.

A Systems Component

For purposes of this chapter, I define a system as a set of variables that have the potential to influence development and that are organized within a conceptually meaningful framework. In part, the idea of a multidimensional system is inherent in the definition of interaction, given that combinations of variables may have unique effects that are not seen when only individual variables are examined. This may be due to the possibility that single measures viewed in isolation may have different meanings than single measures viewed within a system. For example, the implications for development of high activity level per se may be quite different from the implications of early onset, pervasive, high activity level (Rutter & Pickles). Thus, a theory of organism–environment interaction that could be useful in driving research should be centered around an organized set of variables rather than encompassing only one or two developmental determinants. The variables that could be included in this type of system have been discussed earlier in this chapter under environmental and organismic considerations. Obviously, these variables will include environmental factors, such as specific caregiver–child relations, and individual characteristics, such as sex or temperament. However, a systems approach to organism–environment interaction must also include less obvious factors. Context is an example of one such factor.

Contest is defined as the larger setting within which specific organism–environment transactions occur. Context can also be viewed as a higher order environmental measure (macroenvironment) that may interact with individual characteristics (Wachs). An excellent example of the use of context in this fashion is given by Sroufe's illustration of how children with different attachment histories functioned in summer camps having different types of structural characteristics. Other examples, involving interactions between biological parents' history of criminality and type of offspring placement prior to adoption, or between sex of child and maternal employment status, can be found in a review article by Bronfenbrenner (1986).

Obtaining contextual information may also be important when utilizing meta-analytic techniques to integrate across small-scale studies of organism–environment interaction. Cronbach has argued that understanding the context within which data in individual studies were collected may increase researchers' ability to generalize and to understand the conditions in which interactions appear. For example, results from Aptitude × Treatment interaction studies involving mixed versus homogeneous ability groups became meaningful only when the investigator used a nonquantitative, contextual variable: the student's proneness to give or receive help (for a detailed description, see Chap. 6).

In addition, contextual data (''side information''; see Cronbach), if collected, may be important in understanding the processes through which organism–environment interaction occurs. For example, in discussing the classic Cooper and Zubek paper, Plomin argues that although heritability was low in both the enriched and deprived rearing conditions, low heritability per se indicates nothing about the nature of the interaction involved. Only by knowing the treatment context was it possible to determine that deprivation primarily influenced maze-bright rats, whereas enrichment primarily influenced maze-dull rats. Similarly, higher order contextual factors such as social support, stress, or culture may mediate the expression of the microenvironment as it enters into interactions with individual characteristics (Wachs). Knowing the nature of relations between the microenvironment and higher order contextual factors may tell researchers more about the nature of processes underlying environmental contributions to organism–environment interaction than just focusing on microenvironmental variables per se.

Obviously, it is good science to keep as full a record as possible of supplementary variables that occur during the course of individual studies. However, one of the conclusions drawn from the chapters in this book is that an adequate theory of organism–environment interaction should require the systematic collection of contextual information as part of the ongoing research process. Furthermore, adequate theory would not simply dictate that contextual information be collected but would also aid in defining what types of contextual information should be given highest priority for data collection.

Although emphasizing the need to use a systems perspective on organism–environment interaction, a number of chapter authors have also pointed out that using more variables reduces the power to detect interactions. However, I am not advocating that all variables in a system be investigated simultaneously. Rather, what I am stressing is (a) the need to use a systems perspective to determine the

choice of variables to be investigated in studies of organism–environment interaction and (b) the need to interpret observed interactions within the framework
of the system and not in isolation.

A Longitudinal Component

A number of authors in this book (McCall; Rutter & Pickles; Sackett; Sroufe)
emphasize the importance of looking at interactions within a longitudinal framework. Although it is possible to detect an organism–environment interaction at a
given point in time, the meaning of organism–environment interactions observed
at one point in time may be very limited. This is because variables that enter
interactions at one age may not enter into interactions at earlier or later ages
(Sackett). Furthermore, the appearance or disappearance of interactions across
time may not be a random process. Rather, the necessary organismic and environmental conditions that produce interactions may come together only at certain
periods of time (McCall), or the mechanisms underlying interaction may change
across time (Rutter & Pickles, Sackett). Thus, one conclusion is that nonlongitudinal theories of organism–environment interaction will offer less help identifying and illustrating the processes underlying interactions than will theories that
are longitudinal in nature. Indeed, Rutter and Pickles argue that the essential
aspect of a longitudinal theory of organism–environment interaction is an emphasis
on looking for mechanisms that operate across time rather than at interactions
per se.

   Obviously, it is necessary to identify what longitudinal mechanisms need
to be integrated into the theory. There are at least two approaches that are suggested
in this book. First, Sackett has emphasized the necessity of using a temporal
perspective when studying organism–environment interaction. A temporal perspective would include, among other things, an understanding of the nature of
the *maturational stage* of the organism at the time of exposure to specific environmental stimuli. What is also clear from Sackett's chapter is that the range of
relevant maturational stages must be broadened to include prenatal as well as
postnatal development. Furthermore, a temporal perspective would not only include the study of the developing organism but also intergenerational factors such
as the nutritional status or degree of reproductive risk of the organism's parents.

   A second approach is to understand the prior developmental history of the
organism. Using attachment as an example, Sroufe provides a number of illustrations wherein organism–environment interaction at a given point in time can
be traced back to differences in attachment history. Within Sroufe's longitudinal
model, developmental history is viewed as a mechanism through which current
experiences are filtered. It is this ongoing filtering of current experiences that
provides the means for understanding how the objective environment translates
into the effective environment.

An Interaction Component

I have stressed that theory-driven interaction research should involve a system of variables and be longitudinal in nature. It could be argued that these criteria could characterize good developmental research per se, even if the research did not involve the study of organism–environment interaction in any way. Has a component emerged from this book that is unique to the study of organism–environment interaction and that could be used to help develop theories of interaction or theory-driven interaction research? One potential candidate, which appears in several chapters (Rutter & Pickles; Sackett; Wachs), is the idea that there are different types of interactions that are governed by different underlying processes. For example, in synergistic interaction, the presence of a single risk factor such as psychosocial adversity has little effect on risk for psychiatric disorder; however, when a second risk factor co-occurs, its presence potentiates the influence of the original risk factor well beyond what would be predicted from simply adding the effects of the two risk factors (Rutter, 1983). In contrast, in *buffering interactions*, the presence of a nonrisk variable reduces the adverse effects of a risk variable, as in studies showing how social support networks may allow individuals to cope more adequately with stress (Rutter, 1983). Thus, one necessary component for any theory of organism–environment interaction would be the a priori specification of multiple types of interactions and multiple types of processes underlying observed interactions. An adequate theory of organism–environment interaction would not only require researchers to ask what type of interaction they are dealing with but should also force them to determine what process best explains the observed interaction. Examples of different types of interactions have been carefully described by Rutter (1983) and are not repeated here. Rather, primarily on the basis of the chapters by Rutter and Pickles and by Sroufe, I focus on delineating processes that could underlie interactions and that should form a necessary part of any theory of organism–environment interactions.

Differential Vulnerability

One of the defining features of organism–environment interaction is that the objective (observed) environment is not the same as the effective environment. Rather, individuals differ in the salience of any particular stimulus. Thus, one approach is to look for mechanisms through which the objective environment becomes the effective environment. One mechanism could be individual differences in either susceptibility or vulnerability to specific aspects of the environment. The idea that there may be individual differences in sensitivity to the environment is intuitively appealing and can be translated into specific theory-driven research hypotheses. Examples have been noted throughout this book as in the suggestion that men may be more sensitive to stressors than women, or as in Sroufe's hypothesis about attachment history acting as a filter for current experiences.

Empirical support for some type of differential sensitivity underlying interaction has also been reported by Loehlin, Willerman, and Horn (1982) in the area of child psychopathology and by Strelau (1983) and by Wachs and Gandour (1983) in the area of temperament.

Utilization of Environmental Opportunities

A second possible mechanism underlying interactions involves variations in the child's ability to make use of environmental supports. What is meant is not individual vulnerability to risk factors, but rather the individuals' ability to make use of the environment to facilitate their development. Sroufe has provided examples of how children with secure attachments take better advantage of opportunities to interact with peers than do children with less secure attachments.

Whether the child is able to make more or less use of opportunities may well be related to the presence or absence of previous stressors in the history of the individual (e.g., Bronfenbrenner, in press; Werner & Smith, 1982). Similarly, the relative frequency or infrequency of certain types of past experiences may also be important, as in the example given by Rutter and Pickles about positive school experiences having special salience for institution-reared children. However, factors that influence the individual's ability to make use of the environment do not necessarily have to relate to previous experience. Individual characteristics may also play a part. For example, the longitudinal clinical study by Murphy and Moriarity (1976) suggests that one of the factors that predisposed individuals to cope with stress was the energy the child had available to make use of environmental supports. Other examples of internal factors leading to differential utilization of the environment include activity level (Grandour 1989; Wachs, 1987) and sociability (Werner & Smith, 1982).

Differences in Response Pattern

A third alternative is variability in response patterns to various aspects of the environment. Individual differences in reactivity would not necessarily involve differences in degree of response (quantitative differences) as much as differences in the behavior elicited (qualitative differences). For example, the example given by Rutter and Pickles of sex differences in reactivity to family stress (oppositional behavior vs emotional distress) would be one example of a differential response pattern. Another example is seen in the work of Dodge (1986), who showed that aggressive children are more likely to respond aggressively to ambiguous situations than are nonaggressive children.

Although not intended to be an exhaustive list, differential sensitivity, differential utilization, and differential response patterns would appear to be prime candidates for inclusion in theories of organism–environment interaction.[5] What must be stressed again is that a satisfactory theory of interaction should include all of the interactive mechanisms as essential parts of the theory so that research deriving from the theory would involve tests of different processes.

The Current Status of Theory-Driven Research

The use of theory-driven research is more likely to reveal existing interactions, as well as to increase understanding about the nature of the process underlying observed interactions. Furthermore, the use of a theory-driven research strategy can aid in the design of future studies in this area. For example, McCall suggests isolating individuals who fit hypothesized organism–environment combinations, and comparing these individuals to the total sample. Differences in outcome between these individuals versus the complete sample would not only illustrate interaction, but would also illustrate possible mechanisms underlying observed interactions.

In calling for theory-driven research, it is fully recognized that although researchers have a number of promising leads to help define appropriate interaction theories, at present there are no existing sets of ''benchmark'' theories that can be used to guide future research in this area. This is particularly true if one is talking about deductive theories. Thus, Cronbach has suggested that it may be more appropriate to proceed from observation to theory, and not vice versa, when studying organism–environment interaction. Going from observation to theory does not necessarily mean the use of purely atheoretical studies of organism–environment interaction. Rather, what is implied by Cronbach's argument is the formulation of inductive rather than deductive theory-driven studies. One example of how an inductive theory-driven approach might work would be studies of organism–environment interaction that are designed to investigate at least one of the three types of processes previously delineated as integral components of a theory of interaction, using research methods that capitalize on the other recommendations outlined in this chapter. Thus, in addition to taking advantage of the research design suggestions made earlier in this volume, the first generation of inductive studies could be designed specifically to investigate differential sensitivity, differential utilization, or differential response patterns. As replicable interactions are discovered, these would be integrated into inductive ''prototheories'' (to use Wachs's term), which are centered around these three components. Predictions coming from these inductive prototheories could then be used to guide

---

[5] Another potential set of processes are the mechanisms of induction facilitation and maintenance, as described by Sackett. However, the lack of human data on these processes may limit their applicability to studies of organism–environment interaction involving human behavioral development.

the next generation of studies on organism–environment interaction. A focus on
the process dimensions discussed in this chapter would be crucial in accelerating
the transition from purely empirical to prototheory-driven research on organism–
environment interaction.[6]

Conclusion

In the initial chapter of this book, Wachs and Plomin identified what has come
to be called "Plomin's paradox": If interactions are so ubiquitous in nature (see
Rutter & Pickles), why are they so difficult to find in behavioral research studies?
One way to deal with this paradox is to conclude that interactions are not as
important for behavioral development as initially believed. However, at a conceptual level, the salience of organism–environment interaction for behavioral
development has been emphasized (McCall). Similarly, evidence from the ongoing
research reported by contributors to this book (Rutter & Pickles; Sackett; Sroufe;
Wachs) clearly documents the salience of organism–environment interaction for
a variety of developmental outcomes. Thus, researchers are still left with the
Plomin paradox. What I hope has emerged from this book are examples of conceptual and methodological factors that have blocked the ability to reliably identify
existing organism–environment interactions. These include the following:

1. *Power*. Many studies investigating organism–environment interaction
   may not have sufficient power to reliably detect interactions. This is
   particularly true for studies using multiple variables and for studies
   based on small sample sizes.
2. *Oversimplification*. Typically, studies of organism–environment interaction are nonlongitudinal and assess only a small subset of individual
   characteristics or environmental variables. As elegantly pointed out by
   Sackett, organism–environment interactions are probably governed by
   multiple processes, and these processes may be nested within specific
   time periods. Given this degree of complexity, isolated studies may be
   less likely to reveal existing organism–environment interactions. The
   problem with oversimplification goes further, however. All too often,
   other processes such as organism–environment covariance (McCall)
   may mask the existence of organism–environment interaction. Furthermore, researchers interested in main effect models avoid looking for
   existing interactions. Thus, even if interactions exist, researchers may

---

[6] In commenting on this chapter, McCall has raised the point that researchers are not likely to
ever develop a general theory of organism–environment interaction. Rather, he argues that theories
are more likely to be domain specific. McCall may well be correct, but at this point researchers are
so far from having even domain-specific theories that his argument is one that may be better discussed
by future generations of researchers.

view them as noise rather than as a legitimate influence on development.

3. *Statistics.* Standard statistical analyses may be insensitive to some interactions, particularly if interactions are occurring primarily for a subsample of populations or environments under study. The problem is compounded by the use of statistical models that are based primarily on proportion of variance accounted for or that produce a single yes or no decision.

4. *Research strategies.* Interactions are more likely to appear when extreme groups are used. However, extreme groups are often underrepresented in the literature. Furthermore, unstable or inappropriate measures of organism or environment are often used. Under these conditions, the chances of finding organism–environment interactions are considerably lessened.

5. *Atheoretical research.* Researchers cannot expect interactions to appear across all combinations of organism, environment, temporal period, and developmental outcome. Rather, interactions may exist only for certain developmental outcomes, for certain environmental characteristics, for certain organismic characteristics, or at certain time periods. The critical question then becomes what combinations of organism, environment, outcome, and temporal factors are most likely to reveal existing interactions. More appropriate and powerful tests of this type of question are most likely to occur when the researcher is using theory-driven research, particularly if the theory is based on prior systematic descriptive research. However, given the lack of appropriate theory, most approaches to the assessment of organism–environment interaction in human development studies have been atheoretical in nature. The chance of hitting the exact combination of organism, environment, outcome, and time period with an atheoretical study is quite remote.

Given the complexity of the processes underlying organism–environment interaction, both at a conceptual and at a methodoligical level, the authors of this book cannot claim to have solved all of the problems in this area. We do feel that we have made a promising start in documenting the importance of organism–environment interaction for understanding development. We hope that this work will sensitize developmental researchers to the need to think about interaction in their own area of study. In addition, we have also made a start by proposing a set of research strategies that may help to illustrate existing interactions and to understand the processes underlying specific interactions. We also hope that this book will serve as a stimulus for promoting more and better research on organism–environment interaction. However, in keeping with the theme of this book, we do not expect a main effect of this work on the field. Rather, our hope is for a strong interaction that involves at least a few researchers whose developmental course, context, and temperament make them eager to accept the challenge of investigating organism–environment interaction.

References

Bronfenbrenner, U. (1986). Ecology of the family as a context for human development. *Developmental Psychology, 22,* 723–742.

Bronfenbrenner, U. (in press). The ecology of cognitive development. In R. Wozniak & K. Fischer (Eds.) *Specific environments: Thinking in context.* Hillsdale, NJ: Erlbaum.

Crockenberg, S. (1987). Predictors and correlates of anger toward and punitive control of toddlers by adolescent mothers. *Child Development, 58,* 964–975.

Dodge, K. (1986). Social information processing variables in the development of aggression and altruism in children. In C. Zahn-Waxler, E. Cummings, & R. Ianotti (Eds.) *Altruism and aggression* (pp. 280–302). Cambridge, England: Cambridge University Press.

Gandour, M. (1989). Activity level as a dimension of temperament in toddlers: Its relevance for the organismic specificity hypothesis. *Child Development, 60,* 1092–1098.

Kagan, J. (1989). *Unstable ideas.* Cambridge, MA: Harvard University Press.

Loehlin, J., Willerman, L., & Horn, J. (1982). Personality resemblances between unwed mothers and their adopted away offspring. *Journal of Personality and Social Psychology, 42,* 1089–1099.

Maxwell, S. (1990). Why are interactions so difficult to detect? *Behavioral and Brain Sciences, 13,* 140–141.

Murphy, L., & Moriarity, A. (1976). *Vulnerability, coping and growth in infancy to adolescence.* New Haven, CT: Yale University Press.

Rutter, M. (1983). Statistical and personal interactions: Facts and perspectives. In D. Magnusson & V. Allen (Eds.) *Human development: An interactional perspective.* (pp. 296–320). San Diego, CA: Academic Press.

Strelau, J. (1983). *Temperament, personality and activity.* San Diego, CA: Academic Press.

Wachs, T. D. (1987). Specificity of environmental action as manifest in environmental correlates of toddlers' mastery motivation. *Developmental Psychology, 23,* 782–790.

Wachs, T. D. & Gandour, M. (1983). Temperament, environment and 6 month cognitive–intellectual development. *International Journal of Behavioral Development, 6,* 135–152.

Werner, E., & Smith, R. (1982). *Vulnerable but invincible.* New York: McGraw-Hill.

NAME INDEX

Abelson, 93, 102, 128, 131
Agarwal, 107, 133
Ainsworth, 71–72
Aitkin, 131, 141
Allen, 1, 7, 43, 134–135
Anastasi, 31, 41
Anderson, D., 131, 141
Anderson, G., 102
Anderson, N. H., 93, 95, 102
Anderson, P., 55
Anderson, S., 99, 102
Anderson-Goetz, 50
Angold, 109, 135
Appelbaum, 159
Arend, 75
Aristotle, 3
Armitage, 124, 131
Arms, 70
Armstrong, 3, 6
Arnold, 51
Aronson, 7
Ashworth, 57
Auquier, 102

Baade, 109, 136
Babigian, 135
Baker, 131, 141
Bamford, 108, 134
Banta, 75
Barker, 114, 131
Baron, 102
Barron, A., 3, 6
Barron, R., 56
Barter, 3, 6
Baudin, 132
Baynen, 108, 133
Bebbington, 121, 134, 136
Beckwith, 60

Bell, 120, 132
Belmont, 49
Belsky, 50, 56, 72
Bergeman, 35–36, 38, 40–42
Berger, 135
Bergman, 2, 6, 53, 132, 134
Birmingham, 3, 7
Birns, 57
Black, 108, 132
Blakemore, 106, 108, 132
Blehar, 71
Block, 53, 79
Blot, 126, 132
Bock, G., 108, 110, 132, 134, 136
Bock, R., 98, 102, 120, 132, 156
Bohman, 54
Bonnevaux, 5, 7
Bornstein, 1, 6, 41, 105, 132, 143
Box, 132, 139
Bowlby, 70
Bradford, 132
Bradley, 60
Brainerd, 58
Braun, 103
Breen, 125, 132
Breiman, 100, 102
Bresler, 11
Breslow, 132–133, 139
Brice, 53
Bricker, 12
Briner, 53
Brodsky, 53
Bronfenbrenner, 44–45, 48, 56, 175, 178
Broman, 129, 132
Bronn, 136
Brooke, 108, 134
Brown, 8, 116, 121, 123, 132, 138, 141
Brownell, 90, 102

SUBJECT INDEX

190